HIRED!

THE JOB-HUNTING/CAREER-PLANNING GUIDE

THIRD EDITION

Michael Stebleton

Michael Henle

Connie Harris

PEARSON

Prentice Hall

Upper Saddle River, New Jersey
Columbus, Ohio

Library of Congress Cataloging-in-Publication Data

Stebleton, Michael.
   Hired! The job-hunting/career-planning guide/Michael Stebleton,
Michael Henle, Connie Harris.—3rd ed.
   p. cm.
   ISBN 0-13-114965-2
   1. Job hunting—Handbooks, manuals, etc. 2. Career development—
Handbooks, manuals etc. I. Henle, Michael J. II. Harris, Connie. III. Title.
   HF5382.7.S738 2006
   650.14—dc22

                                                        2005023861

Photo Credits

All of the photographs in this book
are from royalty-free disks by the
following sources: BananaStock,
Comstock, Corbis, DigitalStock,
DigitalVision, Dynamic Graphics,
Eyewire, PhotoDisc, Image 100,
Stockbyte, and StockDisc.

Vice President and Publisher: Jeffery W. Johnston
Executive Editor: Sande Johnson
Editorial Assistant: Susan Kauffman
Production Editor: Holcomb Hathaway
Design Coordinator: Diane C. Lorenzo
Cover Designer: Ali Mohrman
Cover Photo: Corbis
Production Manager: Pamela D. Bennett
Director of Marketing: Ann Castel Davis
Marketing Manager: Amy Judd
Compositor: Integra–Pondicherry, India
Cover Printer: Phoenix Color Corp.
Printer/Binder: Banta Book Group

Dedication

*Michael Stebleton would like
to dedicate his work
in loving memory of his sister,
Jennifer H. Stebleton
(1972–2000).
We miss you dearly.*

Pearson Prentice Hall™ is a trademark of Pearson Education, Inc.
Pearson® is a registered trademark of Pearson plc
Prentice Hall® is a registered trademark of Pearson Education, Inc.

Pearson Education Ltd.
Pearson Education Singapore Pte. Ltd.
Pearson Education Canada, Ltd.
Pearson Education–Japan

Pearson Education Australia Pty. Limited
Pearson Education North Asia Ltd.
Pearson Educación de Mexico, S.A. de C.V.
Pearson Education Malaysia Pte. Ltd.

10 9 8 7 6 5 4 3 2 1
ISBN 0-13-114965-2

Contents

4 Exploring Through Experience   99
LEARNING OUTSIDE THE CLASSROOM

UNIT II — CREATING OPPORTUNITIES   123

5 Developing Your Portfolio   125
SELF-MANAGED CAREER PLANNING

6 Connecting to Employers   143
JOB SEARCH CORRESPONDENCE AND JOB APPLICATIONS

7 Marketing Tools   171
YOUR RESUME AND REFERENCES

UNIT III　SELLING YOUR TALENTS　205

8　Networking and Job Sourcing　207
GROW YOUR POSSIBILITIES

9 Interviewing   221
ACHIEVE JOB SEARCH RESULTS

UNIT IV | **BALANCING YOUR CAREER AND PERSONAL LIFE**   **265**

10 Navigating   267
YOUR PROFESSIONAL DIRECTION

Learning Objectives   **267**

11 Cultivating Meaningful Connections   291

PERSONAL GOALS, LIFE BALANCE, AND RELATIONSHIPS

12 Financing Your Life   317
PLANNING AND IMPLEMENTING   317

Preface

The Philosophy Behind *HIRED!*

HIRED!, *Third Edition*, is based on a holistic approach to career–life planning. Incorporating life-planning issues with the techniques of the job search process, *HIRED!* is a resource that can be used in multiple settings with diverse audiences. Students in career-planning courses at a variety of institutions (community colleges, technical programs, four-year degree-granting institutions) will benefit from this comprehensive and practical guide. Due to the wide scope of the audience, we have used a variety of examples that reflect the breadth of the career areas students might pursue. Additionally, *HIRED!* can also be used by individuals who are not enrolled in an academic institution, but who are eager to engage in the process of career–life decision making. Finally, *HIRED!* can be used in nonacademic programs by training professionals, facilitators, and others in business, industry, and nonprofit organizations.

HIRED! focuses on helping readers develop an ongoing, flexible portfolio of information about themselves and their work to prepare them for satisfying and productive lives in an ever-changing world. The third edition provides information on the changing nature of work—including trends in the marketplace and a turbulent post-9/11 world—and enables individuals to actively explore how to thrive in these fluid and dynamic environments.

Individuals graduating in the 21st century will likely be affiliated with multiple work situations throughout their lives. Many workers will "job hop" frequently in order to seek out new and rewarding opportunities. In fact, the average amount of time spent with a current employer for workers from ages 25 to 34 is less than three years. The days of the traditional, loyal employee staying with one equally loyal employer are long gone. You are in charge of your own career.

Although estimates vary, many career experts contend that the average young American beginning his or her career today will hold seven to eight different jobs between ages 18 and 30, and one in four young workers will have more than ten different jobs during this period. Other predictions indicate that individuals will have three or more *careers* before they retire— if they retire at all. Clearly, change and transition will become commonplace as people plan their work in the future. *HIRED!* is designed to help individuals prosper in these turbulent times. Readers learn how to develop their own portfolios to help organize information about themselves and the world of work as they manage career–life transitions in the future.

HIRED! allows readers to actively prepare themselves to confidently take advantage of these changes in work. This textbook is filled with exercises and examples to assist students in their journeys. The exercises build knowledge and skills through doing. In turn, "doing" through writing activities lead to greater understanding. One of the goals of *HIRED!* is to motivate you to become personally responsible for your life and to become an active participant in its process.

This textbook is a hands-on manual combined with a portfolio that you create. *HIRED!* encourages readers to view the term *career* holistically. Often, the concept of career is viewed as paid employment only. We all play multiple roles in our lives, and paid work is just one of those roles. *HIRED!* invites readers to explore those other roles in life. In addition, *HIRED!* promotes balance and harmony in the various components of your life. With the whole-life approach, you can use the past to help you make well-informed decisions about life in the present and the future. *Career decision making is a lifelong process, not a single event. HIRED!* gives readers an ongoing system that works throughout this process.

HIRED!'s four units—Discovering Your Authentic Self, Creating Opportunities, Selling Your Talents, and Balancing Your Career and Personal Life—are designed to build on and interact with one another. Each unit allows you to practice what you learned in the preceding unit. Each includes Personal Think Pieces that will provide you with opportunities to think critically about the issues presented. Finally, each unit serves to build expression, inspiration, and direction.

The third edition of *HIRED!* continues to be holistic in nature, with an emphasis on career–life planning in a changing world of work. Additionally, the tone of the textbook is interactive—including a workbook approach with numerous exercises for the reader to complete. The third edition offers several significant changes:

- First, the edition features a fictitious college student, Mai, who is a 19-year-old sophomore in college. Mai is introduced in the first chapter, and readers journey along with Mai throughout her career decision-making process. Most of the chapters include a segment that briefly describes Mai in relation to the topic of the corresponding chapter. The readers have the opportunity to respond to questions and complete action exercises that are relevant to career decision making. Additional student profiles have been added throughout the textbook.

- Second, "action step" exercises have been added at the conclusion of some chapters. The objective of the action step exercises is to give readers the opportunity to proactively take their next steps toward implementing a plan. Revisions of many exercises were made in this third edition of *HIRED!*

- Third, job search skills, including new examples of resume writing and interviewing, have been updated. Advances in technology that relate to the job search process are included (e.g., Internet resources, electronic approaches, and others).

- Fourth, updated information on resources, Web sites, statistics, diversity, post-9/11 changes, and other trends in the workplace is included.

- Fifth, a streamlined and repackaged table of contents was made for this edition. All chapters were revised and updated.

- Finally, a new and improved chapter on portfolio development and how to use a portfolio was created for the third edition.

The *HIRED!* System

Job-hunting success is not a secret—it is a proactive, organized approach to finding rewarding work. The steps of the system—Discover, Create, Sell, and Balance—build on and interact with one another. No one part stands alone. You stand in the center and are the "manager" of the system. You are the manager of your career and life.

The goals of Unit I, Discovering Your Authentic Self, are awareness and direction (knowing what you want to do, what you have to offer, and where you want to go with your career–life planning). As you complete the exercises in this unit, you will be motivated to move into the detailed work of the next unit.

The goals of Unit II, Creating Opportunities, are expression and creation (capturing who you are and your experiences on paper). Completion of this unit prepares you for the action of Unit III.

The goals of Unit III, Selling Your Talents, are implementation and realization (planning and executing the step-by-step job-hunting process). Once you have achieved these goals, you will be on your way to realizing the career–life fulfillment goals presented in Unit IV.

The goals of the final unit, Balancing Your Career and Personal Life, are balance and harmony (continuous learning and wholeness). Establishing balance and harmony throughout your life brings you back, full circle, to Unit I, Discovering Your Authentic Self.

HIRED! and Your Portfolios

While reading *HIRED!* you will begin to create two portfolios. Use these portfolios to learn more about yourself and the world of work, and to prepare for your job search and your future career:

- **A textbook-based portfolio.** This portfolio will be a collection of exercises, writing samples, and other materials that you complete while reading each chapter. You will want to use a three-ring binder or folder to organize your materials. Each chapter of this book includes several exercises. These activities allow you to record a wide range of personal and professional information that will prepare you for your job search and career. Look for the icon of a briefcase accompanied by the word "portfolio"—this is your cue to complete the exercise and add it to your personal portfolio.

    If you are using *HIRED!* in a career–life planning course, your instructor also may have expectations and recommendations for you regarding what you should save and compile. All of the documents you collect will complement the more formal portfolio you will compile for your actual job search.

- **Your job search portfolio.** Beginning in Chapter 5, you will learn how to develop a professional portfolio. This portfolio will be flexible, expandable, and portable. You will use this portfolio in your job search process, including the resume-writing and interviewing steps. The job search portfolio will be a collection of essential documents that demonstrate your key skill sets. These documents will offer evidence of the value you bring to a potential employer. In some cases, an exercise that you use in your textbook-based portfolio may also be used in your job search portfolio (for example, your final resume).

As you begin your journey into *HIRED!*, relax and enjoy the creative energy and awareness developed by doing the exercises. Apply the new knowledge and skills to all areas of your career and life. Enjoy the journey!

Acknowledgments

We express grateful acknowledgment for permission to reproduce examples of student and client work throughout the text. Without these examples and the permission from the individuals involved, this text would not have been possible. In almost all cases, the names, places, and dates have been altered to protect the privacy of the individuals. In some instances, the examples are compilations.

We also wish to thank the following individuals:

The reviewers, who read this book in earlier forms and offered constructive suggestions: Sally Gelardin, University of San Francisco; Deb Jansky, Milwaukee Area Technical College; Richard Nelson, University of Kansas; and Andy Saucedo, Dona Ana Branch Community College.

Our wonderful spouses, Marvin Harris, Mary Henle, and Rashné Jehangir, who have given us their unending support and love throughout the planning, development, and writing of this textbook.

Our students and clients have been the best teachers, and we will be forever in their debt.

Sande Johnson, Executive Editor at Prentice Hall, and Gay Pauley of Holcomb Hathaway, for their advice and suggestions throughout this revision of *HIRED!*

Connie Harris would like to thank Professor Bern Wisner, Central Oregon Community College, who provided the opportunity to develop the Getting Hired class and the text for that class.

Discovering
YOUR AUTHENTIC SELF

1

Who are you? What do you really want? Where do you want your life to go? What career areas do you want to explore? How might occupational trends affect your decision-making process? These are not easy questions to answer. In fact, your responses may change on a regular basis depending on a variety of factors—and that's okay. The primary objectives of this unit, Discovering Your Authentic Self, are to help you gain more self-awareness and to provide direction.

Thoroughly to have known oneself, is above all art, for it is the highest art.

—*THEOLOGIA GERMANICA*

Additionally, you will have the opportunity to actively explore careers, educational opportunities, and the changing nature of work.

You will be asked to play an active role in this self-discovery process. No one knows you better than yourself, so it makes sense for you to assume this role, right? In this unit, you will be building a personal portfolio of information and knowledge that you can use throughout your lifetime. **It is important to realize that career–life decision making is a process and not a one-time event.** You will revisit this process multiple times throughout your future. Therefore, it is crucial that you have a solid understanding of yourself and how to access career-related information.

The preface of this textbook mentioned that the average young American will have seven to eight different jobs between ages 18 and 30, and some will have more than 10. Many people will have three or more careers before retiring. This trend of change and transition is vastly different from previous work patterns.

In the past, many employees devoted their entire work lives to one employer—a mutually beneficial arrangement based on loyalty. Now there is a new, more short-term employment agreement that is based on the understanding that the employee will move on to new opportunities. Because you will hold numerous work positions, it is important that you have a thorough assessment of the interests, values, skills, and experiences you bring to a prospective work situation.

The portfolio that you will create as you work through the textbook is unique in several ways. This document offers at least three important traits:

- The portfolio will be flexible, dynamic, and expandable. You and the file's "contents" will change over time. Expect these changes, and learn from them.

- The portfolio is unique to you. You can be as creative as you wish to be.

- It is a file that you can use in many situations—including getting a job.

Your D.A.T.A.

Because the employee–employer agreement has changed, it is likely that you will work for multiple employers for shorter periods of time. But what about the actual jobs themselves? How will they change in the future?

William Bridges, author of *JobShift* (1994) and a leading consultant on workplace transition issues, believes jobs have changed already and will continue to do so. According to Bridges, the world of work as we have known it in the past is no longer the same. Well-defined jobs with detailed task descriptions are fast becoming a thing of the past. Many "jobs" are now undefined, while others are gone completely—a process Bridges refers to as "de-jobbing." In order to succeed in this de-jobbed environment, we must know ourselves and what we bring to a work situation, and adjust quickly to the multitude of changes. Flexibility is vital if we are to thrive in this new work environment.

In terms of knowing ourselves, Bridges advises us to "survey our D.A.T.A." (a comprehensive self-assessment of Desires, Abilities, Temperament, and Assets). He encourages workers to survey and recycle their D.A.T.A. on a regular basis in order to identify what they bring ("their product") to a prospective employer. Today's employees need to be able to identify and articulate their value (in terms of skills, experiences, services provided, and values) to those who have the power to hire them.

In this Discovering Your Authentic Self unit, you will complete several self-assessment activities so you can articulate who you are and what contributions you bring. This unit is about knowing your authentic self.

The Chapters

Career—life decision making involves cycling and recycling through three main steps. First, individuals must thoroughly assess themselves by examining their interests, values, skills, personality, needs, lifestyle, and experiences. Second, they must gain a solid understanding of the world of work by assessing such areas as career opportunities, education or training involved, and trends affecting the marketplace. What academic and career options are available? Finally, individuals must make decisions, set goals, and test opportunities based on the integrated information generated from steps one and two. The organization of Unit I follows this traditional and practical career—life planning model.

Chapter 1, Know Yourself: A Self-Awareness Journey, allows you to do exercises spontaneously, without being concerned about results or performance. Through these exercises, you will discover invaluable information about yourself that will help provide direction in your life. The goal is to know yourself and find your path to fulfilling, meaningful work.

Look within. Within is the fountain of good, and it will ever bubble up, if thou wilt ever dig.

—MARCUS AURELIUS

Chapter 2, Charting the Future: Goal Setting and Decision Making for Life, helps you identify your long-term life and career goals through building goals around the main areas of your life: professional, personal and social, and financial. You will also explore the issue of balance in your life roles.

Chapter 3, Researching Careers: The Changing Nature of Work, provides an opportunity to actively explore career and educational options using a variety of research tools, including the Internet. You will also learn about work environments and the importance of keeping a cautious eye on trends in the workforce.

Chapter 4, Exploring Through Experience, shows you how experiential educational opportunities, such as internships and study abroad options, can help you in your academic and professional life.

Through the exercises in this Discovering Your Authentic Self unit, you may find that you're pointed in the right direction. Or you may find that you've been traveling away from your true desires and should reevaluate your direction choice. It should be noted that the unit exercises serve as a catalyst for thoughtful life and career decision making. They are not intended to replace the comprehensive career and personality assessments provided by college career development centers and other professionals.

Whatever the case, be assured that all of your experiences will establish a strong base for building the future you want, deserve, and can create. So relax, complete each exercise, and allow the experience to enrich your self-awareness and understanding. Discover your direction for life.

REFERENCES

Bridges, W. (1994). *JobShift: How to prosper in a workplace without jobs.* Reading, MA: Addison-Wesley.

Know Yourself

A SELF-AWARENESS JOURNEY

chapter

1

learning objectives

1. To understand how writing can assist you in the self-discovery process

2. To assess what you enjoy by exploring your interests and passions

3. To gain knowledge about your skills, including transferable and life skills

4. To assess the importance of values and lifestyle preferences in decision making

5. To explore how personality and "fit" can make a difference in your work

chapter

1

Life is either a daring adventure or it is nothing.

—HELEN KELLER

Introducing Mai. Meet Mai, a college sophomore who is making relevant decisions about her future. Like many students, she feels overwhelmed by choosing a career. In fact, many of the questions she is addressing may be similar to those that confront you. In many of the chapters, Mai will be featured along with several discussion questions for you and your classmates to ponder. Mai is typical of many college students—she is bright, articulate, and undecided. Following are some details about Mai so that you can better understand her. Consider how her situation may be similar to or different from your own.

MAI'S STUDENT PROFILE:

- She is a 19-year-old sophomore enrolled at a midsized university in the Southwest.

- Mai is undecided about her major. She is interested in business, art, psychology, and sociology. Her adviser has encouraged her to declare a major, but she is reluctant to do so given her diverse interests. Her parents are encouraging Mai to consider a business degree so that she can contribute to the family income.

- Mai is a first-generation student (i.e., she is the first in her family to attend college). She comes from a middle-class family and grew up in a large, urban environment. Mai graduated in the top 15 percent of her class of 425 students, and she enjoys learning. Her current grade point average is 3.3.

- Her father works for the U.S. Postal Service and her mother is an administrative assistant for a law firm. Mai has two younger brothers who attend high school.

- Mai has worked part-time in several retail jobs including food service and clothing. She has no internship experience so far, but intends to seek out opportunities next summer. Mai has expressed an interest in working in the areas of accounting and marketing but is still undecided.

- Mai is starting to get involved in on-campus activities. She holds a leadership position in her residence hall council. Mai joined a business club through the school, and she volunteers for a city arts program associated with the university.

One of the first tasks Mai wants to address is self-awareness. She has multiple interests but is unclear about how these interests might translate into a chosen major or career.

Before moving into the rest of the chapter, consider the following questions about your situation now that you've met Mai.

It took me almost three years to decide on a major. I was worried about making the "wrong" decision. Eventually, I decided on a psychology major after consulting with my academic adviser and exploring various resources. (Actually, she told me I had to make a decision now.) I encourage students to do extensive research prior to making this important decision.

—MICHAEL STEBLETON

- Are you undecided about your career direction? If so, what steps might you take to help you with the career decision-making process?
- What are some of the barriers you are facing at this time in your life? What is your biggest obstacle?
- What is the most important decision you hope to make in the next 6 to 12 months?

There are no easy answers to these questions; however, this textbook will help with the career decision-making process.

Like Mai, you must be active in this process of career–life decision making. Ultimately, you are responsible for the direction your life takes. This is your opportunity to get to know *you*: your interests and passions; your unique skills; where you want to live and how you want to live out your life.

How do you get to know yourself? Disconnect the phone, turn off the TV, and tell everyone to stay away for a short while. Find a quiet, peaceful place. Then, take a pen and paper and start working through the exercises in this chapter. Begin today to plan for your future.

Methods for Self-Analysis

The primary method used in this chapter for achieving self-awareness is writing. Desires, ideas, and concepts shift, disappear, and change in thought form. They are fleeting and difficult to analyze. The act of writing puts these thoughts into a form that can be analyzed and reviewed over the years. Writing is stationary. Furthermore, writing serves as a useful reminder or confirmation of a decision you made in your life. In times of doubt, you can go back to what you were experiencing at that time and be reminded of why you made the choice you did.

For the next few days, work through exercises designed to make you think on paper. You will be using the following methods to capture your reflections:

- Creating thought clusters (this approach is similar to brainstorming)
- Writing spontaneously

The primary method used in this chapter for self-analysis will be writing.

- Making intuitive lists of items
- Completing sentences spontaneously

Other writing strategies that you might add to the preceding list include:

- Keeping a journal of your insights
- Creating a scrapbook of writings, pictures, quotes, and other items that inspire you
- Visualizing yourself leading the career–life that you really desire and putting those images down on paper
- Completing several self-assessment inventories— including interest and personality surveys (discussed later in the chapter)

Clustering: A Thought Picture

Because many of us have difficulty expressing ourselves articulately in writing, the clustering method has been selected to assist you with this task. You will find this technique called for throughout the text, not only to help you write but also to help you analyze a job advertisement and use other job-hunting strategies.

Clustering is similar to brainstorming in that you never rule out ideas when they come to you. No matter how crazy the idea may seem, you record it. Because clustering may be new to you, here are the general principles of clustering as described by Gabriele Lusser Rico in her book *Writing the Natural Way* (2000).

> To create a cluster, you begin with a nucleus word, circled, on a fresh page. Now you simply let go and begin to flow with any current of connections that come into your head. Write these down rapidly, each in its own circle, radiating outward from the center in any direction they want to go. Connect each new word or phrase with a line to the preceding circle. When something new and different strikes you, begin again at the central nucleus and radiate outward until those associations are exhausted.
>
> As you cluster, you may experience a sense of randomness or, if you are somewhat skeptical, an uneasy sense that it isn't leading anywhere. That is your logical Sign mind (left, logical brain) wanting to get into the act to let you know how foolish you are being by not setting thoughts down in logical sequences. Trust this natural process, though. We all cluster mentally throughout our lives without knowing it; we have simply never made these clusterings visible on paper.

In other words, follow these steps:

1. Begin with your central thought or theme—a word or phrase—circled in the center of the page. An example is "career interests."

. . . we do not write in order to be understood; we write in order to understand.

—C. DAY LEWIS

2. Write down all impressions generated from this central thought.

3. Connect each impression to the central circle or an outlying circle. (See Figure 1.1 for an example.)

4. Write each impression (thought) quickly, connecting it to the circle before it.

5. When a new thought hits you, begin again at the central thought and radiate outward until all associations about this new thought are spent.

6. When you exhaust all impressions of the central thought, review your thought cluster and begin writing spontaneously.

7. You may write about all the thoughts on the page, or you may find that you only want to write about some of the ideas generated. Let the writing lead you through the cluster or off on its own.

8. After writing, read what you have written aloud. The ear hears what the eye does not see. Spend a minute or two making any changes you feel will enhance your writing.

9. Now, lay the writing aside for an hour or a day or two. Then, review it again for any changes you feel will strengthen it.

figure **1.1**

Dream cluster, courtesy of a student.

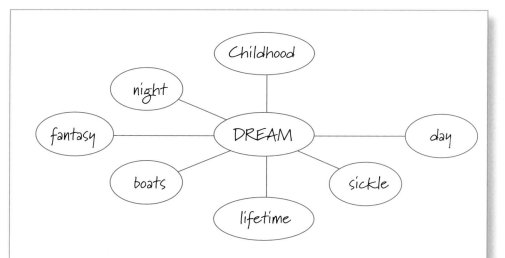

Childhood dreams—nurse, living in Africa with the wild animals, living on a ranch raising cattle . . .

Day dreams of travels, hikes, interesting conversations, quiet times . . .

Nighttime dreams of the daily living often given a strange twist.

figure **1.2**

Thought cluster, courtesy
of Josephine Manes.

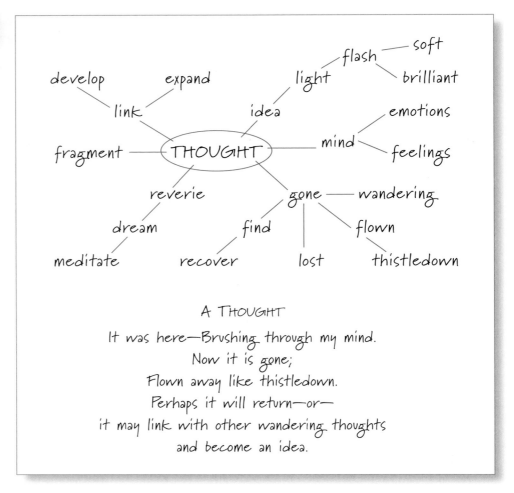

A THOUGHT

It was here—Brushing through my mind.
Now it is gone;
Flown away like thistledown.
Perhaps it will return—or—
it may link with other wandering thoughts
and become an idea.

The example in Figure 1.2 is clustered using just lines. There is no one "right" way to cluster. Whatever seems to work best for you is what you should use.

Clustering is an easy way to see your thoughts on paper. You may opt to use it to explore "passions," "interests," or "skills that you hold," among others. It's a natural way to write, to script telephone conversations, to analyze complex writing, and to draft resumes—it is a simple tool to use once you master it. Use clusters to write naturally. They're fun, and they enhance your writing.

Writing is a creative way to learn about yourself, but it is not the only method. Self-assessments and inventories also provide valuable information.

Self-Assessments and Inventories: An Introduction

In the remainder of this chapter, you will have an opportunity to participate in numerous exercises and activities. These activities are designed to assist you with the career–life decision-making process. Inventories and assessments serve as helpful tools; however, they will not tell you what to do or not do with your life. Instead, they serve as catalysts for organizing information that you learn via self-reflection. The exercises are not intended to replace the comprehensive career and personality assessments provided by schools, career education centers, and other professionals.

Consider these points prior to completing the exercises and inventories:

- There are no right or wrong answers. Attempt to respond honestly to the questions. Honest responses produce more accurate and helpful information.

- Go with your first response. Your initial instinct is usually the most sincere. Try not to spend too much time overanalyzing a particular question. Move through the exercise or inventory quickly yet carefully.

- Inventories are not crystal balls. They will not tell what you should do with your life. They will, however, provide new insights about you.

- Because each person is unique, everyone has different answers to and interpretations of the questions.

The way you happen to feel at the time you complete a self-assessment exercise or inventory could affect the outcome. It is possible to complete an assessment on one day and then repeat it another day with contrasting results. Your mood may influence the results slightly. So, don't be surprised if you repeat an exercise later and the results vary.

Use Your Native Language

You may be introduced to these exercises in a language other than your native language. If this is true, do the exercises in the language that you are most comfortable working in, the language you automatically think in. Doing so keeps your answers spontaneous and helps you intuitively respond to each exercise.

"To Be" vs. "To Do": A Matter of Perspective	Dr. John Holland, a pioneer in career development, believes "despite several decades of research, the most efficient way to predict vocational choice is simply to ask the person what he/she wants to be." Madhu Bhat, academic adviser at the University of Minnesota–Twin Cities, tells her students, "Don't tell me what you want *to be*, tell me what you want *to do*." What is your perspective?

The Self-Awareness Section of the Portfolio

You will use some of the exercises from Chapter 1 in your portfolio (to be discussed in more detail in Chapter 5). You will also complete exercises directly in the textbook. You can tear out these activities and place them in your portfolio or leave them in the text—it is your choice. Following are some suggestions to consider:

- To keep Chapter 1 organized, make a chapter divider and file the completed exercises behind it. You will be using your own paper to complete many of the exercises.

- Keep these exercises and similar ones in this section for future reference.

- If and when you redo these self-awareness exercises, file the new ones with the prior ones. As the years go by, it will be helpful and informative to compare the answers from a prior time to the answers of today. You may want to examine any significant changes and explore what might have contributed to those differences.

- If any portfolio section becomes large and unwieldy, put it in a separate notebook.

Good luck. Have fun. And enjoy discovering your authentic self.

Exploring Your Passions and Interests: What Do You *Really* Want?

ow many times has someone asked you, "So, what do you want to do when you grow up?" If you are a traditional student (age 18 to 22), you've no doubt encountered the perennial holiday dinner interrogation from visiting relatives. It goes something like this: "So, what are you planning to major in?" "What kind of job can you get with that degree?" Those who are not in that traditional student age range are *still* grappling with the same initial question: "So, what do I want to do when I grow up (if that ever really happens)?"

A musician must make music, an artist must paint, a poet must write, if he is to be ultimately at peace with himself. What one can be, one must be.

—ABRAHAM MASLOW

We, the authors of HIRED!, are convinced that the ongoing questioning of "what do I want to do?" is a natural component of healthy career–life development. In today's ever-changing world, you will likely be faced with transitions where you ask yourself, "What in the world do I want to do next?" You can expect that a continual exploration of your interests and passions will be critical to your own happiness. One of the authors asked students in his career planning course why a thorough assessment of interests and passions might be helpful. Their responses included the following:

- Pinpointing certain preferences regarding a major and an occupation helps narrow down the available options.

- Identifying interests can lead to choosing more engaging and rewarding careers. (In fact, research shows that people who are interested in their work report greater satisfaction and happiness on the job. The more your interests can be incorporated into your work, the more fulfilled you will be with your career–life.)

- Identifying personal passions can be fun and perhaps financially rewarding.

Exploring your passions and interests is a crucial part of answering the question "What do I want to do?"

You may be wondering, what is the difference between an interest and a passion? Actually, there is considerable overlap between the two terms. *An interest is simply something you like to do or would like to explore.* It can be an activity, a hobby, or a particular discipline or occupation. It is a preference for one option over another based on the pleasure or fulfillment received from that choice. *A passion is an extension of an interest—it is something that you love to do and must explore.* Some define *passion* as a compulsion—an urge or desire that one cannot turn away from no matter what the consequences. For example, think about some of your favorite musicians or performing artists. Maybe it is a rapper, entertainer, or music group that you enjoy. It is likely that these artists really enjoy what they do. They discovered their passion and can earn a living doing what they love to do. Do something that you love.

If you are interested in reading personal stories about passions, check out a fun book called *Roadtrip Nation*, about several recent college graduates who went on a nationwide quest to find meaningful and passionate work (Marriner, Gebhard, & Gordon, 2003; Marriner, McAllister, & Gebhard, 2005).

The Pursuit of Vocation

What do you really want to do with your life? For many people, a passion is a special "calling." They intuitively know that a certain area of work is meant for them. We often hear religious leaders, teachers, and social workers, to name a few, refer to their "vocation"—a calling that they heeded. Historically, the term *vocation* comes from the Latin, *vocare*, or "to call." However, a calling is not restricted to the ministry or one of the helping professions. It refers to any area you are particularly drawn to for any reason. The following excerpt provides additional insight into the concepts of passion and vocation.

Vocation is "the place where your deep gladness and the world's deep hunger meet."

—FREDERICK BUECHNER

In a culture that sometimes equates work with suffering, it is revolutionary to suggest that the best inward sign of vocation is deep gladness—revolutionary but true. If a work is mine to do, it will make me glad over the long haul, despite the difficult days. Even the difficult days will ultimately gladden me, because they pose the kinds of problems that can help me grow in a work if it is truly mine. If work does not gladden me in these ways, I need to consider laying it down. . . . (Palmer, 1998, p. 30)

What might bring you deep gladness? It could involve turning a hobby into some type of paid work. Not surprisingly, some up-and-coming businesses are owned by inspiring individuals who have a passion. Can you think of two people in your life who are pursuing their passions? Listen for that voice of vocation (Palmer, 2000).

How do you find your passion? Often, a passion will find you. You may have heard the advice to "follow your bliss." Simply put, it means following your heart as you make career–life decisions. Joseph Campbell, author and philosopher, was one of the first to use the term in his discussions on mythology and life purpose. He offers this piece of advice: "I feel that if one follows what I call one's bliss—the thing that really gets you deep in the gut and that you feel is your life—doors open. They do! . . . Put aside the passing moment that says you should live this way. Be informed and go where your body and soul want you to go" (Campbell & Moyers, 1998).

personal THINK PIECE

Your calling. *What do you think your bliss might be? What interests and activities might your bliss involve? What are you passionate about?*

_____

_____

_____

_____

_____

Does This Path Have a Heart?

by Carlos Castaneda

Look at every path closely and deliberately. Try it as many times as you think necessary. Then ask yourself, and yourself alone, one question. . . . It is this. . . . Does this path have a heart? All paths are the same. They lead nowhere. There are paths going through the brush or into the brush. Does this path have a heart is the only question. If it does, then the path is good. If it doesn't it is of no use. Both paths lead nowhere, but one has a heart and the other doesn't. (Castaneda, 1968)

Does the path you are pursuing have a heart?

A Closer Look at Interests

It may be helpful to assess your interests by looking at your preference for working with one or more of the following:

- Data (e.g., accounting, computers, and office practices)
- People (e.g., teaching, counseling, and sales)
- Things (e.g., machinery, working outdoors, and using tools in your work)

Many individuals prefer working with *data*. These people enjoy computing, analyzing, manipulating, or synthesizing facts and related information. Does this sound like something you would enjoy?

Others prefer working with *people*—they want extensive interaction with others in their work, whether it is with coworkers, clients, students, or audiences. Some individuals wish to teach or serve other people in some way. Others want to negotiate, persuade, or sell products or services to clients.

The third major preference is working with *things*. Many people want to use equipment or machinery in their work, whether this involves driving a bus, operating a drill, or using a computer.

Most people enjoy a combination of working with data, people, and things. We all have our own preferences.

personal
THINK PIECE

Do what interests you. *In the space below, briefly describe your interests as they relate to data, people, and things. What are your personal preferences?*

_____

_____

_____

_____

_____

_____

_____

_____

_____

Childhood dreams are the fantasies you held as a child. Exploring these past dreams can lead to insights you have as an adult. First, look at your early years, and then proceed to the present. Using the clustering technique you learned earlier, follow these steps:

Dreams are the seedlings of realities.

—JAMES ALLEN,
AS A MAN THINKETH

1. Label a blank page with the headings shown in Figure 1.3, and title it "Lifelong Dreams."

2. Begin clustering your early childhood dreams. Don't worry about making sense; just write as fast as you can. The goal is to be as spontaneous and creative as possible. Attempt to answer the recurring question: "What do I want to be or do when I grow up?"

3. Next, cluster the dream jobs you had as a teenager. List all of the jobs you ever dreamed about, regardless of how foolish or unrealistic they may appear now.

4. Now, cluster the jobs you have considered as an adult. This cluster should include all of the jobs you have held and those you have considered.

5. Finally, cluster all of your fantasy jobs—anything you would like to do. Remove any limitations by including whatever you would like to do. Don't worry about whether training is required or the job is practical or whether it seems impossible.

6. Now, write a paragraph or two about your dreams. Write quickly and spontaneously, letting the cluster lead your writing. Be creative and expressive. You won't turn in this exercise, so don't be concerned about limiting your ideas. Your only audience is yourself, so don't write about what you think is important or what might impress someone else.

7. After completing the exercise, respond to these questions: What was it like to do this exercise? What did I gain from this activity?

Add this activity to your portfolio.

---

figure   **1.3**   *Example of Exercise 1.1, Lifelong Dreams.*

CHILDHOOD	Truck driver	Engineer	Police officer	Rancher	TV Star	Coach
TEEN YEARS	Guitar player	Astronaut	Computer programmer			
ADULT YEARS	Business owner	Counselor				
FANTASY JOBS	Olympic athlete	Folk singer	World traveler			

When I was a kid, I always dreamed of following in my dad's footsteps . . . he was a rancher with lots of cattle. I felt this would be a perfect life. I also dreamed of being a TV star and a police officer, among others. Now I think I'm more practical. Ranching really isn't for me. I love computers and I enjoy helping others. I enjoy working independently, and I may want to own my own business someday.

Also, I love to travel, participate in sports, and play the guitar. Maybe I can combine all these things into a career. There's so much that I could do. I'm just beginning to dream . . .

1.2   25 Things I Love to Do

This is an opportunity to explore your passions and interests—what you really love to do. Make a list of 25 activities you really enjoy. Include activities from all arenas of your life. The exercise will not be turned in, so let the list be exactly what comes to mind. Keep going until you have at least 25 things on the list. Follow these steps:

To be successful, you must love what you do.

—DOTTIE WALTERS

1. Take a blank piece of paper and title it "25 Things I Love to Do."

2. Begin making your list of activities. Write as fast as you can. It doesn't matter what particular activity you like to do, why you enjoy doing it, or how minor or trivial it seems to be—just write it down.

3. Keep going until you have 25 activities. It may seem like a lot, but be creative and spontaneous. If you think of more, make the list longer.

4. Don't try to list the activities in order of ability or preference. Just write as fast as you can. (The example in Figure 1.4 shows a variety of activities.)

5. After completing the list, record your feelings about this exercise.

6. Jot down your reactions to the following questions: Did you notice any themes or connections between your ideas? If so, what are the similarities? Are there any connections that you might build on in terms of career–life planning?

7. How do you think this exercise will help you with your career–life planning process? Write your answers on your sheet. What did you learn?

PORTFOLIO

Add this exercise to your portfolio.

figure **1.4**   *Example of Exercise 1.2, 25 Things I Love to Do.*

25 THINGS I LOVE TO DO

1. Play my guitar
2. Read science fiction novels
3. Hike in the woods
4. Ride horses
5. Browse through bookstores
6. Save money for future investments
7. Organize social events

8. Tell jokes and stories
9. Visit friends and family members
10. Go swing dancing
11. Eat my favorite foods
12. Shop at the mall
13. Watch sporting events
14. Walk in the snow
15. Help other people
16. Fish with my friends

17. Drive my car
18. Sleep in on weekends
19. Attend classes
20. Research on the Internet
21. Play board games
22. Go to the movies
23. Listen to live jazz
24. Travel to new places
25. Run with my dog

I found this exercise . . .

Assessing Your Skills: What Are You Good At?

It is important to analyze your interests and passions as critical pieces in the career–life decision-making process. Perhaps equally important is an accurate assessment of your skills. (You may have the desire to be the next LeBron James or Kevin Garnett on the basketball court, but unless you have the necessary skills, it probably won't happen for you.) As with interests, if you are using your skills in a satisfying and productive way, you will likely find more happiness in your work. In other words, a "good fit" with both your interests and skills leads to greater fulfillment in your life.

Let's examine several different skill sets. First, look at *natural* skill areas. What are your natural gifts? Perhaps you have artistic abilities or mechanical skills. Genetics does play a significant role in terms of skill development. To return to the example of LeBron James, he no doubt is naturally gifted with exceptional athletic abilities. Granted, he worked diligently to develop those skills, yet genetics also played a major part in his rise to basketball stardom. You will have the opportunity to assess your own natural talents later in this chapter.

A second question to ask yourself is: "What skills do I want to use?" Think back to the previous discussion about working with *data, people,* and *things*. Of these three primary areas, where might your skills best fit?

If you use your skills in a satisfying and productive way, you are likely to find more happiness in your work.

Data: Skills include analyzing, organizing, computing, managing, assessing, interpreting, manipulating, investigating, and calculating.

People: Skills include teaching, counseling, selling, negotiating, persuading, public speaking, debating, caring, treating, and entertaining.

Things: Skills include lifting, operating, drilling, cutting, driving, loading, installing, removing, building, and constructing.

personal THINK PIECE

You are skillful. *What general skills do you see yourself using? There may be other skill areas that are not listed above. Feel free to include them in your answer here.*

_____

_____

_____

_____

personal THINK PIECE

Travel expert. *Maria is thinking about going into the travel industry. She is considering a training program in travel planning at her technical college. What three skills might Maria need to be a successful travel planner?*

1. _____

2. _____

3. _____

You may have some general ideas about what industry or business you wish to enter. It's also possible that you are considering several different industries. As part of your skill assessment, you should think about industry-specific skills. What skills are needed to be successful in a particular job? Do you have those skills? If not, can you gain them either before or once you enter that industry?

 your turn . . .

1. List at least one occupation or industry you are considering:

_____

2. Next, write down which of the three main directions (data, people, things) this industry best fits into (remember, it can be a combination of the three):

_____

3. Jot down at least five skills necessary to be successful in that work:

_____

_____

4. Do you have the skills to be successful in this occupation? If not, what might you need to do to develop or hone the necessary skills? Explain.

_____

_____

_____

_____

You Can Take Them with You: A Look at Transferable Skills

You may have read the career planning book *What Color Is Your Parachute* in which the author uses a term he calls "transferable skills" (Bolles, 2005). *Transferable skills* are those abilities that you can transport from one work environment to another. More specifically, they are skills that you can use in most job positions, regardless of the industry. These skills are learned both through formal courses, such as the ones you may be enrolled in at your educational institution, and through informal learning that occurs through life experiences.

If you are a student, you are currently honing your transferable (or portable) skills. Did you ever question the benefit of a certain written project?

Or did you ever pause to question the worth of that dreadful group work you had to endure last term? The good news is that you were developing your written communication and teamwork skills, respectively. Transferable skills are more important than ever in the new millennium, especially because you will enter numerous work situations throughout your lifetime.

Your Toolkit of Skills: An Overview

- *Critical thinking and reflection skills:* the ability to use higher-level problem-solving skills to address a variety of issues and dilemmas

- *Information management skills:* the ability to organize and synthesize data and other information in order to research, present information, and solve problems

- *Interpersonal skills:* the ability to get along with people, articulate your ideas, empathize with others' points of view, and be understanding

- *Techno-literate skills:* the ability to use the Internet, use the computer for basic skills, and communicate using technology (such as e-mail, fax machines, and so forth)

- *Communication skills:* the ability to write and speak effectively (including speaking in public) and to interpret nonverbal communications from others

- *Learning to learn:* the ability to learn how you learn best in a new situation, to adapt to new learning situations, and to be flexible and open to new information and learning methods. Also called *"learning agility."* (Eichinger, Lombardo, & Raymond, 2004)

Another portable skill is what we refer to as *navigational skills.* Navigational skills include the ability to become familiar with a new system in order to meet your objectives. It is the ability and resourcefulness to be able to "navigate" one's way through a bureaucracy or complex system. Navigational skills can be used in almost any daily life experience, including work. These skills are crucial as you acclimate to multiple new work environments in the future.

Finally, all individuals must develop solid *transitional and adaptation skills.* It is vital that you know how to manage your own transitions. You have to become flexible and learn how to cope with transitions in times of personal and professional change. Readers interested in transition management are encouraged to read *Managing Transitions* by William Bridges (2003). Transferable skills are invaluable to all of us for successful employment because they serve as anchors as employees change jobs more frequently in the future.

In today's marketplace, it is important that employees know how they learn best in new work situations. Feller and Whichard (2005) refer to workers of the 21st century as "knowledge nomads," or global pioneers (p. 48).

In addition to "learning how to learn," most knowledge nomads possess several additional abilities, including:

- abstraction
- systems thinking
- experimentation
- collaboration (p. 49)

Furthermore, several character traits are typical of knowledge nomads. These include comfort with being contract workers or temporary employees, comfort with ambiguity, lifelong learning, the ability to thrive on pressure, mobility, thirst or yearning for adventure, and a propensity toward entrepreneurship and creativity in work (Feller & Whichard, 2005, pp. 50–51).

In order to be successful in the workplace, today's employees need to develop and practice these traits. Consider strategies that help you gain these valuable abilities (e.g., internships, volunteer experiences, and work opportunities).

What Do Employers Want?

What do employers expect from you in terms of skills? According to the National Association of Colleges and Employers (NACE) Job Outlook 2005, employers want new graduates to have strong communication skills—both written and verbal. In fact, since 1999, communication skills have been at the top of the list (in 2005, communication was tied with honesty/integrity). Ironically, "communication skills" is the skill most employers say graduating college students lack.

Following are the most important skills/traits in order of importance:

1. **Communication** (written and verbal)

2. **Honesty/integrity**

3. **Interpersonal skills**

4. **Strong work ethic**

5. **Teamwork**

your turn . . .

1. What skills are your strengths?

   _____

   _____

2. What skill areas need some improvement?

   _____

   _____

3. What can you actively do to intentionally develop these skill sets? Think about specific activities such as internships, community service, and so forth.

   _____

   _____

   _____

You are encouraged to learn more about assessing your skills by completing Exercises 1.3, 1.4, and 1.5.

What natural talents do you have? This is a question that may best be asked in your teenage years because you are more likely to select the skills most natural to you rather than choosing skills you acquire through training and education. Your natural skills are the skills you were born with. They are the skills that you most likely use well and enjoy using most. Later in life, with education and training, you acquire additional skills.

1. Imagine yourself at age 13. Remember the activities you enjoyed doing most and the games you played. Did you love to play sports? Did you sing or dance? Did you enjoy spending time on a computer or solving puzzles? The answers to questions like these will help you assess the skills that come to you naturally.

2. On a piece of paper, title this exercise "Natural Talents." Write down at least five natural talents you have. What talents have you had since you were a small child? These should be talents you've always possessed—not ones you've acquired. For help, refer to *Your Natural Gifts: How to Recognize and Develop Them for Success and Self-Fulfillment*, by Margaret E. Broadley (1991).

3. Answer the following questions: How are you using your natural talents in your current work? How might you apply those talents to future career–life planning decisions? What skills or talents that you are not presently using could you use in the future?

Add this exercise to your portfolio.

1.4 | 12 Things That I Am Good at Doing

In this activity, focus on the things that you are really good at doing—your skills. This list should include acquired skills, ones that you have learned through experience or training.

The first work of the Artist is Herself.

—LAWRENCE G. BOLDT

1. Take a piece of paper and title it "12 Things That I Am Good at Doing."

2. Start by writing down what you do best. Your goal is to make a list of 12 things you do really well. Your list can be longer, but include at least 12 skills. Do not censor your thoughts. Write down everything you do well. (See Figure 1.5 for an example of such a list.)

3. If you have difficulty generating enough items, ask a friend, parent, sibling, teacher, or supervisor. Before asking, first make an effort to do it on your own.

4. Next, write down your reactions and feelings about this exercise. How do you think it may have benefited (or even hindered) you? Your feelings may be positive or negative.

5. If it is easier for you to do this exercise by clustering, please do so.

This is no time for modesty. In an interview situation, you must to be confident and comfortable discussing your skills and how you can contribute. Don't be shy or reticent about what you are good at. You have talents and abilities that are uniquely yours. Brag about them.

Place the results of this exercise in your portfolio.

figure **1.5** | *Example of Exercise 1.4, 12 Things That I Am Good at Doing.*

12 THINGS THAT I AM GOOD AT DOING

1. Riding and training horses
2. Telling interesting stories
3. Using the computer to find useful information
4. Playing the guitar and singing
5. Changing parts in automobiles
6. Organizing data and systems
7. Planning social activities
8. Writing short stories
9. Teaching others
10. Giving presentations in public
11. Cooking new dishes
12. Driving my sport utility vehicle

I found this exercise . . .

1.5   My Five Greatest Achievements

Another strategy you can use to assess skills and interests involves examining your greatest achievements. You used certain abilities to earn those accomplishments. By analyzing your achievements, you will be able to accurately assess what skills you possess. What is an achievement? It's an activity that gave you a sense of pride, a feeling of fulfillment. Where do achievements come from? Everywhere! Look for achievements at home, at school, on the job, through a hobby, or in a club or organization.

1. Title a piece of paper "My Five Greatest Achievements."

2. Describe five accomplishments in which you felt good about the outcome. Include the value or benefit derived from each activity. Here are some examples: helped my residence hall council reach its charity goals, improved the environment through active participation in the Sierra Club, helped serve dinner for the homeless, improved morale and production at my work site, and so forth. You get the idea.

3. Look for achievements from home, school, and community.

4. If you have worked, look for the work experiences that gave you real satisfaction.

   - Concentrate on specific projects. Spend some time writing out the details.

   - Include percentages, numbers, dollars, and dates. You want to quantify your accomplishments whenever possible. This activity will also help when it comes time to create your resume.

   - Use action verbs; be explicit.

   Place the results of this exercise in your portfolio.

After completing the exercise, record your feelings about this activity here.

_____

_____

_____

_____

_____

_____

_____

_____

_____

Values Assessment: What Is Important to You?

Why might it be important to examine values in this process of self-assessment? A *value* is simply defined as "that which is important to you." We all have different values, and we are all driven by a different combination of motivators. Additionally, all of us have different lifestyle preferences. A *lifestyle preference* can be viewed as an integrated component of your value system. In this section, we will explore life and career values and lifestyle preferences.

Values. *Career counselor Howard Figler (1999) believes that "values are at the center of every career-related decision." Do you agree or disagree? Explain.*

_____

_____

_____

_____

Although there is no "right" answer to this question, we agree with Howard Figler. Values are at the center of every career decision. We place varying levels of importance on a variety of values, or qualities, that are important to us. As we make decisions about entering a particular career or changing positions, we inevitably return (whether consciously or unconsciously) to our value systems, personal systems that have been shaped and reshaped over our lives. We all have been influenced by a person, a situation, or perhaps a series of events. Parents tend to be powerful influences when it comes to shaping our value systems, as in the case of Caryn.

> *Career planning and management done without taking into account your life mission and values is work resting on a weak foundation.*
>
> —M. L. BURTON AND R. A. WEDEMEYER, *IN TRANSITION*

student profile

Caryn. Caryn is a sophomore at a small private liberal arts college. She wants to teach elementary education in the inner city. She has always been an outstanding student, and she loves the pursuit of knowledge. She values education and learning, and she wants to share both with young children in a challenging work environment. Where did Caryn acquire these values? She does not need to look far. Both of her parents are educators. Her father is the principal of the high school in her hometown, and her mother is an art teacher in the middle school. Caryn has been around education her entire life, and her parents emphasize the importance of a good education.

personal THINK PIECE

Exploring values: Impact of the events of 9/11. *Most of us remember the tragic events of September 11, 2001. About 3,000 people lost their lives as a result of the events of 9/11, and many people reported that the tragic day changed their lives forever. For example, a significant number of people said that they planned to make changes in their lives—including personal relationships and work/career decisions. Similar feelings have been inspired by the Hurricane Katrina disaster.*

Many people say that "doing work that is personally meaningful to me" is very important. They want to engage in work that provides them with a sense of meaning and satisfaction. How did the events of 9/11 impact you? If you do not remember the actual day, how do your parents or teachers talk about the day and its impact on them? How did the events of Hurricane Katrina affect you?

_____

_____

_____

_____

_____

_____

_____

_____

your turn . . .

Briefly respond to the following questions regarding values:

1. How important is it for you to do work that is meaningful?

   _____

   _____

2. What might you choose to do that would give you a sense of meaning and satisfaction?

   _____

   _____

3. If you were to list your top three to five values (things that you had to have in a job), what would they be?

   _____

   _____

   _____

Some individuals place a high value on money and material possessions. Others place a low value. The following anecdote depicts one young recent college graduate and her priorities.

I'LL TAKE THE RED ONE, PLEASE

A young female college graduate in engineering is searching for her first full-time job. She is in the final stages of the interview process. At the end of the graduate's last interview, the human resources representative asks the engineer from Stanford, "What starting salary were you thinking about?" The engineer responds, "In the neighborhood of $95,000 a year, depending on the benefits package." The interviewer says, "Well, what would you say to a package of 5 weeks' vacation, 14 paid holidays, full medical and dental, a company matching retirement fund to 50 percent of salary, and your own car, say, a black or red BMW Z3 2.3, depending on your personal preference, of course?" The engineer sits up straight in the chair and reacts instantly, "Wow! Are you kidding?" The interviewer quips, "Yeah, I am kidding, but hey, you started it."

Granted, we all like to be compensated for our good work. But there is more to the story, right? Money is one reason we work, but it isn't the only reason. For many people, in fact, the pursuit of money and material wealth is not even the primary reason for choosing a career, or for accepting a particular position, or for working so arduously. What might be other reasons?

A person is rich in proportion to the number of things he (she) can do without.

—HENRY DAVID THOREAU

In responding to this question, consider what is most important to you in terms of work. Again, your personal value system will influence how you make career–life decisions. Work values that may be given the most attention could include creativity, independence, prestige, salary, and stability. Keep in mind that each individual is motivated by different factors. It is important that you give considerable thought to what is important to you. Not surprisingly, if you have a clear idea about your own value system, you will make future decisions more confidently.

personal **THINK PIECE**

What motivates you? *Take three minutes to respond in writing to the following question: What motivates you (other than the money and the $30,000 red car)? Realize that there are no right or wrong responses to this question.*

_____

_____

_____

_____

Taking a Look at Lifestyle Preferences

In the previous section, we discussed values as they relate to work and career. It is also important to explore lifestyle preferences, or nonwork issues. However, be careful not to view "work" issues separately from "nonwork" issues. *HIRED!* takes a holistic approach to career–life planning and acknowledges that all issues are interrelated.

Lifestyle preferences can include whether or not you want to travel as part of your job.

Lifestyle preferences include the type of residence you have, the size of the place (city versus rural) where you live, the possessions you own, the climate in your part of the country, the community activities you participate in, and other aspects of your life. Your lifestyle preferences may affect the type of job you have and vice versa. Let's take a closer look at one of the lifestyle preferences mentioned—where you live. In other words, geography matters!

Your preferences regarding where you want to live are extremely important, and young people are making this important lifestyle decision. Consider a recent study on creative, young knowledge workers, whom economist Richard Florida (2002) refers to as the "creative class."

Over 40 million people work in the "creative" sector. This includes professions fueled by innovation such as education, science, business, the arts, and health care, to name a few. Many of these individuals choose to live in cities and urban areas that value individuality, creativity, tolerance (including lifestyle choices regarding sexual orientation), and artistic expression. According to Florida (2002), individuals in the creative class tend to move to geographic areas, known as creative centers or creative hubs, that embrace and foster these traits. Examples include Boston, Seattle, San Francisco, Austin, and Minneapolis–St. Paul as well as other national and international (e.g., Dublin, Toronto, and Sydney) creative hubs. Many individuals are also choosing a more mobile lifestyle.

It is important to consider where you live. In other words, place matters.

personal **THINK PIECE**

Oh, the places I could go. *Do you agree with the perspective that the first element of career happiness is geography? Explain. In terms of geography preference, where do you see yourself living and working in the future? Use the space below to write down your preferences.*

_____

_____

_____

You are encouraged to explore other lifestyle variables by doing the exercises throughout this textbook.

1.6 Values Clarification

How do you determine what values are most important to you? You have already had the chance to complete a short inventory on lifestyle preferences. Another strategy is to do a values clarification exercise in which you assess each value in terms of its importance to you.

1. Take a piece of paper and title it "Values Clarification." Place it lengthwise. At the top margin, from left to right, write "ALWAYS VALUED," "OFTEN VALUED," "SOMETIMES VALUED," "SELDOM VALUED," and "NEVER VALUED." Each title should have its own column.

2. Your task is to assess each value presented below and write it under the title that seems most appropriate to you.

3. Go through the list value by value until all have been entered in the columns according to your personal value system.

LIST OF VALUES: WHAT DOES EACH MEAN TO YOU IN TERMS OF YOUR VALUES?

Accomplishment	Safety	Aesthetics	Cooperation	Travel
Developing New Skills	Education	Economic Return	Environment	Family
Working Outdoors	Health	Helping Others	Independence	Integrity
Community Service	Loyalty	Management	Pleasure	Power
Persuading Others	Prestige	Recognition	Teamwork	Spirituality
Raising a Family	Security	Having a Partner	Physical Fitness	Adventure
Supervising Others	Status	Ethics/Morality	Artistic Creativity	Fame
Working w/ tools	Variety	Leisure Time	Material Wealth	Religion
Intellectual Stimulation	Respect	Challenge	Honesty	Comfort
Personal Appearance	Organization	Productivity	Time to Yourself	Patriotism
Entertaining Others	Opportunity	Freedom	Advancement	

Include other values not listed that are important to you. Address the following questions:

1. Did any of your results surprise you? Explain.

2. Do you see these values changing in the future? Which ones? How so?

3. What themes emerge from your results (e.g., valuing security and structure over change and variety)?

4. How might this exercise benefit you in your career–life decision-making process? What did you learn about yourself from this activity?

5. In 25 words or less, write a brief description of your value system.

Good work! **Place this exercise in your portfolio along with the other activities you have completed.**

PORTFOLIO

Assessing Personality and
Work-Style Preferences

What work environment do you think would be ideal for you? Do you get energy from being around people or from finding more privacy? How do you best make decisions? All of these questions relate to personality preferences. Like interests, skills, and values, your personality profile is unique to you. There is no perfect or model personality type. In fact, the world would be an extremely boring place if all of us had identical personality characteristics.

To find out what is truly individual in ourselves, profound reflection is needed: and suddenly we realize how uncommonly difficult the discovery of individuality in fact is.

—CARL JUNG, PSYCHOLOGIST

Knowing your personality preferences as you progress through your lifelong decision-making process is important. Work environments vary tremendously. For instance, some work situations are extremely structured, while others are more spontaneous and fluid. Your personality preferences will help determine what environment is a good fit for you. In turn, your comfort level with the personality fit between you and the work environment will affect how happy and satisfied you are with your work.

There are many instruments used to assess personality types. The most commonly used instrument is the Myers-Briggs Type Indicator® (MBTI). You should consider taking the MBTI at your college career center or via a career counselor. A brief overview will be presented here, but this information should not serve as a substitute for the actual assessment.

The Myers-Briggs Type Indicator® is based on the psychological theories of Carl Jung. Isabel Myers and Katharine Cook Briggs, a mother–daughter team, constructed the instrument, which is a personality inventory based on how you fit along four dimensions:

- *Extroversion/Introversion refers to where you focus your attention.* In other words, do you get energy from being with others or from being alone?

- *Sensing/Intuition refers to how you prefer to take in information.* Individuals who prefer Sensing like to take in information that is tangible and real (i.e., through the five senses). People who prefer Intuition tend to take in information by viewing the big picture.

- *Thinking/Feeling refers to how you make decisions.* People who prefer the Thinking dimension examine the logical consequences and implications of an action or selection. Individuals who prefer Feeling in decision making tend to get others involved and make decisions based on compassion and empathy.

- *Judging/Perceiving refers to who one deals with the outer world.* Judging types prefer to live in a planned and predictable manner with a high degree of order. Perceiving types like to live in a more flexible and spontaneous way.

The MBTI scoring is based on a continuum for each scale, with an individual having a preference in one direction over the other on each dimension. The scoring results in a four-letter type based on the preferences (there are 16 different types). The assessment helps you understand how you function in different work environments, how you work, how you make decisions, and how you assimilate information. It does not measure interests, skills, values, or motivation to succeed. Nor does it directly recommend career fields or suitable occupations.

The MBTI is used for individual awareness as well as in team situations. Numerous organizations are using the MBTI to enhance teamwork in the workplace as they move to a team-based approach to projects.

| Where Can I Go for More Information about Personality Assessment? | The following resources can provide more Information about personality and work:

• *Please Understand Me: Character and Temperament Types* (1984) by David Keirsey and Marilyn Bates

• *Please Understand Me II: Temperament, Character, and Intelligence* (1998) by David Keirsey

• *Do What You Are: Discover the Perfect Career for You Through the Secrets of Personality Type* (2001) by Paul D. Tieger and Barbara Barron-Tieger

• Keirsey Character Sorter, www.keirsey.com or www.advisorteam.com

• Riso–Hudson Enneagram Type Indicator, www.enneagraminstitute.com

• Self-Directed Search, www.self-directed-search.com

Note: Some of the Web site assessments may require a fee to access, and links may change over time. |

How Does Personality Apply to Today's Workplace?

It may seem that we are belaboring the point of the changing workplace. However, it is worth mentioning again in terms of personality assessment. You will be entering multiple work situations in the future, and it is critical that you have an accurate understanding of your personality preferences and the work environments in which you will thrive.

The workplace has changed dramatically in recent years. We will address trends in more depth in Chapter 3, but consider here some of the developments in workplace environments.

- More and more employees are telecommuting; many work from homes or even from a ski lodge in the middle of the mountains.
- Work can be 24/7. Given the development of communication technology, many employees have a "virtual" office; they can work anytime, anyplace—day or night.

- Many workers don't have an actual office space. They are out in their respective fields attempting to serve their clients directly, on-site.
- Flattened organizational structures and smaller staffs result in more cross-functional teams.
- Many of an organization's services and functions are being out-sourced. Many individuals are working as independent consultants (free agents) or external vendors who sell their products and services to potential employers.

Another question that you should ask yourself is, "Do I want to work in a small, medium, or large organization?" Your personality preferences will affect how you answer that question. For example, if you seek a great deal of interaction with people and see yourself thriving in a structured work environment, you may opt to work in a larger organization.

In reality, however, the number of people seeking work in smaller organizations has increased significantly. For example, after 2005, 80 percent of the labor force will be working for firms employing fewer than 200 people (Cetron & Davies, 2003). Many young graduates will not be looking for employment at Fortune 100 companies, but rather at smaller and midsized organizations.

personal
THINK PIECE

Big or small? Office, home, or virtual? *Do you think you would be more comfortable in a small, medium, or large organization? Perhaps you do not want work directly for an organization at all, but rather want to be an independent consultant. Could you see yourself telecommuting or working in a "virtual" organization? Or do you prefer the advantages of having an office space at a place of work? Explain.*

_____

_____

_____

_____

Exercise 1.7, Work-Style Preferences, will help you assess your own needs and desires regarding your work situation.

Your work-style preferences indicate how and where you like to work. They can include the type of structure you like to work in, the size of the organization, the number of hours devoted to work, the type of environment, whether you prefer to work alone or on a team, the flexibility of your work hours, and so forth.

This exercise on work-style preferences will help you gain an appreciation of how your personality can influence the work environment you seek. For each statement, put a 1 if it is a factor you DON'T SEEK MUCH in a work situation; a 2 if it is a factor that you SEEK in a work situation; or a 3 if it is a factor that you SEEK VERY MUCH in a work situation.

_____ 1. Own office: Work in a setting where I have my own private office

_____ 2. Work alone: Do projects by myself, with limited contact with others

_____ 3. Set own hours: Have the flexibility to come and go as I wish

_____ 4. Work under pressure: Work under deadlines where pressure is common

_____ 5. Decision responsibility: Have to make significant hiring and firing decisions

_____ 6. Teamwork: Work on projects with team members

_____ 7. Working unplugged: Be able to work on a computer away from an office

_____ 8. Casual attire: Decide what I want to wear to work (within reason)

_____ 9. Uncertainty: Expect every day to be different; have frequent change in routine

_____ 10. Compensation: Have a stable rate of pay regardless of effort; earn no commissions

By identifying your most important and least important work-style preferences, you can focus on career directions, specific jobs, and work settings that suit your personal style. Almost as important, you will be able to eliminate those careers or work situations with which your style might conflict. As with all aspects of self-assessment, work-style preference is another piece of the overall career–life jigsaw puzzle.

 follow-up questions

1. What were the items that you indicated you "SEEK VERY MUCH"?

   _____

   _____

2. What were the items that you indicated you "DON'T SEEK MUCH"?

   _____

   _____

3. How might this activity on work-style preferences help in the decision-making process for a new job or a job change?

   _____

   _____

1.8 Analyzing the Holland Personality Types

John Holland (1997), a pioneer in the field of career development, developed a theory in which he described six different personality types: realistic, investigative, artistic, social, enterprising, and conventional. He theorized that each individual has a preference for one type over another. Individuals can have a combination of preferences that is called a theme. One example of a theme is SAE, with social the most preferred, artistic second, and enterprising third. Holland also generated personality code themes for occupations. Once you know your personal theme, you can gauge your "fit" with various occupations of interest. The Strong Interest Inventory (SII) is based on Holland's personality types. You can complete the SII through your career development center or a trained career counselor.

1. Read the descriptions below of each type. Rank the types from 1 to 6, with 1 being most like you and 6 being least like you.

2. After ranking the types, generate a code based on your top three rankings (i.e., rankings 1, 2, 3). This is your informal Holland code.

3. Now, go to your career center and inquire about computerized assessment programs, or take the SII. Obtain the results from either exercise.

4. Compare your own rankings with the results from the software program or inventory.

5. Address the Follow-Up Questions. **Place the results of this exercise in your portfolio.**

HOLLAND PERSONALITY TYPES: GENERAL DESCRIPTIONS

_____ *Realistic.* You like to work with things. You enjoy working with your hands and fixing things. You prefer things that seem real rather than ideas or concepts. You enjoy mechanical and/or athletic tasks.

_____ *Investigative.* You enjoy logical thinking and like to understand how things work. You like scientific tasks, mathematical problem solving, and research.

_____ *Artistic.* You enjoy art, dance, acting, and music. You appreciate creativity and free expression. You may oppose conformity and structure.

_____ *Social.* You enjoy working with others. You like to solve problems by talking about them. Your work with people often includes helping, counseling, and teaching.

_____ *Enterprising.* You like to lead people and are comfortable supervising others. You like to be in control and often thrive on competition. You enjoy talking, persuading, selling, and negotiating.

_____ *Conventional.* You keep things in order and appreciate rules and instructions. You tend to be good with details and are very careful and accurate with numbers, measurements, accounting, and so forth.

follow-up questions

1. What is your three-letter theme code? How does your personal ranking compare to the assessment ranking from the software program or inventory?

   _____

2. Were you surprised at any of the results? Explain why or why not.

   _____

   _____

3. Based on these results, what careers do you plan to research more thoroughly?

   _____

   _____

4. How did the results confirm what you already knew about yourself?

   _____

   _____

5. Briefly describe how you plan to use the results of this inventory in your major and career-planning process.

   _____

   _____

What Do You Bring to a Work Situation?

The final two areas of assessment involve *experiences* and *advantages*— what you bring to a work situation. This component of self-assessment often gets overlooked because individuals don't realize its importance when looking at work opportunities.

Experiences include anything in your past that you can use to market yourself. For example, many nontraditional students have many years of work and life experience that can help them in their job searches.

Monica is a 40-year-old mother of two who is returning to college to complete her degree in psychology. Prior to returning to school, she worked for over 15 years in a social service agency interacting with underserved clients in the inner city. Monica will market those years of learning experience to a prospective employer.

During his junior year, Mark decided to participate in his college's national student exchange program. He studied at an institution in California. During his experience, he met people from across the world. Mark gained a greater awareness of diversity issues and realized that he enjoyed working with diverse populations. During his job search, Mark should emphasize the awareness he gained through his exchange experience.

Experience is a plus. *What experiences have you had that you can bring with you? Think about how you might market these experiences in an interview. Attempt to name at least three.*

_____

_____

_____

You also bring **advantages** with you. Management consultant William Bridges (1994) uses the comparable term *assets*. An advantage is any characteristic, life event, or circumstance that you can use in your favor. It may not get you the job on its own, but coupled with other highlights in your portfolio, it will give you a leg up on the competition. Consider the following types of advantages:

- *Connections.* Knowing someone at a place of employment where you wish to be hired. For example, Julia has a friend who works in the human resource division of XYZ organization.

- *Ethnicity/Culture.* For example, Juan is a multiracial graduate student. He knows three languages and hopes to work with the growing Hispanic population.

- *Special Skills.* For example, Mike, who works in the hospitality field, is looking for a part-time job to supplement his income. Mike has played the piano for 20 years. He meets a colleague who is a member of a dinner club that is looking for someone to play piano on the weekends. Mike now has a part-time job plus the chance to network.

personal **THINK PIECE**

Advantage: You! *What advantages do you bring to a work situation? Think about special circumstances, skills, or life events that you could turn to your favor. Remember—the key is to market these advantages to a potential employer.*

_____

_____

1.9 | Chapter 1 Action Steps

Choose a job you love and you will never have to work a day in your life.

—CONFUCIUS

1. After reading through Chapter 1, how well do you think you know yourself— that is, your interests, abilities, values, and so on?

   _____

   _____

   _____

2. What steps can you take to get to know yourself even better?

   _____

   _____

   _____

3. Briefly outline two or three concrete action steps that you intend to take within the next few months.

   _____

   _____

   _____

   _____

   _____

4. What are the obstacles or barriers toward taking these action steps and meeting your goals?

   _____

   _____

   _____

   _____

   _____

5. What might you do to overcome these barriers? Identify two or three strategies that might work.

   _____

   _____

   _____

   _____

   _____

Summary

Y ou have thoroughly assessed your interests, passions, skills, values, personality preferences, and other variables. You have successfully completed your first significant step in finding rewarding and meaningful work. Next, you will have the opportunity to explore goal setting and decision making. You will have the chance to practice setting goals, including identifying potential barriers. Finally, you will be introduced to new decision-making models that will assist you.

REFERENCES

Bolles, R. N. (2005). *What color is your parachute?* Berkeley, CA: Ten Speed Press.

Bridges, W. (1994). *JobShift: How to prosper in a workplace without jobs.* Reading, MA: Addison-Wesley.

Bridges, W. (2003). *Managing transitions: Making the most out of change* (2nd ed.). Reading, MA: Addison-Wesley.

Broadley, M. E. (1991). *Your natural gifts: How to recognize and develop them for success and self-fulfillment.* McLean, VA: EPM Publications.

Burton, M. L., & Wedemeyer, R. A. (1991). *In transition.* New York: HarperBusiness.

Campbell, J., & Moyers, B. (1998). *The power of myth* (B. S. Flowers, ed.). New York: Doubleday.

Castaneda, C. (1968). *The teachings of Don Juan.* Berkeley: University of California Press.

Cetron, M. J., & Davies, O. (2003). Trends shaping the future: Technological, workplace, management, and institutional trends. *Futurist, 37*(2), 30–43.

Eichinger, R. W., Lombardo, M. M., & Raymond, C. C. (2004). *FYI for talent management.* Minneapolis, MN: Lominger Limited.

Feller, R., & Whichard, J. (2005). *Knowledge nomads and the nervously employed: Workplace change and courageous career choices.* Austin, TX: Pro-Ed.

Figler, H. (1999). *The complete job search handbook: Everything you need to know to get the job you really want* (3rd ed.). New York: Holt.

Florida, R. (2002). *The rise of the creative class: And how it's tranforming work, leisure, community, and everyday life.* New York: Basic Books.

Holland, J. (1997). *Making vocational choices: A theory of vocational personalities and work environments.* Odessa, FL: Psychological Assessment Resources.

Lusser Rico, G. (2000). *Writing the natural way* (2nd ed.). New York: Tarcher/Putnam.

Marriner, M., Gebhard, N., & Gordon, J. (2003). *Roadtrip nation: Find your path in life.* New York: Ballantine Books.

Marriner, M., McAllister, B., & Gebhard, N. (2005). *Finding the open road: A guide to self-construction rather than mass production.* Berkeley, CA: Ten Speed Press.

National Association of Colleges and Employers (NACE) Press Release (2005, January 20). Communication skills, honesty/integrity top employers "wish list" for job candidates. Retrieved February 15, 2005, from www.naceweb.org.

Palmer, P. J. (1998). *The courage to teach.* San Francisco: Jossey-Bass.

Palmer, P. J. (2000). *Let your life speak: Listening for the voice of vocation.* San Francisco: Jossey-Bass.

Charting the Future

GOAL SETTING AND DECISION MAKING FOR LIFE

learning objectives

learning objectives

1. To review your life line in order to acknowledge important people and events in the past, the present, and the future

2. To learn how to establish short- and long-term goals in your life

3. To introduce decision-making models and discover your preferred styles

4. To learn how to write affirmation statements as they relate to the three areas of your life—professional, personal/social, and financial

5. To learn how to visualize your future success

chapter

2

A goal without a plan is just a wish.

—ANTOINE DE SAINT-EXUPERY

student profile

Mai. Remember Mai from Chapter 1? Mai is becoming more confident in herself. During the last semester, she learned a great deal about who she is as a person. She identified some of her interests, abilities, and experiences. In addition, she started to think about what really matters to her, both in her personal life and her academic- and work-related lives. Mai is beginning to define her personal values and her belief systems; her self-identity as an emerging adult is starting to take shape. Also, she is starting to think more concretely about setting short-term and long-term goals for herself. Mai is making tentative decisions and working toward meeting those goals; however, she realizes that making important decisions is not always easy. It takes time and energy to decide what is relevant and what is not. Plus, she continues to get pressure about making those decisions from friends and family members.

In this chapter, you will have the opportunity to think more concretely about what is important to you! What values define you as an individual? Furthermore, like Mai, you will learn about goal-setting and decision-making strategies. You will learn about rational, planful approaches as well as intuitive strategies toward making decisions. And at the end of the chapter, you will have the chance to concretely set some of your own personal and professional goals that will guide you toward success in the future.

We should all be concerned about the future because we will spend the rest of our lives there.

—CHARLES FRANKLIN KETTERING, *SEED FOR THOUGHT*

Goal Setting: Planning the Adventure

Do you remember the last time you planned a trip? You may have traveled to an exciting, balmy destination with your family or friends. If you were actively involved in the planning for this trip, you no doubt put a great deal of effort and time into making it a reality. During the planning process, you likely mapped out places and people you wanted to visit along the way and scheduled certain activities based on your expectations for the journey. In other words, you created an itinerary for the trip. You probably did some research on the destination before you embarked in order to gain a better understanding of what you were to experience.

As with any planned event, there were likely several details of your trip that did not work out as expected. To compensate for the unplanned events, you made some adjustments and carried on with your trip. Some of these changes may have even presented unexpected benefits and pleasant surprises. In any event, your trip ended up being a learning experience in numerous ways.

Goal setting for your life and career is comparable to embarking on an adventure to an exciting destination. You need to plan carefully yet still be

Goal setting for your life and career is comparable to embarking on an adventure to an exciting destination.

flexible if you intend to meet your objectives. Research and active exploration are vital keys to success throughout the process. Also, you must make decisions at multiple points in your journey. This chapter introduces the concepts of goal setting, affirmations, and decision making. You will have the opportunity to apply these concepts to your own life through various exercises.

You decide how you want to live your life and how much time and effort you are willing to commit to acquiring the knowledge and skills necessary to achieve your goals. Goals require action if they are to become reality. When you think of goals, you may feel a bit uncomfortable if you are skeptical about their effectiveness. If you have difficulty motivating yourself to set goals, consider the obstacles these people overcame to become successful.

- Walt Disney was told that he lacked ideas, and he was fired from his newspaper job. He also went bankrupt several times.

- Jon Hassler, author, did not begin writing until later in life, and many of his stories were rejected initially.

- Beethoven's teacher called him hopeless because he preferred playing his own compositions to improving his technique.

- Rapper Eminem struggled as a young artist in Detroit, Michigan, before getting his first recording deal and making it big.

- Lance Armstrong overcame cancer in 1999 to go on to win seven consecutive Tour de France titles.

So relax, this chapter is designed to be enjoyable. It's a time for visualizing your success. This does require work, but it is creative work. Before beginning the exercises, consider the time you have to accomplish your dreams. Now, let's begin with a review of your life—past, present, and future.

Review Your Life Line

How many productive years do you have left? If we view every year as "productive," you likely have many years remaining in this lifetime. Let's begin by reviewing your life line. It's important to examine the past, the present, and the future. Most importantly, you should focus on reaching your goals of the future. Several hundred years ago, the average life span was less than 30 years. Today, it's 77 or more. Individuals will continue to work into their sixties and seventies—often in both paid and unpaid opportunities.

So the odds are with you. Hopefully, you will enjoy life much longer and more vibrantly than your ancestors. Examine the lives of the following people who contributed to society later in their lives:

- Einstein was 60 when he started work on atomic nuclear fission.
- Grandma Moses was in her seventies when she began painting.
- Van Gogh had numerous unsuccessful careers until he decided to become a painter.
- Famous aviator Amelia Earhart worked as a schoolteacher and career counselor prior to becoming a pilot at age 30.

Two themes emerge from these examples. First, what you initially decide to do with your life and career may change (and change can be a positive and welcome occurrence). Second, you still have time to achieve your goals. Time is most likely on your side.

Often, we learn from our mistakes over the years, and we can use this knowledge as we plan for the future. A life line allows us to look at our entire lives—past, present, and future.

Constructing a Life Line

In this exercise, you will construct your own life line. The life line will allow you to reflect on your life up to now as well as provide an opportunity to visualize your career–life in the years to come. Think back to your earliest memories as a small child. Your task is to write about the significant events, people, situations, and achievements that shaped you. Events can also include nonevents, events that you expected to happen but that did not for whatever reason. Often, nonevents are just as significant as events that actually occur.

Step 1. On a piece of paper, draw a line horizontally across the middle of the page.

Step 2. On the left side of the paper, write "birth"; on the right side, write "death."

Step 3. Starting with birth, indicate your earliest memories and what was most significant about each. Put an "X" on the line and jot down your thoughts above and below.

Step 4. Continue chronologically down the line until you reach the present. Significant events could include divorces, marriages, graduations, and reunions. Also, include any career changes or other decisions that affected your career–life up to now.

Step 5. Take a look at the future. What do you want to happen? Write down events, job titles, hobbies, and so forth that you hope will be part of your life in the future. You may wish to draw a symbol that represents your future life. For example, other students have used various symbols, such as a dollar sign or a bird, to represent their visions. One female student depicted a butterfly trapped in a net. She explained it in the following manner: "I know I want to fly like a butterfly, but I feel trapped because I don't know where to go." You may feel the same way. This same student said at the conclusion of the course that she felt "as if the net had been lifted" and that she now had a greater sense of clarity about what she wanted to do with her life.

Step 6. Respond to the following questions after completing the exercise.

 follow-up questions

Write your responses on a piece of paper.

1. What experiences, lessons, or events from the past have influenced where you are currently in your career–life?

2. Describe where you are presently. How are your current activities and plans preparing you to reach future goals?

3. If your life line includes a symbol of the future, describe what the symbol means to you.

4. What did you learn from this exercise?

File this exercise in your portfolio.

Strategies for Goal Setting

Goals serve as powerful motivators—especially as you chart your future life and career plans. Goals help ensure success on the job. The following statement by Ethleine Desir, a recruiter who works with job candidates, illustrates the importance of setting goals: "One of the most critical things in your career is to understand that it is your responsibility to know what you want and to write down your goals and how you will accomplish them" (Malone, 1997).

When you set a goal, determine whether it's a long-term (lifelong) goal, a midterm (one to four years) goal, or a short-term (a week to a year) goal. In this section, you will work primarily with long-term and short-term goals. Beverly Kaye (1997), organizational career consultant, recommends that individuals construct goal statements that are "SMART." The acronym stands for the following:

Specific: name the competency, project, position you want to accomplish

Measurable: yardsticks for assessing success are clear; you will know when you succeed

Attainable: the goal is relatively within your grasp, yet provides opportunity for growth

Relevant: the goal is in sync with the organization, industry, and profession trends

Time-bound: time frames and deadlines are stated and specific

Long-Term Goal Setting

Life goals provide the general direction for your life. They are the basis for setting all other goals. To use an analogy of a house, your long-term goals form the foundation that your life rests on. They guide you along your journey. Furthermore, they are used for all short-term goal setting and for all decision making. Consider the following three points when setting long-term goals:

- Long-term goals are your life's major goals.
- Long-term goals can be broad, general, and nonspecific.
- Long-term goals often have no set time frames because they are lifelong goals.

Review the following student profiles.

student profiles

Ricki. Ricki has always enjoyed learning. In addition to her formal education, she likes to read on her own (she has an affinity for psychological thrillers) and she keeps up with current developments in her career area. Ricki considers herself a lifelong learner, and she is eager to follow up on new innovations. Learning is one of her long-term goals.

Marcus. Marcus works in the area of wildlife conservation. He recently earned his two-year degree in forestry resource technology. As a child, Marcus loved being outdoors with his family. He especially enjoyed their camping trips. A strong environmentalist, Marcus has committed himself to preserving the great outdoors and considers this to be one of his lifelong goals.

You will notice that in both examples the long-term goals are general, nonspecific, and lifelong. Both Ricki and Marcus focused their goals on passions. They believe in their goals, and these goals serve as significant motivators in their lives.

personal THINK PIECE

Your lifelong goals. *What are the lifelong, long-term goals that you base your life around? Attempt to name at least three goals. Write your responses in the space below.*

1. _____

2. _____

3. _____

Short-Term Goal Setting

Your long-term goals should help shape your short-term goals, which are objectives that can typically be reached within a year. When setting short-term goals, consider the following characteristics:

- Short-term goals are specific, timed, and measurable.
- Short-term goals fit into the overall plan of your long-term goals.
- Short-term goals complement one another and move you closer to your long-term goals.

As you think about your own short-term goals, also look at how you intend to meet those goals. What actions will you take to meet your goals? It is critical that you have a plan.

For example, Adela, a returning adult student, intends to bring up her grade point average to 3.4 by the end of the spring semester (short-term goal).

She wants to maintain a competitive grade point average so that she can apply for graduate school to study history. Her long-term goal is to work in an academic setting. How will Adela meet her goals? She mapped out an action plan. In order to raise her grades, she prepared the following:

1. Use the tutorial services on campus
2. Study on a regular schedule in a quiet space
3. Visit the professor if I have problems with any of the material
4. Join a study group with other students in class
5. Get regular feedback on my progress

Adela clearly stated a specific, timed, and measurable short-term goal: raising her grades. She then established a detailed action plan to accomplish this goal.

personal **THINK PIECE**

What is one of your short-term goals? *Think about a short-term goal that you hope to accomplish within the next year. It can be related to work, school, or your personal life. In the space provided, write down your specific, timed, and measurable objective. Also, include five steps in an action plan that you could take in order to meet that objective.*

Short-term goal: _____

Action Plan

1. _____
2. _____
3. _____
4. _____
5. _____

Identifying and Overcoming Barriers

As is the case with most short- and long-term goals, there will be certain hurdles, or barriers, that you need to clear en route to fulfilling your objective. If you are able to identify the potential barriers ahead of time, you can plan for them—you can avoid the barriers, or at least be better prepared to manage them. Some barriers are real and others merely perceived, but all barriers are important to address because they may impede your progress.

Attempting to identify barriers at the time you set your goals can help. Granted, most paths to success don't follow a straight line. More often, the path to your goals will twist and involve diligent work. However, some obstacles can be identified with some foresight.

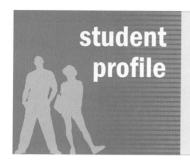

Candace. Candace wants to attend a professional psychology program. She intends to begin classes in the fall semester. Candace has been admitted to the program, which is the first step to reaching her goal of becoming a therapist. However, there is a significant roadblock in her way. She wonders how she will pay for expensive private school tuition. What should Candace do?

Candace successfully identified the primary obstacle: money. The second step to overcoming barriers is to explore resources, including support systems, to help manage the problem. Candace could investigate numerous options to help with her tuition costs, including the following:

- Looking to the institution for financial aid, including grants and scholarships
- Exploring off-campus national scholarship and award competitions
- Investigating organizations that would help pay off her loans
- Asking family members for assistance (if that is a viable option)

Ideally, Candace could use one or more of these options to help her with the high cost of tuition. By planning wisely—identifying the barrier (money) before starting classes—she has time to explore resources that could help her. With careful planning and some luck, Candace will be able to meet her goal of becoming a therapist.

personal
THINK PIECE

What are your barriers and resources? *Look back at the long-term goals you identified on page 45. Select the goal that is most important to you. Next, identify three potential barriers that could prevent you from reaching that goal. Additionally, think of three resources or support systems that could help you overcome the three barriers.*

Goal: _____

_____

Potential Barriers Toward Goal

   1. _____

   2. _____

   3. _____

Possible Resources to Help Overcome the Barriers

   1. _____

   2. _____

   3. _____

When you stand at a crossroads in your decision-making process, ask yourself, "Does this interirm goal take me closer to my major life goals?"

Rewarding Yourself

Be sure to reward yourself when you reach your short-term goals. Establish the reward at the time you set your goals so that you have a "prize" to strive toward throughout the process. You also may want to reward yourself for smaller accomplishments en route to the final goal.

Despite your hard work, you may not always reach your final goal. Evaluate your progress along the way. Perhaps you will need to reshape your objectives. Additionally, try not to punish yourself for not meeting the goal. Depending on your personality type, you may find it difficult to live with imperfection. Finally, remember that plans change. Be flexible and open to alternatives or new possibilities that may present themselves unexpectedly.

When you stand at a decision crossroad, ask yourself this question before proceeding: "Does this goal take me closer to or farther from my major life goals?" If your answer is closer to, continue on. If you answer farther from, rethink your decision. Reaching a decision is not an arbitrary process. There are numerous decision-making styles and, like personality styles, we all have preferences.

A Note on Goal-Setting Exercises

Refer to Exercise 2.4 later in this chapter. If you wish, that list of goals can be placed in your portfolio, which we will cover in Chapter 5. You will have a chance in Unit IV of this book to set long- and short-term goals for the different areas of your life.

Decision-Making Styles

How do you go about making decisions? What steps do you follow to reach a decision? Research on decision-making styles and how people make decisions has identified the specific steps that individuals use (or don't use) when making decisions. Lillian Dinklage (1966) identifies eight decision-making styles as follows:

Planful. A planful decision involves approaching a decision rationally. Thoughtful and well-researched, planful decisions involve a healthy balance between following the "heart" and following the "head."

Agonizing. This style involves much time and effort in gathering data and exploring options. The decision maker feels overwhelmed by the process and essentially "decides not to decide"—never reaching the decision point.

Impulsive. Impulsive decision makers often pursue the first option presented. They don't necessarily follow the age-old advice of "look before you leap." They make the decision without exploring other opportunities.

Intuitive. This style involves listening to one's intuition. Some describe it as following a gut feeling or listening to your heart to make a decision that "just feels right."

Delaying. In a delaying scenario, the individual does not want to face the decision for any reason. This style can be compared to the procrastinator—"I'll do it later."

Fatalistic. This approach involves no proactive effort. The fatalistic decision maker doesn't set goals to be reached. Instead, he leaves the decision up to fate—"it's out of my hands; I'm not in control of the situation."

Compliant. The compliant decision maker follows the advice of others without taking into account what she really wants. This is also known as dependent decision making.

Paralytic. The paralytic decision maker accepts responsibility for the need to make the decision but can't seem to move toward actually making it. She is "paralyzed" by the decision point.

Which decision-making style(s) can you best relate to? Keep in mind that we all use several different styles depending on the situation and the decision to be made. Explore the following exercise.

Given a decision to be made in your career–life, how do you reach it? Do you have a preferred style for making certain types of decisions? This activity allows you to examine your own decision-making style preferences. An understanding of your preferences will help you make decisions in the future.

Step 1. Take out a sheet of paper and title it "How Do You Make Decisions?"

Step 2. Think about a decision that you made within the past month. Describe it briefly. Write down the final outcome of this decision. It can be an academic- or career-related decision or an everyday personal choice.

Step 3. Address the following questions:

A. Which of the eight strategies described in the previous section did you primarily use when making this decision? Did you also use secondary styles?

B. What were some of the advantages of using the style(s)? Disadvantages?

C. How effective do you think this strategy is for making decisions? If you had to make a similar decision again, what would you do differently?

D. In what types of situations might the styles be most effective? In career and life decisions?

E. What did you learn from this activity?

Place this exercise in your portfolio.

Is One Decision-Making Model Better Than the Others?

It can be argued that the planful decision-making model is most effective for making academic, life, and career decisions—the types of decisions that have greater implications (as opposed to picking out your attire for the day). There are at least eight steps in the planful decision-making model. Ideally followed in a sequential manner, the steps include the following:

- Identify the decision to be made
- Gather information
- Identify alternatives
- Weigh the evidence
- Choose among alternatives
- Take action
- Review the decision and its consequences

The planful decision maker uses all of these steps. Individuals who use other styles, such as agonizing, impulsive, or intuitive, typically do not progress through all the steps. What steps might some of the other styles not include?

Planned Happenstance: A Nontraditional Approach to Decision Making

Is it really just luck? Do you ever notice how sometimes your well-intended "plans" do not go as planned at all? Or maybe something positive happens in your life that is "unplanned," but it leads to a wonderful outcome (e.g., new job, meeting someone new, etc.). In *Luck Is No Accident* (2004), authors Krumboltz and Levin refer to these unplanned circumstances as *happenstances*. Krumboltz and Levin argue that you can intentionally turn these happenstances into positive life and career choices. Planning is still a wise strategy. However, they suggest the following six strategies to make the most out of unplanned events in your life:

- Take advantage of unexpected disappointments (e.g., not getting your first choice of an internship but discovering another possible option that interests you).
- Be open to changing locations and occupations.
- Share your interests and experiences with people you meet (e.g., on a plane ride).
- Convert frustrations into opportunities.
- Realize that unplanned events result in more unplanned events.
- Make the job fit you.

According to the planned happenstance theory, five other traits, or strategies, are effective. Using these techniques, you can create "planned" occurrences in your life that will benefit you and your career. These strategies include:

- *Curiosity:* actively exploring new opportunities to learn.
- *Persistence:* moving forward with your goals despite obstacles.

- *Flexibility*: changing your attitudes according to the circumstances presented.
- *Optimism*: keeping a positive attitude and seeing goals as attainable.
- *Risk taking*: taking proactive action despite not knowing the outcomes.

 your turn . . .

1. Think about an event or outcome in your life that was not "planned" but turned out to be positive. How did that outcome happen?

_____

_____

_____

2. What action might you take in the future that could open up new opportunities—even though you don't know the outcome at this time? You will have a chance to do an exercise at the end of the chapter using planned happenstance as an approach.

_____

_____

Now that you have looked at the years you have to accomplish your life dreams, have studied the goal-setting and decision-making concepts, and understand the guidelines for setting goals and making decisions, let's look at life roles and balance.

Exploring Life Roles

Do you ever feel as if you are juggling several responsibilities at one time? If you are like most busy individuals, you are wearing multiple hats at once. At times, it might seem as if this juggling act is an overwhelming endeavor. In order to find balance with your many commitments, you need to establish priorities.

Donald Super, a career development theorist, believes that all of us have multiple roles that we play over the course of a lifetime. In fact, Super (1980) defines the term *career* as the combination of roles played during a lifetime and the pattern in which those roles fit together at a given time. He differentiates the term *job* from *career*. Super believes that a job is a combination of work tasks; a series of activities carried out in the worker role. On the other hand, he defines a career as "the integration of personality with work activities."

Super (1980) conceptualizes a life role theory that he depicts through a career–life rainbow. He believes that most individuals play a combination of eight roles throughout the course of a lifetime. These roles include the following:

Life without endeavor is like entering a jewel mine and coming out with empty hands.

—JAPANESE PROVERB

- Son or daughter
- Homemaker
- Student
- Parent
- Worker
- Citizen
- Spouse or partner
- Leisurite (what you do for fun and relaxation)

Many returning adult students fulfill the multiple roles of employee, parent, and student.

Super believes that individuals cycle and recycle through various roles throughout a lifetime. Which of the above roles do you assume? What are some other roles that you play? Additional options include lifelong learner, grandparent, and caretaker for an elderly parent.

Roles that you assume today may be different than the ones you will assume in the future. As you explore your life roles, you may find that you have a multidimensional career based on the many roles of your "career" as defined by Super. Instead of viewing your job as "physical therapist," you may see your life and career in a more holistic light. For example, your career could be parent/spouse/son/therapist/citizen. You have multiple roles that make up your holistic approach to your career–life.

Many individuals are assuming the role of returning adult student. The number of nontraditional students has increased significantly, as reflected in the list below. According to Super, they are recycling through the student role at a "later" time in life.

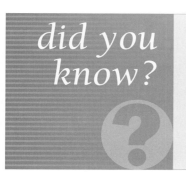

did you know?

- Students of Hispanic origin are the fastest growing racial/ethnic group at community colleges.

- 32 percent of community college students are 30 years of age or older; 46 percent are 25 or older.

Source: McPhee, S. (2004). *Hot programs at community colleges.* Retrieved February 16, 2005, from American Association of Community Colleges Web site: www.aacc.nche.edu.

Identity, Life Roles, and Decision Making: Emerging Adulthood

If you are like most students, you probably lead a busy life. You may be undecided about the big questions in life: work, love, faith, and other commitments—consider yourself normal. In fact, new research indicates that most young people are in a period of transition. In other words, young people are in a time of exploration before making long-term commitments.

If you are between the ages of 18 and 25 and are still undecided about what you want to do in life, you are not alone. Researcher Jeffrey Jensen Arnett (2004) calls this developmental period *emerging adulthood*. Individuals in this period are not adolescents any longer. However, most 18- to 25-year-olds are waiting to make "adult" type decisions such as marriage, lifelong partnerships, children, and commitment to a long-term job.

As Arnett (2004) states, this period is the age of *feeling in-between*, in transition, neither adolescent nor adult. It is a time of exploration, or identity exploration. Most individuals who are emerging adults are asking serious questions about who they are and where they want to go in life:

- What do I really want to do?
- What am I best at?
- What do I enjoy the most?
- How do my abilities and passions fit with the various opportunities available?
- Overall, what type of person do I want to be?
- Who do I want to spend my life with?

Are you in transition?

- Based on Arnett's description, what do you think of this developmental period called *emerging adulthood*? Does it seem to describe you? If yes, how so?

  _____

  _____

- What types of identity questions are you currently facing? What questions seem to be the most pressing for you at this time?

  _____

  _____

2.3 What Roles Do You Play?

SETTING PRIORITIES

You have an opportunity in this exercise to examine your life roles. Think about the many hats you wear today. Conflicts and stress often arise when balancing roles and life goals. To avoid major setbacks, it helps to establish a set of priorities from which to operate. One way to establish priorities is to review your life roles. This activity may be especially useful for nontraditional adult learners. After reviewing your roles, prioritize each, making the most important number one. Using a separate sheet:

Step 1. List all the roles that you have in your life (e.g., paid and nonpaid roles, student, daughter/son).

Step 2. Prioritize each role according to its importance in your life at this time.

Step 3. What roles are most important? Least important? How would you like this to change in the future?

 follow-up questions

1. What are the top three roles in your life currently?

   _____

   _____

   _____

2. What do you think your primary roles will be in 5 years? In 10 years? In 20 years?

   _____

   _____

   _____

3. How does this activity influence the decisions you might make in the near future?

   _____

   _____

   _____

Place this exercise in your portfolio.

The Power of Goals and Affirmations

We will next look at your long-term goals as they relate to the three major life areas. You will also have the chance to learn how to create affirmations and visualizations of what you want.

Long-Term Goals and Affirmations

To ensure compatibility (balance and harmony) between your goals, consider the three main life areas:

- *Area 1:* The *Professional* area.
- *Area 2:* The *Personal and Social* areas (cultivating meaningful connections with self and with others)
- *Area 3:* The *Financial* area

By examining each area, you can set goals that will provide a positive base from which to plan your life. Identify what you want to accomplish in each area. Keep in mind that goals serve you best when they are compatible and mutually supportive of one another. Ask yourself these four questions for each of the areas of your life:

1. What do I want professionally? What goals do I want in my professional or worker role? What kind of goals regarding job, education, employer, salary, and geographical area do I have?

2. What do I want personally? What are the goals that are important to me as an individual? These goals can be physical, mental, spiritual, or emotional.

3. What do I want socially? What do I want from interpersonal relationships? Family and friends? Personal relationships? Community, professional, political, and religious/spiritual involvement?

4. What do I want financially? What are my long-term financial goals? What does financial independence mean to me? How much available cash and personal assets would make me comfortable?

Writing Affirmations

Affirmations are the power behind your goal statements. Using the power of positive thinking, they help program your mind for success. Affirmations can have a significant impact on your positive thinking and mental attitude. It is important that you write out affirmations and state them verbally as you visualize meeting your goals. Following are several guidelines for writing affirmations so you can draft your own.

Affirmations should be:

- Mutually supportive, compatible, and in balance with your major life goals.

- Stated in personal form. For example, write: "I enjoy writing every day. Writing is fun for me."

- Stated in the first person. For example, "I weigh 128 pounds."
- Stated in present tense. See yourself accomplishing your goal. For example, "I am a certified public accountant," or "I am a college graduate."
- Stated positively. For instance, "I eat only healthy foods," instead of "I don't eat junk food."
- Written down. Your statements must be written down in order to be effective.

What do you visualize yourself doing in the future? What kinds of goals do you want to be striving toward in the long term? Now is your opportunity to visualize your plans. On a separate sheet of paper, record answers to the following:

Step 1. Write out your life goals, listing several goals for each life area.

Step 2. Visualize your goals. Once you establish your long-term goals, visualize them as having already been accomplished. Then, you can put power behind them by writing affirmations.

Step 3. Write affirmations to cover the three life areas: the Professional, Personal and Social, and Financial. "I am" statements, such as "I am prosperous," can be especially powerful.

Step 4. Say the affirmations. Affirmations must be spoken—and spoken often. Repeat them to yourself several times each day to help instill them in your mind and in your actions.

Place your long-term goals with their corresponding affirmations in your portfolio.

Reminder: Goals and affirmations should reflect your deepest values, your individualism. Program your mind for success by using the affirmations you create. Chart the effectiveness of this technique as you continue to move toward your long-term goals.

Cognitive Imagery: What Do You See?

Visualization, also known as cognitive imagery, is a powerful tool for reaching your goals. Read the steps below and follow through with the experiential activity.

- Take a few quiet moments to yourself. Sit in a comfortable position. Concentrate on your breathing.

- Imagine that the date is exactly five years from now.

- What are you doing? Try to imagine a typical workday.

- Visualize yourself doing whatever you hope to be doing in three to five years. Refer back to your long-term goals for ideas. Be creative.

- See yourself fulfilling those goals with complete success.

- Imagine your home life. Where are you living geographically? Is anyone with you? Are you in a big city, in a small town, or in the country? Are you in an apartment, a house, or another living arrangement?

- What is taking place in the varied roles in your life? Are you a student? A parent? A caretaker? A partner?

- What else is going on in your life?

After your visualization, spend five minutes writing spontaneously about what you imagined. Capture the ideas that went through your head. Use a separate piece of paper for this part of the activity, and **file your response in your portfolio.**

personal **THINK PIECE**

My next job. *What do you want to do? Only you can decide.*
After all of the exercises and planning, it's time to create your ideal job. You may wish to write a job objective, or you can be more subjective in your description. Imagine that you need to search for work today. What job or area of work would you begin your search with? Write your description below.

_____

_____

_____

_____

Remember to stay focused on your goals, but also remember to enjoy the journey. Often, we can get so involved with reaching our final destination in the future that we miss the joys of today.

Planned Happenstance: Creating Possibilities

Record your answers to the following questions on a separate sheet of paper and/or discuss with a partner or classmate.

1. Discuss an instance or decision that you made that was impacted by a chance event.

2. What factors may have led to a chance event occurring?

3. Did you do anything proactively to influence this happenstance? If yes, please describe.

4. What might you do in the future to create more chance events in your own life? Write down at least one or two ideas or activities that you can implement this semester/year. Examples of ideas: informational interviewing (to be discussed in more detail in a subsequent chapter), surfing the Internet, taking classes in an interest area, and sending e-mails to people who have similar interests.

5. Obstacles may stand in your way. Identify at least one significant roadblock in your path to meeting your goals.

   • How have other individuals overcome these types of roadblocks to action?

   • Is this obstacle temporary or permanent? How could you find out?

   • What concrete steps might you take to overcome this obstacle? Write down at least two or three steps or actions that you could take within the next year.

File this exercise in your portfolio.

2.7 Is This Really an Obstacle?

Overcoming Obstacles, Real or Perceived

Identify an obstacle (use the example from the previous exercise if you wish). Now, let's examine this particular roadblock more closely. Sometimes, obstacles can be real and permanent; other times, perceived and temporary.

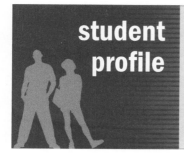

student profile

Mai. Let's return to Mai. Mai has some career anxiety because she feels that she "must make the correct decision now or it will be too late to go back." Is her obstacle real or perceived? It is certainly real for Mai. However, many career counselors agree that most of us will have multiple careers and jobs—and it is never too late to switch directions.

1. Write down the most significant career-related obstacle currently in your life.

   _____

   _____

2. How permanent is this career obstacle? (10 = definitely permanent; 1 = not permanent at all.)

   _____

3. How realistic is this barrier? In other words, if you asked five friends about this obstacle, what would they say? Is it possible that you perceive this block as being more overwhelming than it really is? *Hint:* Go ahead and share your obstacle with several friends or classmates, and ask them to rank it. (10 = very realistic; 1 = not realistic at all.)

   _____

4. What did you learn from this activity? Briefly describe your response below.

   _____

   _____

   _____

   _____

PORTFOLIO

File this exercise in your portfolio.

Summary

Congratulations! You successfully completed the work of Chapter 2, Charting the Future. You learned how to identify roles, set short- and long-term goals, write affirmations, and visualize your goals happening. In addition, you learned more about decision-making preferences and reflected on your life through the life line activity. You are now ready to move to Chapter 3, Researching Careers.

Enjoy your journey!

REFERENCES

Arnett, J. J. (2004). *Emerging adulthood: The winding road from the late teens through the twenties.* New York: Oxford University Press.

Dinklage, L. (1966). *Adolescent choice and decision making: A review of decision making models and issues in relation to some developmental tasks of adolescence.* Cambridge, MA: Harvard University.

Kaye, B. (1997). *Up is not the only way.* Palo Alto, CA: Davies-Black.

Krumboltz, J. D., & Levin, A. S. (2004). *Luck is no accident: Making the most of happenstance in your life and work.* Atascadero, CA: Impact Publishers.

Malone, B. L. (1997, January 30). Career cartography: A professional development plan just might be the most valuable tool for your career. *Equal Opportunity Career Journal, 28*(3), 24.

Super, D. E. (1980). A life-span, life-space approach to career development. *Journal of Vocational Behavior, 16,* 282–298.

Researching Careers

THE CHANGING NATURE OF WORK

chapter

3

The wrong job or work environment is like wearing shoes two sizes too small; it's deforming.

— UNKNOWN

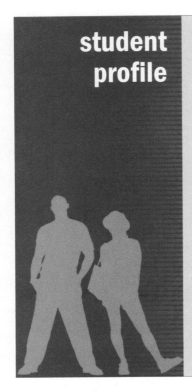

student profile

Mai. It is the beginning of the semester and Mai is starting to think more about choosing a major. In addition, she realizes that she should begin to consider different career options. Her parents are starting to apply some pressure on her as well. Mai decides it is time to take some action.

On one of the bulletin boards in her residence hall, Mai notices that there is a posting from the career development center on campus. In particular, the flier reads that there are several workshops designed for exploring major and career options. Furthermore, Mai heard from one of her friends that there are counselors at the career center who will meet with her individually. In fact, a friend from her business class met recently with a counselor to talk about internships for the following summer.

After reviewing her schedule for the week, Mai contacted the career development center and signed up for several workshops. She also decided to take an interest inventory to better assess her own interests. Finally, she scheduled a time to sit down with one of the counselors in order to talk about the decisions facing her.

The career development center on campus is an invaluable resource for all students—even first- and second-year students. Often, students wait until their senior year to explore the many career center resources; this can be a huge mistake. In this chapter, we will examine the changing nature of work and explore the many tools that you can use to examine career options—including the on-campus career development center.

Start exploring your career options as soon as possible. Career development expert and best-selling author Richard Bolles provides a basis for job and environment selection in his book *What Color Is Your Parachute?* (2005). He asks you to think of yourself as a plant and to consider in what environment you will thrive. He makes the point, "It is easier to make the environment conform to you, rather than you to the environment."

In Chapter 1, you had the opportunity to thoroughly assess yourself, including your personality and work environment preferences. In this chapter, you will continue on the path of self-awareness by examining the changing world of work and your place in it. We will build on the exercises begun in Chapters 1 and 2 and help you integrate these concepts into your career–life decision-making process.

You will learn how to use a variety of resources to research educational programs and career options. You will examine job characteristics and employer environments, and look at occupational trends and how they may affect you and your planning. The exercises in this chapter will facilitate your self-discovery process, helping you make choices that match you with your work.

The Value of Doing Research

Most of you have engaged in some form of research in the past. Perhaps you had to do a research project for class or an assignment at work. Obviously, the purpose of your research was to find out more information, to gain more knowledge so that you could reach some objective or make some decision. Similarly, you should do extensive occupational research so that you have adequate information on which to base your future career-related decisions.

The time and energy you put into honing your occupational research skills now will benefit you throughout your life.

Unfortunately, many individuals do not conduct the active research needed prior to making life and career decisions. Ironically, many of us put more effort into planning for an exotic vacation or a big purchase than we do into planning for our own careers! We diligently research the travel guidebooks or consult the consumer reports, yet we don't go to the library or tap into the Internet to use helpful occupational resources to plan our own careers. That doesn't seem quite right, does it? Many people who do not actively engage in the necessary research process end up with regrets later.

A survey by InsightExpress, a research company, found that only 1 in 3 employed 20-somethings are happy with the current status of their career. Nearly half of 20-somethings in the workforce (48 percent) are not working in a career they envisioned in college. Four in 10 employed 20-somethings say that "knowing what they know now" they would have majored in something different when they were in college (Yin, 2003, p. 13).

What are your reactions to these results? Do you think the results might have differed if individuals spent more time figuring out their interests and skills as undergraduates?

Clearly, the importance of research cannot be overestimated. Furthermore, researching occupational information is a skill that you will use throughout your lifetime. The time and energy you put into honing your research skills now will help you make current decisions (e.g., choosing a major or a career direction) as well as help you with future life and career decisions (e.g., changing employers or deciding to retire). Remember—you will be changing careers and employers multiple times throughout your lifetime.

First, visit your career development center or a library. Here you will learn about the resources available for job hunters. You will use the Internet to explore options, and will investigate other methods of research, including informational interviews. These resources will provide you with specific information about occupations, such as job outlook, compensation, working conditions, and training or education needed. All of these factors are important when making work and employer choices. Your decisions inevitably affect your self-esteem, your work life, and your personal life—including your health. The exercises in this chapter supplement the comprehensive assessments that should be available through your career development center or library.

Check Out the Career Development Center

The on-campus career development center is a useful resource. The resources available are designed to help all students—including first-year students. If you have not had a chance to visit your career center, make it a point to visit soon.

Both a person's desires and her/his abilities need to be considered in finding the rightness of career. . . . most people often mismatch both areas.

—GUNN

Myth: Some students believe that a career development center is designed to help graduating students find jobs. This is simply not true. Most career development centers do not serve as "placement" centers. Instead, the primary mission is to help students prepare for lifelong employment by teaching them a wide variety of useful skills (e.g., interviewing, resume writing, and job search strategies).

If you are using this textbook in a career planning course, you likely know something already about the career development center on campus. Listed below are several resources that may be available to you. Explore the options.

- Workshops (job search skills, negotiating job offers, resume and cover letter writing)
- Individual career counseling with a career counselor
- Assessment inventories (i.e., to learn more about your interests, personality, skills, and value preferences)
- On-campus job interviews
- Panel presentations about specific career areas (e.g., what can you do with a major in history, philosophy, or art?)
- Graduate and professional school reference files
- Career and graduate school publications to help you explore your options
- Courses related to internships and career planning
- Student exchange programs
- Off-campus civic involvement options
- Access to alumni connections and other directories for contacts
- Internship and job opportunity listings

The resources available in the on-campus career development center are designed to help all students, including first-year students.

The list of services continues, but you probably get the point. The career development center exists to help you—the student. As one of the authors of this textbook

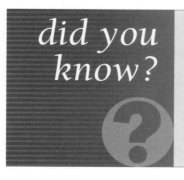

jokes with his students each term: "You inevitably pay for the career center through your tuition dollars and student fees; you should *definitely* use it since you are supporting it." The next section introduces assessment tools and other occupational resources to help you with your decision-making process.

Assessment Tools

The career development center or library may offer certain types of assessments. Some of these assessment tools are free, while others charge a fee. For a broader self-assessment, consider trying an inventory. Listed below are three inventories that may be available at your career center.

1. *Myers-Briggs Type Indicator® (MBTI).* This personal inventory was introduced in Chapter 1. You may recall that it measures personality preferences along four dimensions.

2. *Strong Interest Inventory (SII), 2004 Revision.* This interest inventory assesses your interests (likes and dislikes) according to Holland's six personality types, which were introduced in Chapter 1. Your responses are scored on basic and occupational scales. For example, Nichel is interested in being an engineer. He will get a score comparing his interests on the "engineer" scale to other engineers successfully employed in that field.

3. *Kuder Occupational Interest Survey.* This inventory, which compares your interests with the interests of others by field, can recommend many occupational fields and suitable college majors. Also, this inventory includes skills and values inventories.

Exploring Careers and Self-Awareness

Do your best to complete all of the exercises in this chapter. Several of the activities have to be done at your career development center or lab where computerized information programs are available. Others can be completed using the information in the textbook. Complete the exercises on separate pieces of paper, then file them in your portfolio where appropriate.

Occupational Resources

Computerized Career Information Delivery Systems

Computerized career information delivery systems (CIDS) are software programs that provide current information on occupations and the job market. They are designed to help you with educational planning and career decision making. Much of the information is built on the occupational categories found in the *Dictionary of Occupational Titles (DOT)* and combines information found in the *Occupational Outlook Handbook (OOH)*. In other words, the delivery system is a computerized *DOT* and *OOH* with additional features. (The *DOT* and *OOH* are discussed later in this section.) See a counselor at the career or workforce center for assistance.

Most states have a computerized database system that includes occupational data, self-assessment activities, and information about educational programs offered around the state and nationally. For example, the Career Information System (CIS) in Oregon covers at least 268 occupational categories, or about 95 percent of the employment found in the state and the major types of work found elsewhere in the country. The Micro-Skills program used in conjunction with the CIS program helps the user analyze 72 specific skills that are contained in various categories.

Locate this resource for your state. By using this program, you will learn the following:

1. Which skills you enjoy most and want to use in your work

2. Which occupations include the skills you enjoy using

3. Your Holland personality code as it relates to your interests (recall that the six personality types are realistic, investigative, artistic, social, enterprising, and conventional)

4. Which CIS clusters best match your skills

5. Which specific skills may cause you to be uncomfortable in an occupation you are considering

6. New information about several occupations that may be suited to you

Career and Job Reference Books, Compact Disks, and the Internet

Your career center or local library likely has the resources listed below, or comparable ones, in book form as well as on compact disk (CD). Review this list. Becoming familiar with each source will greatly assist you in your occupational search both today and in the future.

The Dictionary of Occupational Titles *and* O*NET

The *Dictionary of Occupational Titles (DOT)*, originally published by the U. S. Department of Labor in 1939, provides concise job descriptions for over 12,000 jobs. Although many counselors feel that the *DOT* is an overwhelming tool to use due to its complex coding system, it does provide relevant information about a wide variety of occupations.

To help users with the *DOT*, the Department of Labor designed an electronic version called the Occupational Information Network (O*NET). The O*NET database is billed as "the nation's new resource of occupational information" and includes an extensive data dictionary and database to help users with self-assessment and exploring occupations. The resource also reflects current changes in the marketplace. In order to access O*NET, point your browser to http://online.onetcenter.org. Students who want to learn how to use the numbering system in the *DOT* book version should consult a career counselor.

The Occupational Outlook Handbook

The U. S. Department of Labor, Bureau of Labor Statistics, publishes the *Occupational Outlook Handbook (OOH)* every other year. Because it is printed in a narrative format, most users find it easier to use than the *DOT*. The *OOH* describes over 250 occupations in 35 major industries, including descriptions of work, working conditions, employment statistics, training and other qualifications, job outlook, earnings, and a list of related occupations. It cross-references its job descriptions with the more than 7,000 job descriptions contained in the *DOT*. The *OOH* Web site is located at www.bls.gov/oco/home.htm.

A caveat: readers should be cautious when interpreting job outlook predictions. As is the case with any future prediction, the outcome frequently differs from what was initially projected. Outlook information should be used in conjunction with a comprehensive self-assessment involving information about the world of work.

Guide for Occupational Exploration

Often used as a supplement to the *DOT*, the *Guide for Occupational Exploration (GOE)* can sss an important reference tool when exploring occupational information. The United States Employment Service (USES) recently devised an interest inventory and checklist to be used with the GOE. The GOE is not used as often as the *OOH*, but you should ask about it during your visit to the career development center or library. A career counselor trained to use the GOE should be able to give you an overview of how to use the coding system.

Books on Corporations, Manufacturers, and Associations

There are many books that describe corporations, manufacturers, and associations. By understanding what's available in this category, you can easily research a specific company or organization, locating the names of officers, addresses, and general company information. This type of information is

The library and career development center house many books describing corporations, manufacturers, and associations. Many of these resources are also available online.

key for researching organizations. Following is a list of the most common reference books:

Standard and Poor's Register of Corporations, Directors and Executives. This resource has three volumes and is updated annually.

- Volume 1: Corporate Listings
- Volume 2: Directors and Executives
- Volume 3: Indexes

Thomas Register of American Manufacturers. This reference book is published annually and contains 21 volumes.

- Volumes 1–12: Products and services listed alphabetically
- Volumes 13–14: Company profiles
- Volumes 15–21: Catalog file alphabetized by company name and cross-referenced to the first 14 volumes

Dun and Bradstreet Million Dollar Directory. This directory lists corporations with sales of $1 million or more. It is similar to *Standard and Poor's Register of Corporations, Directors and Executives.*

Encyclopedia of Associations. This resource is your guide to over 25,000 national and international organizations.

Directories of State Manufacturers. Most career centers have listings of state manufacturers. If not, check the local library, chamber of commerce, or state economic development agency. If you are considering work out of state, it may be possible to view the directories from other states on the Internet or use the resource through an interlibrary loan program. For readers who are on a college campus, you can get career assistance at a One-Stop Career Center near you. Call toll-free, 1-877-US2-JOBS (872-5627).

Biographical Sketches of People and Careers. Reading biographical sketches of people involved in the organization you are pursuing can provide useful information. The *Who's Who* directories come in several volumes, each depicting a different category of persons. This reference contains biographic data on 72,000 influential people. Entries provide names, addresses, positions, vital statistics, education levels, family status, career and career-related activities, civic and political activities, and writings.

Readers may also want to look into the "Careers In" series of resource books published by VGM. This reference gives an overview of various career options in a particular area of interest (e.g., health sciences or working outdoors). Several texts provide real-life descriptions of individuals who work in the featured occupations. Examples of fun titles include: *Careers for gourmets and others who relish food* and *Careers for hard hats and other constructive types.*

Professional Associations and Trade Unions. Trade unions and professional associations can be a useful resource for administering training. Interested readers can access the O*NET database online at www.onetcenter.org or contact the One-Stop Career Center number listed earlier.

Other resources are available to help you with your exploration process. The ones just described were selected to give you an overview of the many options available. Given the advances in technology and the proliferation of the Internet, more and more job and career seekers are also turning to the World Wide Web as a resource tool.

Research Using the Internet

It is probably safe to assume that you are familiar with the Internet and the World Wide Web. Although Internet use did not become commonplace until the 1990s, it is now difficult to imagine life without "surfing the Net." The Internet is invaluable to most people—including those who access job and career sites.

The advantages of using the Internet as a career resource tool are numerous. What do you think some of the advantages might be? Write down at least three ideas.

1. _____
2. _____
3. _____

You probably generated responses similar to the following:

- Information is easily accessible. I can tap into valuable resources without leaving my home. (I don't need to spend countless hours in the stacks at the library.)
- Data can be updated on a regular basis.
- Many career sites are interactive and engaging.
- Most sites include links to other locations that have related useful information.

Clearly, using the Internet as one of your resources is a wise idea. However, you should heed certain warnings about using career sites on the Internet. What do you think some of those potential disadvantages might be?

1. _____
2. _____
3. _____

Warnings users should be aware of when using the Internet as a resource tool include the following:

- Information on many sites is not monitored, and any user can put up a Web page. Be critical when reviewing information—especially occupational outlook data because it may be inaccurate.

- Sites may include information that is outdated.
- On-site inventories and activities should not be substituted for the actual assessments. However, they can complement the work that you do in the career center or library.
- Web site addresses change frequently. For this reason, this textbook provides some addresses but not an extensive list. The bulk of the surfing is up to you. Now is your opportunity to do some research on your own.

The *Occupational Outlook Handbook (OOH)*, published by the U. S. Department of Labor, Bureau of Labor Statistics, is a helpful resource that you should familiarize yourself with. Your task is to embark on an occupational scavenger hunt using the handbook as a guide. Use either the paper version found in your career center or the electronic version found on the Internet at www.bls.gov/oco/home.htm.

Step 1. Gain access to the *OOH*. Review the table of contents and become familiar with how the resource is organized.

Step 2. Label a sheet of paper with the title of the exercise—"Using the *Occupational Outlook Handbook*"—and date it. **You will put this exercise in your portfolio upon completion.**

Step 3. After briefly reviewing the *OOH*, select an occupation you wish to learn about. Enter the title of that occupation at the top of your paper (e.g., physical therapist, carpenter, cook).

Step 4. Answer the following questions about your selected occupation:

A. Describe the nature of the work you would be doing.

B. Describe the work environment and conditions. Are there any physical demands? If so, explain what they are.

C. Describe the educational requirements. What is the necessary training? Will you need special training? A four-year degree?

D. Describe the job outlook. Remember, this is only a prediction for the future based on past and present conditions. What do the trends look like at this time?

E. Briefly include the salary, typical hours, and other benefits.

 follow-up questions

1. Based on your research, does this occupation interest you? What aspects are most and least appealing at this time?

_____

_____

_____

_____

_____

_____

2. What other career areas might you research?

_____

_____

_____

_____

_____

3. What are your reactions to using the *OOH* as a tool? How do you think it is most useful?

_____

_____

_____

_____

_____

4. Briefly describe how this exercise helped you with your decision-making process.

_____

_____

_____

_____

_____

3.2 Using the Internet to Explore Career Sites

You need access to the Internet in order to complete this exercise. Your task is to research a career site of your choice. You may need to use a search engine in order to come up with a list of possible links, or you could use the Web address of your career center and link into one of the sites included on its Web page.

Step 1. Choose a site that might help you with your greatest career needs. For example, if you want suggestions on how to write a resume, select a site with that type of information.

Step 2. Spend some time researching the site you selected. Your objective is to learn something new from this activity.

Step 3. Take some notes as you surf the site. Write down the site's URL. Feel free to link to other sites. If possible, print out the site's title page.

After you are done, complete the following questions on a sheet of paper and **include the responses in your portfolio.**

1. What is the name and URL of the site you selected?

2. Briefly describe what you learned from this site. How did it help you?

3. What type of career information did the site focus on (e.g., self-assessment, resume writing, and so forth)?

4. What are the advantages of this site? Would you recommend it to others who are doing career-related research? Explain why. What are its possible limitations?

5. What did you learn from this exercise? Explain.

Ideas to Get You Started	America's Job Bank, www.ajb.org
	Career Builder, www.careerbuilder.com
	CareerMagazine, www.careermag.com
	Employment Guide, www.employmentguide.com
	The Monster Board, www.monster.com
	Vault, www.vault.com
	WetFeet, www.wetfeet.com

Researching Career Training and Educational Options: A Key to Success

By now you have realized the importance of researching career-related information. Hopefully, you are becoming comfortable using a wide variety of resources, both written and electronic. You have used the OOH to determine what training you need for certain careers. Now, how do you go about selecting a major or training program in order to reach your goal? Here are two student profiles.

student profiles

Tamika. Tamika is a 33-year-old returning, nontraditional student. She is changing careers and is considering several training options at her local technical college. She knows she wants to go into the health sciences, but is unclear about her direction. Her choices include emergency medical services, medical assisting, dental assisting, and health information technology. How does Tamika go about making a choice?

Manuel. Manuel is an 18-year-old student at a large four-year degree-granting institution. His long-term goal is to become a successful lawyer. He is taking a career–life planning course in order to explore majors at his university. Manuel was told that he can pursue any undergraduate degree and still go on to law school, but where should he start? There are over 60 different majors at his school.

Although Tamika and Manuel have different career goals, they are both faced with similar decisions. They need to choose an educational option. *What do you recommend they do to get started? What would you do in this situation?*

First, Tamika and Manuel need to determine what they want from an educational program. In other words, they should set their own criteria for a good major or educational program. The second step is to determine whether the program under consideration meets those criteria.

For example, Takima knows that the program she selects must meet the following criteria:

1. The courses must be offered in the evening because she works during the day.

2. The program must be short-term (one to two years at the most).

3. The job outlook must be promising in her geographic area.

Manuel determines that his choice of major must meet the following criteria:

1. The undergraduate degree must be in a liberal arts area that will give him the transferable skills for law school (e.g., public speaking, writing skills, and others).

2. The degree must not involve a great deal of math (the thought of taking calculus makes Manuel feel suddenly ill).

3. The degree must be completed in four years.

 your turn . . .

Now it is your turn. What is most important to you when you consider educational options? What training do you need to meet your goals? Think about several options that interest you. Your task is to establish five criteria a program must have in order to meet your needs. Feel free to look back at the examples of Tamika and Manuel for ideas.

Establish at least five of your own criteria for choosing an educational program.

1. _____

2. _____

3. _____

4. _____

5. _____

By establishing your own criteria, you can rule out certain options while keeping others open for consideration. It is important that you ask yourself some key questions before embarking on a program. Use your research skills and seek out additional information about schools, specific programs, and departments.

Listed below are some questions that you should answer as part of your decision-making process. Some of these questions are similar to the examples of Tamika and Manuel.

- How long will it take me to complete the program?
- How many credits do I need to obtain the degree?
- Will previous credits transfer into the program (if returning to school)?
- Can the degree be completed on a part-time basis? Or is it full-time only? Evenings?
- Can requirements be completed through independent study or distance learning?
- How challenging is the program? How much does it cost per credit?

In addition to answering those questions, also consider some job-related questions when making decisions about educational options.

- What is the job market like for this career area in my geographic region? (This is especially relevant if you are looking at a specific vocational program.)

- How much money can I expect to earn in this occupation? What are the starting salaries in this line of work? (Consider the cost of living in your area.)

- What is the demand for workers in this occupation?

- Will this education be transferable if I want to continue my studies? For example, an Associate of Arts (AA) degree will likely transfer to a four-year university.

Choosing Your Academic Major

What's your major? Every undergraduate hears this question multiple times throughout the course of her or his undergraduate career. The question seems to have universal exposure. It's a question that is asked around the dinner table at family holidays and at social events across campus.

Is your academic major or program really that important? According to economist Thomas Harrington, your decision on a major may be the most important decision you make as an undergraduate (Fogg, Harrington, & Harrington, 2004).

So, how do you go about choosing a major? Listed below are five recommendations.

- Know who you are, including your interests, values, and skills as they relate to work.

- Talk to other students who are majoring in areas that interest you. Ask them about what they like and dislike about the major.

- Do some occupational research about what graduates do in terms of work options with their major at your school. There are a wide variety of Web sites and other resources to help you with this process.

- Gain some experience in the areas that interest you. Experience can be the best teacher. Find out what you like and what you dislike.

- Follow your intuition. Eventually, you need to feel comfortable with your decision (and your plans may change—that's okay).

Kathleen Mitchell, A. S. Levin, and psychologist John Krumboltz (1999) suggest that you look at this scenario from a different perspective. Rather than asking, "What is your major?" try asking: *"What questions would you like your education to answer?"* How do you want to use your education, and how can your acquired knowledge help answer the questions you might have about a certain area of interest?

did you know?

It's okay to be undecided . . . for now!

- Being "undecided" about your major and career plan is not that unusual. Government statistics indicate that approximately 40 percent of students change their major at least once. A record 8.5 percent of entering first-year students were undecided about their career choice in 2001.

- Choosing a major should be less about preparing for one specific career and more about preparing for many future options. Most of us will have multiple jobs and several careers in the course of a lifetime.

- *Cool majors:* Listed below are several specialty majors at several U. S. campuses. Explore them but proceed with caution. It is useful to look at societal factors and events that may influence major and career decisions. As you probably know, what is cool today might not be in a few years. . . .
  - Videogame development
  - Gaming/casino management
  - Tourism planning
  - Homeland security, counterterrorism
  - Disaster management
  - Sports sales

Source: Connors, L. L. (2004, October 5). Specialty majors are the rage on some campuses. *Christian Science Monitor*, p. 15.

Are there other questions that you should ask prior to making a decision? You may have special circumstances or needs that require special attention. For example, one of the authors works at an urban institution that serves returning adult students. These adult learners have needs that many traditional students don't have. Adult student needs include the following:

- Transportation and day care (many students are parents)
- The opportunity to take classes via independent study
- Accessibility in terms of class times and locations

personal THINK PIECE

I need answers. *What specific questions regarding educational programs do you need to ask? Think about special circumstances that might be unique to you.*

_____

_____

_____

We've already identified several resources to help you answer your questions related to career outlook. Many additional resources and strategies are available to research educational programs, including these:

- Talk with an adviser or faculty member in the program. Attend open houses and informational programs.

- Obtain and read departmental literature. Most educational departments publish information about degrees offered, services provided, and other aspects of their programs. Explore Web sites from the department.

- Attend informational meetings sponsored by your career center or other local organizations.

- Consider job shadowing a professional. Observe the day-to-day responsibilities of someone who currently works in the profession you aspire to.

You will doubtless discover many other resources, but this should provide a start.

This exercise gives you an opportunity to do some research on the Internet. The objective of this exercise is to use the Prentice Hall Student Success Supersite to locate information about educational majors. Follow the steps described below, and then answer the follow-up questions.

Step 1. Obtain access to the Internet. You can use your own computer or one on campus or in the public library.

Step 2. Log onto the Prentice Hall Student Success Supersite at www.prenhall.com/success.

Step 3. Follow the steps shown on the screen to get to the section on exploring majors.

Step 4. Start by selecting one program area of interest. Spend some time reading the entry.

Step 5. Select at least two additional programs of study. Feel free to take notes throughout the exercise.

Step 6. Review the other useful information on the site.

Step 7. Address the following questions and **file this exercise in your portfolio**.

 follow-up questions

1. What areas of interest did you research?

_____

_____

2. What did you learn from your research in this activity?

_____

_____

3. What interests you most about this area of study? What interests you the least?

_____

_____

4. Do you think you will pursue more information about any of the options you researched? Explain.

_____

_____

5. How do you think this exercise helped you with your decision-making process?

_____

_____

Managing Your Career: Preparing for Stable Work in Unstable Times

You do not need to be an economist to know that work patterns have changed in recent years. In fact, all you need to do is pick up the business section of a newspaper on any given day. There will most likely be at least one article about some company that has decided to cut costs by downsizing, laying off hundreds of workers at a time. It is safe to say that no one is "guaranteed" a job for life. Lifelong employment with a single company has become an artifact. Lifelong learning and the willingness to be flexible now take the place of the outdated "single employer" mentality, and many workers are embracing this new approach to work and career mobility. In fact, many workers are taking a proactive approach toward change.

In today's economy, most workers enjoy their work, but are not afraid to make a move to a better opportunity. Clearly, current workers are taking the approach that loyalty to one's professional development and personal happiness is replacing loyalty to a particular organization.

Ready for a Change?	Oh, how times have changed: "We used to say a job was like a marriage, Not now. These days a job is like a roommate. You share friendships, discoveries, plans, and then move on" (Dauten, 1994). Barbara Moses (2000) says that while we used to compare a job to a marriage, the new economy's view of a job is more like a date. There are pros and cons of both options.

In the past, the organization was responsible for your career development. If you were loyal to the company, they would make sure that you were rewarded with the appropriate promotion up the ladder. Today, employees realize that they need to manage their own careers; the organization is no longer looking out for them. This new model requires workers to be more proactive, flexible, and vigilant of their life and career directions. Many people are embracing this new philosophy, although others are not welcoming it with open arms. In short, workers have to learn how to be flexible as well as comfortable with uncertainty.

What Ever Happened to Good Ol' Loyalty?	In one study, employees revealed the following regarding loyalty and their current jobs: 55 percent don't feel a strong personal attachment to their companies, 58 percent don't believe their companies deserve their loyalty, 66 percent don't feel an obligation to stay with their companies, and 50 percent feel other jobs would be available to them if they left (Hymowitz, 2000).

Chutes and Ladders: Are They Gone?

Do you remember the board game Chutes and Ladders? We have all heard about "career ladders." As with lifelong employment with one company, vertical career ladders will soon be an artifact (if they are not gone already). Your career will most likely include more lateral moves than vertical ones. Many employees will need to consider changing organizations if they want to move into more prestigious positions. Granted, promotions will still come internally for the fortunate few, but significant vertical leaps to the upper levels will be less common.

Career consultant Barbara Moses (2000) writes about this trend in her book, *The Good News About Careers*. According to Moses, "new career patterns reflect this shift from the old straight-line career. Instead of a predictable stride up a linear ladder, people will zigzag between different kinds of work situations, continually redeploying themselves in new ways as their work changes. Instead of, for example, being a corporate lawyer working your way up to partnership in the firm, you may be a recruiter specializing in hiring legal professionals, a legal textbook writer, or a corporate treasurer" (pp. 213–214).

Moses (1997) compares this zigzag movement to a lattice: "There are no career ladders anymore. But neither are there any obvious images to describe the shape of the new career. Think of a lattice, perhaps, or a child's game of hopscotch, zigging and zagging along, or a game of move from side to side at least as much as you move up and down—not only in your work, but between other life domains as well, such as education, leisure, and volunteer work" (p. 119). In other words, you may have to move horizontally before you move up to the desired position (Moses, 2003).

You may be creating your own career, wearing several "hats" at one time as you assume various career–life roles. It is likely that many of us will return to school at some point in our lives either to complete a degree or to take a class for personal enrichment. In fact, there are more adult learners today than ever before. Clearly, this trend toward lifelong learning will continue. More importantly, lifelong learning—either in school or on the job—will be vital to your success.

Keeping an Eye on the Future: Workplace Trends

Technology and Trends

Advances in technology over recent years made some professions virtually obsolete. On the other hand, developments in technology created a host of new work opportunities that never before existed. Technological services proliferated since the Internet became widespread in the 1990s. This interest in and reliance on the Internet and technology resulted in a significant increase in small businesses within this sector.

In fact, many career futurists predict that a significant number of jobs have not yet been created. The job you will hold 10 or 20 years from now quite possibly has no title and is not in existence today. Consider the teacher who asked a young student, "So, what do you want to do when you grow up?" The astute student responded glibly, "It would be foolish for me to target a specific occupation at this time—there is a chance that the job I hold might not exist until years from now." This is another reminder of the importance of being flexible and having the ability to learn. Granted, we can't predict the future; however, we can make wise decisions about our careers by taking the time to explore trends, including technology and its impact on careers.

The Top Cutting-Edge Programs Added by Community Colleges	1. Biomedical Engineering/Biological Technology; health care programs
	2. Homeland Security (training for first responders, cybersecurity, security and protective services, and scientific programs)
	3. Internet Technologies
	4. Computer Networking
	5. Law Enforcement
	6. Multimedia

Source: McPhee, S. (2004).

Nursing, biomedical technology, and other health care programs are among the top programs being added by community colleges.

Warning: Proceed with Caution! Changes May Occur

We discussed some of the changes in the workplace in previous sections, including an increase in technological advances, a new revised model of career development, and an increase in job hopping with less loyalty to a single employer. In this section, we continue to discuss workplace trends and their effects on your career–life planning process.

A word of caution about occupational trends is called for here. Remember—predictions are simply predictions. They may or may not be accurate. Although it is useful to consider trends as you make plans, be careful not to place too much emphasis on them because change is inevitable.

Before you pursue a "hot" career area, consider your responses to at least two questions:

1. Do you have a genuine interest in the career? (For example, if you don't enjoy working with computers, you probably won't make a very good Webmaster.)

2. What happens if the trend in your area "cools"? Be sure your specific skills will transfer to other areas of interest.

The bottom line is: "Two small jumps are sometimes better than one big leap" (fortune cookie saying).

Occupational Trends Over the Next Decade

What trends have you noticed in the workplace? The *OOH* includes information about industry-specific trends as well as general national trends in employment. Revisit this valuable resource for supplemental information about work patterns and changes in the workplace. The statistics below represent current or likely trends. The information comes from the U. S. Department of Labor, Bureau of Labor Statistics and the *OOH*.

- Total employment is expected to increase from 144 million in 2002 to 165 million in 2012, or by 14.8 percent.

- Service-providing industries are expected to grow. The long-term shift from goods-producing to service-providing employment is expected to continue.

- Health care and social assistance—including private hospitals, nursing and residential care facilities, and individual and family services—will grow by 32.4 percent and add 4.4 million new jobs. Employment growth will be driven by increasing demand for health care and social assistance because of an aging population and longer life expectancies.

- Some of the fast-growing information/data–based computer-related industries are software publishers; Internet publishing and broadcasting; and Internet service providers, Web search portals, and data processing services.

- Personal care services will be the fastest-growing industry at 27.6 percent.

- Education is essential to getting a high-paying job. In fact, for all but one of the 50 highest-paying occupations, a college degree or higher is the most significant source of education or training.

- Among the 20 fastest-growing occupations, a bachelor's or associate degree is the most significant source of education or training for 10 of them.

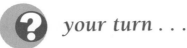

your turn . . .

- What conclusions (if any) can you make from the above predictions?

_____

_____

- How might these predictions impact you and your choices about work?

_____

- What is the value of a college education in the future workplace?

_____

_____

did you know?

Businesses Owned By Women of Color Growing Faster Than Overall Economy

- According to the Center for Women's Business Research, the number of privately held firms that are 51 percent or more owned by women of color grew by 54.6 percent between 1997 and 2004, while all privately held firms in the United States grew by only 9.0 percent.

- As of 2004, an estimated 1.4 million privately held firms are majority-owned by women of color and these firms employ nearly 1.3 million people and generate $147 billion in sales.

- Native American and Asian/Pacific Islander female-owned business has increased by 69 percent; African Americans by 32.5 percent; and Hispanic women by 63.9 percent.

Source: Center for Women's Business Research, www.womenbusinessresearch.org. Release date: 11/16/2004.

Other Trends That Will Impact Work in the Future

1. Baby boomer/Generation X/Generation dot-com demographics will impact work. Plus, there will be generational differences in the workplace (e.g., management styles). More people will make mid-life changes in occupations. One in three 40-somethings opt for a second career rather than head for retirement (Reynolds, 2004).

2. Safety, terrorism, and fears related to personal safety will persist (e.g., effects of terrorism).

3. Universal connectivity will continue to evolve. By 2010, all long distance calls, plus a third of all local calls, will be made via the Internet, while 80 to 90 percent of all Internet access will be made from Web-enabled phones, PDAs, and wireless laptops (Snyder, 2004).

4. Lifelong learning will be vital. Distance education will continue to grow. By the year 2014, distance education will be the primary method of instruction on college campuses, comprising approximately 30 percent of all courses, according to Snyder (2004).

5. Offshoring, outsourcing—jobs going overseas to other countries such as India—will continue. This will lead to greater globalization. Many other jobs will become automated. Jobs in our society will move from an information age to a conceptual age with an emphasis on work that cannot be replaced through automation (Pink, 2005). High conceptual abilities that rely on non-linear, right-brained functions will be highly valued in the future (e.g. helping skills, design, art, and others).

6. Project-based work and the use of temporary workers will proliferate (e.g., the use of adjunct instructors on most college campuses). Organizations are able to save on full-time salaries and the cost of benefits.

7. The boundaries between work and leisure will continue to blur. Work can be 24/7 with the use of e-mail, fax, and other technology. The globalization of most countries worldwide increases work demand and production.

8. Telecommuting will grow from around 15 million today to over 50 million by the year 2010.

9. Jumping industries is a popular job-hopping trend. For example, a systems analyst in banking decides to become an analyst in health care. Self-employment will be a primary choice of work for many younger workers, and creative workers will move overseas to pursue work opportunities (Florida, 2005).

10. There will be an increase in leisure and learning. Elder products, health and medicine to promote longevity, and activeness will be prominent.

3.4 | What Do Occupational Trends Mean for You?

So, what do all of these trends actually mean for you? Your task in this exercise is to analyze several of these trends and identify some implications. By giving some thought to occupational trends, you will better understand them and integrate the implications into your planning process.

Step 1. On a sheet of paper, write the title "What Do the Occupational Trends Mean for Me?"

Step 2. Choose at least three of the trends listed in this section. You may want to add trends that you've noticed to the list.

Step 3. Separate your paper into three sections, and list each trend at the top of a section.

Step 4. Answer the following questions for each trend. **File the answers in your portfolio where appropriate.**

A. What might be some possible causes of the trend?

B. What are some positive aspects of this trend?

C. What are some negative aspects of this trend?

D. How might the trend affect you as an employee?

E. What strategies or solutions could you use to address the trend favorably? How might it impact you?

Current Events and Reading as Planning Strategies

A daily newspaper is a helpful career resource that is often overlooked. Current events on any given day affect numerous industries and organizations. Reading a newspaper could help you gain a perspective on how these events influence workers in those areas. Here are several examples:

- In many metropolitan areas, the housing market is booming. Homes tend to sell quickly. What might this mean for someone who is exploring options in real estate appraisal, real estate finance, or real estate/property management? The Las Vegas, Nevada, area is one of the fastest-growing areas for new homes. What might be the implications for a carpenter who is looking for work in this geographical area?

- A student named Anne is taking a massage therapy course. She hopes to take advantage of a current trend toward "wellness" and "simple luxuries"—targeted toward the Baby Boom generation. What impact does demographics have on her business?

- Other current events and trends could result from layoffs, restructuring, or consumer behavior that affects spending habits.

personal **THINK PIECE**

Impact of events. *Think about one of the career directions you are considering. How might events (current, past, or future) affect this profession? Next, how does this make you feel about a tentative decision to pursue this career area (e.g., does it cause you to be hesitant)?*

_____

_____

_____

_____

Staying Current

- Read local, national, and alternative newspapers.
- Watch news channels and programs that deal with newsworthy events.
- Talk to people in the profession that interests you; develop a network.
- Belong to a professional organization related to your career interests.
- Read journals and publications sponsored by your occupation of interest.
- Read outside of your field; keep on top of current events.

Reading in Your Industry

It is crucial that you stay current in your chosen profession. This is true whether you are pursuing an advanced professional degree or are working in a technical trade area. By staying current, you can identify trends and perhaps take advantage of them. Consider embarking on a short research expedition regarding your area of interest. Find out the answers to the following questions:

- What are the main publications, journals, and newsletters in your area of interest? Begin your search on the Internet.
- What are some of the trends, issues, and topics mentioned in these publications?
- What other trends are you noticing? What are possible trends that may result based on the economy, popular culture, or other factors?

An Example of an Avid Reader	A colleague makes it a goal to read one book per week about new issues in his field of organizational development. He believes that reading publications and keeping abreast of current work in his occupation is time well spent. He also happens to do a significant amount of entrepreneurial work. In fact, many innovators and entrepreneurs spend approximately one-third of their time reading!

The Trend Toward a Multifaceted Career

In the days of our ancestors, work was often unpredictable and variable (sounds like the new workplace, right?). Due to unforeseen circumstances (e.g., droughts, natural disasters, migration), people did not always know where their next source of income would be found. To prepare for this uncertainty, our ancestors had to rely on multiple income streams. In fact, many of our famous historical icons, including Benjamin Franklin, had multiple careers at one time.

Some career counselors believe that we should return to this type of career–life planning. Our multiple streams can come from various projects within our primary profession, or they can be nonwork-related money-making ventures. Many individuals are turning hobbies into part-time entrepreneurial opportunities. This multiple income stream approach also provides variety for those individuals who thrive on constant stimulation in their lives. Other workers are developing "portfolio" careers, selling their skills and services to a variety of employers. In a sense, they are becoming contract workers, moving from one project to another. We will discuss portfolios in an upcoming chapter. Madu's Student Profile helps illustrate this concept of a multifaceted career.

student profile

Madu. Madu is going back to school to get her AAS degree in the travel planner program at her local community college. She wants to learn to market herself in several ways. Madu hopes to generate income from a variety of sources—all related to her interest in travel. She does not want the traditional 40-hour-per-week, 9-to-5 job as a travel agent in an agency. By following recent Internet trends, Madu learned that more and more travelers are bypassing the agent and purchasing tickets directly over the Internet. For this reason, Madu wants to identify supplemental ways to earn her living. She took out a sheet of paper and wrote down all of the ideas that came to mind. Her brainstorming list includes:

- Working as a part-time travel planner for an agency
- Writing a column for the travel section of her local paper
- Doing contract work for small companies
- Organizing business trips and private excursions
- Doing presentations at travel bookstores
- Offering a travel-related course for community education (e.g., "Journey to South America")
- Setting up a Web page and responding to travel-related inquiries
- Writing a book based on her extended travels to Argentina
- Doing individual consulting and trip planning

Madu's list could go and on, but you get the picture. She has options and so do you! The lesson to be learned for tomorrow's workplace: don't put all of your eggs in one basket!

What Might Your Multifaceted Career Look Like?

Imagine that, like Madu, you are preparing for a multifaceted career with income streaming in from multiple sources. What might your career look like in the future? Be creative here. There are no boundaries to your imagination in this exercise. Think about various ways to bring in income—work-related, nonwork-related, or a combination of the two. As with the other exercises, **include this activity in your personal portfolio.**

1. What job/career would be your primary source of income?

   _____

   _____

2. Brainstorm other ideas of how to diversify your career (use Madu as an example).

   _____

   _____

   _____

   _____

   _____

3. What are your reactions to this idea of multiple sources of income?

   _____

   _____

   _____

   _____

   _____

4. Find and talk to someone—a friend, family member, or colleague—who is practicing this philosophy. What is this person doing to bring in multiple sources of income? Describe below.

   _____

   _____

   _____

   _____

   _____

   _____

   _____

The Diversification of America's Workforce

The final trend to be discussed deals with the workforce becoming more diverse. Perhaps you are actively involved with groups on campus or in the community that help promote diversity awareness.

Diversity can be defined in a variety of ways. It involves an acknowledgement and appreciation of differences among all individuals, including differences in gender, age, race, ethnicity, religion, physical and mental ability, military status, sexual orientation, class, and educational level.

The workforce is becoming more diverse than ever before. The development of your "relational" skills—the ability to get along with others and to be culturally competent—has become even more critical than it was in the past.

Let's look at several trends relating to diversity. Think about how each might affect the workplace. Unless otherwise noted, the estimates come from the *Occupational Outlook Handbook* and U. S. Department of Labor, Bureau of Labor Statistics (2004–2005).

- By 2050, the U. S. population is expected to increase by 50 percent, with immigration accounting for almost two-thirds of that growth. About half of all Americans will belong to what are now considered minority groups.

- Only 37 percent of individuals with disabilities are employed. Many of these individuals believe there are no appropriate jobs available (52 percent) (U. S. Dept. of Labor, 2005).

- The U. S. Census Bureau estimates that the nation's foreign-born population in 2003 numbered 33.5 million, or 12 percent of the total U. S. population. The foreign-born population is comprised largely of young adults, with 45 percent between the ages of 25 and 44, compared with 27 percent of natives.

- Twenty-seven percent of the foreign-born age 25 and over had a bachelor's degree or higher education—not significantly different from the native population (*Foreign-born population reaches 33 million*, 2004).

- Based on current U. S. census data, over 57 million immigrants and their children (i.e., first-generation residents of the United States) comprise over 20 percent of the total U. S. population—the highest overall number in history.

- The Asian labor force and the Hispanic labor force are projected to increase faster than other groups—40 percent and 37 percent, respectively—because of high net immigration and higher than average fertility rates. The African American labor force is expected to grow by 20 percent, twice as fast as the expected 10 percent growth rate of the white labor force.

How culturally competent are you? Take the short survey by indicating your comfort level using the scale. The range extends from 5 = very comfortable to 1 = not comfortable at all. Respond to each item directly in this textbook.

_____ 1. How do you feel working with someone who is of a different race than you are?

_____ 2. You have learned that you will be working for a supervisor who is a lesbian. How comfortable will you be working with this person?

_____ 3. Your new manager is at least 20 years younger than you are. She is probably the age of your own children. How comfortable are you with this situation?

_____ 4. You share an office with a colleague who uses a wheelchair. How comfortable are you with this scenario?

_____ 5. During your evening shift, you are one of the only employees on the floor who speaks English. How would you rate your comfort level?

_____ 6. You are a manager at a prestigious firm. You recently learned that one of your new partners is HIV positive. How comfortable are you with this situation?

_____ 7. At your new job, you are responsible for supervising a group of employees. Your boss informs you that not many of your staff received any formal education and that some have difficulty reading. How do you feel?

_____ 8. You are an international student from India. You want to wear a traditional Indian sari (dress) to school, but you wonder how your classmates will respond. As the student, how comfortable do you feel wearing your traditional attire?

_____ 9. You overhear several colleagues making jokes about a new staff member's religious beliefs. You think that you should intervene and say something. How comfortable would you feel taking action?

_____ 10. You are a man who works in a field predominately occupied by high-powered males. Your new boss is a high-powered female. How does this make you feel?

Add up your total score on the cultural competence scale. How did you do? Analyze your responses for all 10 statements. There may be areas of growth and awareness that you could improve on in the future. Again, the lesson behind this activity is to illustrate the importance of embracing and celebrating differences in the world. The ability to get along with others, regardless of your occupation, is paramount and will continue to be so in the future.

File this exercise in your portfolio.

It is important that we not only acknowledge differences in the workplace but also celebrate them and make diversity work as an advantage, not a disadvantage. Ideally, the richness in backgrounds and perspectives should contribute to a healthy work environment.

Clearly, the world is getting smaller even though the total population is increasing. Read the short excerpt in the box below. As you read it, think about its implications.

A Summary of the World

If we could shrink the Earth's population to a village of precisely 100 people . . . with all existing human ratios remaining the same, it would look like this:

- There would be 57 Asians, 21 Europeans, 14 from the Western Hemisphere (North and South), and 8 Africans.
- 51 would be female; 49 would be male.
- 70 would be non-white; 30 white.
- 70 would be non-Christian; 30 Christian.
- 10 would be gay, lesbian, bisexual, or transgender.
- 50 percent of the entire world's wealth would be in the hands of only 6 people and all 6 would be citizens of the United States.
- 80 would live in substandard housing.
- 70 would be unable to read.
- 50 would suffer from malnutrition.
- 1 would be near death, 1 would be near birth.
- Only 1 would have a college education.
- No one would own a computer.

—Author Unknown

What does the "Summary of the World" excerpt mean to you? In your opinion, what is the message?

_____

_____

_____

_____

There is no right or wrong answer to this question. One interpretation could be that when one considers our world from such a global perspective, the need for embracing differences and understanding and appreciating others becomes alarmingly apparent.

Like our student, Mai, you decide that it is time to visit your career development center (if you have not done so already). Your task is to create an action step plan to visit the center, including a timeline with specific dates.

- *Goal #1.* I will go to the career development center: _____

- *Goal #2.* Include various resources you will explore at the center. Identify at least three resources that you want to check out. Review the activities and resources listed in the chapter. Examples could include meeting with a counselor, attending a workshop, using the alumni directories, etc.

  Resource A: _____

  Resource B: _____

  Resource C: _____

Finally, after you make your visit, jot down a few ideas about what you learned.

- What was the most important concept or insight learned from this activity?

  _____

  _____

  _____

  _____

- Identify other resources that you could explore at the career development center.

  _____

  _____

  _____

  _____

- What might you tell your friends or classmates about your visit?

  _____

  _____

  _____

  _____

Include this exercise in your portfolio.

Summary

We covered a number of significant concepts in this chapter on researching careers and options. Our review included resources to use in your search, with a focus on the Internet, as well as various strategies for researching educational programs and career interest areas. We addressed trends in the workplace, including changes in career development and specific occupational trends. The final section was devoted to diversity issues, the changing workforce, and its impact on you as an employee.

REFERENCES

Bolles, R. N. (2005). *What color is your parachute?* Berkeley, CA: Ten Speed Press.

Boyett, J. H., & Boyett, J. T. (1995). *Beyond workplace 2000: Essential strategies for the new American corporation.* New York: Penguin Group.

Connors, L. L. (2004, October 5). Specialty majors are the rage on some campuses. *Christian Science Monitor*, p. 15. Retrieved from ProQuest Newsstand database on October 29, 2004.

Dauten, D. (1994, October 19). It's time to face up to the reptilian economy. *Star Tribune*, section D.

Florida, R. (2005). *The flight of the creative class.* New York: HarperBusiness.

Fogg, N. P., Harrington, T., & Harrington, P. (2004). *College Majors Handbook: The actual jobs, earnings, and trends for graduates of 60 college majors* (2nd ed.). Indianapolis, IN: Jist Publishing.

Foreign-born population reaches 33 million. (2004, August 5). U.S. Census Bureau News. U.S. Department of Commerce: Washington, D. C. Retrieved October 10, 2004, from http://www.census.gov.

Hymowitz, C. (2000, January 2). Loyalty goes both ways. From Walker Information 1999 survey. *Wall Street Journal Sunday*, p. B1.

McPhee, S. (2004). *Hot programs at community colleges.* Retrieved February 16, 2005, from American Association of Community Colleges Web site: www.aacc.nche.edu.

Mitchell, K. E., Levin, A. S., & Krumboltz, J. D. (1999). Planned happenstance: Constructing unexpected career opportunities. *Journal of Counseling & Development, 77*(2), 115–124.

Moses, B. (1997). *Career intelligence: The 12 new rules for work and life success.* San Francisco: Berrett-Koehler.

Moses, B. (2000). *The good news about careers: How you'll be working in the next decade.* San Francisco: Jossey-Bass.

Moses, B. (2003). *What next?* New York: DK Publishing.

National Association of Employers (NACE) (2004). Retrieved on July 24, 2005, from www.naceweb.org.

Occupational Outlook Handbook (2004–2005). U. S. Department of Labor, Bureau of Labor Statistics. Retrieved on July 24, 2005, from www.bls.gov.

Pink, D. H. (2005). *A whole new mind.* New York: Riverhead Books.

Reynolds, C. (2004). Boomers, act III. *American Demographics, 26*(8), 10–11.

Snyder, D. P. (2004). Five meta-trends changing the world. *Futurist, 38*(4), 22–27.

U. S. Department of Labor (2005). Statistics about people with disabilities and employment, Office of Disability Employment. Retrieved July 24, 2005, from www.dol.gov/odep.

Yin, S. (2003). The road not taken. *American Demographics, 25*(9), 13.

Exploring Through Experience

LEARNING OUTSIDE THE CLASSROOM

chapter

4

learning objectives

1. To describe experiential education and discuss its importance

2. To explore various experiential options for students

3. To learn more about the value of internships

4. To help students make the most out of their learning experiences outside the classroom

5. To highlight the advantages of participating in a range of opportunities, including doing informational interviews as a strategy to meet people and explore options

Life is experience and experience is education.

—JOHN DEWEY

student profile

Mai. It is the beginning of spring semester, and Mai is starting to think about her plans for the summer. Some of her friends did internships in the past. Mai realizes that she needs to get some hands-on, practical experience in her field of interest. An internship opportunity over the summer is an ideal way for her to get that experience and allow her to keep exploring her options.

Mai is also thinking about studying overseas. She heard about a business study abroad program in London. It is a three-week program that starts right before the following fall semester. Mai decides that she will explore both opportunities—internships and study abroad options. She knows that the career development center on campus will help her find an internship. A friend informs her of the advising resources at the global campus office on campus.

In this chapter, you will learn about different strategies to get valuable experiences. Many of these experiences will occur outside of the classroom. For example, you will read more about the value of internships and begin the initial steps toward securing your own internship. All of the experiences outlined in this chapter are to help you learn more about yourself and to explore the many opportunities available to you.

One must learn by doing the thing; for though you think you know it, you have no certainty until you try.

—SOPHOCLES

In the previous chapters, we focused on self-assessment, goal setting, and job search preparation. We discussed the value of assessing the experiences and advantages that you have in your life. In particular, we talked about the importance of sharing your stories with a potential employer. As discussed in a previous chapter, some of your experiences in life are planned and others are unplanned. This chapter discusses how you can build planned learning experiences—experiential education—into your exploration process as an integral part of your learning. The experiences that you have as a student, and your life experiences, will help prepare you for satisfying work in the future.

personal **THINK PIECE**

Active learning. *What educational experiences have you had outside the classroom? Describe at least two experiences where you learned "by doing." It could be a part-time job or a related activity. Describe the experiences and what you learned below.*

_____

_____

_____

Learning Outside the Classroom

For some of you, learning by doing is your preferred way to learn. You will recall from Chapter 1 that we all have unique learning preferences. The valuable skill "learning to learn" means finding out how we learn best. Historically, learning occurred primarily in the classroom, with students dutifully ingesting information provided by the instructor. Perhaps not surprisingly, research indicates that many students learn best not in the classroom but outside in the "real world." Academic institutions have responded by incorporating more practical, hands-on learning into the curriculum. Students now have the chance to apply classroom knowledge to real-life situations. Your academic institution likely has numerous experiential educational opportunities available. You may be familiar with some of the options.

Below is a list of experiential learning opportunities often provided to students. Put a checkmark next to the options available on your campus. Put an "X" next to the options you have participated in. Don't worry if you are not familiar with one or more of the choices.

_____ internships/co-ops

_____ study abroad

_____ domestic student exchange

_____ volunteer work/community service

_____ work study

_____ part-time jobs

_____ research work

What other experiential options not listed are you aware of?

_____

_____

_____

_____

_____

_____

Studying Overseas

Get involved and see the world! More and more college students are taking the opportunity to travel and earn academic credit at the same time. There are numerous advantages of participating in a study abroad program. Students learn more about themselves as well as become familiar with another culture. In fact, a greater number of students are taking shorter trips to international destinations (although only about 1 percent of all students currently participate in study abroad options).

As reported by Teicher (2005), the Institute of International Education (2004) indicates that about 50 percent of students who took courses abroad in 2002–2003 did so for less than a semester. The programs tend to be short yet intense experiences, leading to personal growth and a greater appreciation of others. One advantage is that a short trip may be a good introduction to studying abroad. In fact, many students decide to do another study abroad for a longer period of time later in their undergraduate career.

Explore some of the examples of international study abroad programs (Teicher, 2005, p. 11):

- Journalism, geopolitics, and wildlife photography in Antarctica through the University of Delaware
- Tradition and change in China through DePauw University
- Screenwriting in Antigua through Ithaca College

A student of one of the coauthors, Kelly, went to London for a theatre program her junior year and then decided to travel to Ecuador during J-term of her senior year. She had a wonderful time, met new friends, and earned credits toward her business degree. Visit the study abroad office on your campus to explore the many options available to you. Here are two additional examples of students who decided to leave their home campuses and experience a new environment.

student profiles

Ker. **Study Abroad in Spain.** Ker decided to go to Spain her junior year to study the language and culture. While making her decision, she listed the following as advantages of participating in a study abroad program:

- Chance to study a new language and culture
- Chance to meet new people
- Chance to travel
- Chance to get away from the cold weather months of the Midwest
- Chance to get credit toward her majors in Spanish and history

(Continued)

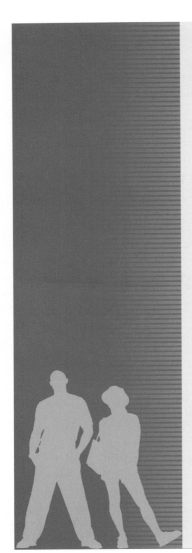

(Continued)

What are other reasons you would add for doing a study abroad opportunity? List them below. If you were planning to study abroad, where might you go?

_____

_____

_____

Miguel. **Domestic Exchange Program.** Miguel is planning to participate in the National Student Exchange program for a semester. Under this program, he can go to another school and pay in-state tuition. He decided to go to the University of Oregon to study history next spring term. Here are his reasons for participating in the program:

- To check out the graduate program in history at the University of Oregon
- To explore the West Coast
- To add some variety to his life
- To meet new people and learn how to rock climb and white-water raft

What do you see as other advantages of participating in a domestic exchange program? What colleges might you explore if you participated in this program?

_____

_____

_____

_____

Exploring Internships

In this section, we take a close look at internships—short-term work experiences that are usually in a student's area of study. Internships are familiar to most students. In fact, many students do at least one internship during their undergraduate years, while others take advantage of multiple opportunities.

Is an Internship in Your Future?

In the past, the best and brightest students on college campuses commonly did internships. According to Porter and Winter (2004), internships are becoming more prevalent among college students, including students in the liberal arts majors. A survey done by job search software company Experience, Inc. (2004) found that approximately 64 percent of graduating college students held at least one internship, 12 percent more than the previous year. The number of students who have held at least three internships doubled from 2003. What is the message here? Get involved with internship opportunities early and often.

Individual students are not the only ones taking note of this trend. Many academic institutions actually require students to complete an internship as part of their degree programs, including both small and large, and private and public institutions.

did you know?

The Time Is Now to Find an Internship. A study by Vault.com (Chatzky, 2003) found that 86 percent of college students have done at least one internship and 69 percent of students completed multiple internships. According to the *Job Outlook*, a survey done by the National Association of Colleges and Employers, HR staffing managers state that their own internship programs are the ideal sources of full-time employees among recent graduates. In other words, when organizations look to hire, they often look at student interns! So, what are you waiting for? Even if you are a first- or second-year student, now is an ideal time to start getting internship experiences!

your turn . . .

In your opinion, what are the advantages of doing an internship? List at least five below.

1. _____
2. _____
3. _____
4. _____
5. _____

Let's explore some of the benefits of internships in more detail.

Reality Testing

If you are buying a new car, you would test drive it, right? Likewise, if you are shopping for a pair of new running shoes, you'd try them on before making a decision. This is a reasonable expectation. It makes sense then that you would "test drive" or "try on" a career before making a commitment to it. An internship allows you to explore a career interest area and gives you the chance to answer the following questions:

- Is this line of work enjoyable?
- Can I see myself making a long-term commitment to this work?
- Will this work be personally fulfilling to me?
- Does it make use of my interests, skills, and values?
- Are the environment and culture comfortable?

Typically, an internship is a short-term arrangement with distinct starting and ending dates and no long-term commitment. Students can do some active reality testing and explore whether the career area is a good fit for them.

Applying Classroom Knowledge

Ideally, an internship allows you to apply theories and concepts learned in the classroom to the work situation. For example, psychology majors may be required to do an internship in order to graduate. The internship is done near the conclusion of the major program, giving students the opportunity to apply the psychology theories learned (e.g., abnormal psychology, social psychology, and others) to an actual setting. Many students, after the internship experience, comment: "Now this concept makes sense to me. I didn't understand it before, but now I do."

A positive learning experience at the internship site allows the student to take new learning back to the classroom. The transfer of learning goes in both directions (i.e., classroom to worksite, and worksite to classroom).

Helping You Enter the Job Market

Students have many reasons for doing an internship, but preparing for a job may be the most popular one (whether they admit it or not). Most organizations want students to have some type of experience prior to hiring them. The internship allows students to gain that exposure to the work world by learning about the organization's culture, how to interact with others, and how to be part of

A positive learning experience during an internship allows the student to take new learning back to the classroom; thus, the transfer of learning goes in both directions.

a team. For this reason, interning improves your value to a prospective employer.

You may have heard about other students who got full-time jobs through their internship experiences. Although we don't recommend that you take an internship solely for the purpose of getting a job offer, it is possible that you may get the chance to stay on with the organization. The statistics tend to support this trend:

- According to a survey conducted by the National Association of Colleges and Employers (NACEWeb Press Release 2004), employers report that on "average they extend offers for full-time employment to nearly 58% of the students who served internships with their organizations, and to more than 60% of those who have taken part in co-op assignments with them."

- Employers indicate that internship and cooperative education programs are among their most effective methods of attracting and hiring new college graduates. So, it pays to get involved in various learning experiences as an undergraduate.

The odds are in your favor. Get actively engaged in internship experiences. Try to avoid taking an internship in order to get a full-time job; however, if you do outstanding work, you may just receive an offer after graduation.

Honing Your Transferable Skills

Recall our earlier discussion in Chapter 1 about the workforce skills of the future and the value of having a variety of transferable skills. Depending on the experience, you should be able to foster those skills by doing an internship.

personal **THINK PIECE**

Portable skills. *Consider an internship that you have now or would like to have in the future. What transferable skills do you intend to develop during this internship experience? Generate at least five ideas.*

1. _____
2. _____
3. _____
4. _____
5. _____

Potential transferable skills acquired in an internship are similar to the skills employers are looking for in new college graduates. College graduates should have the following skills when looking for a full-time job: communication, honesty/integrity, interpersonal, strong work ethic, teamwork, analytical, motivation, flexibility/adaptability, computer, detail-oriented, leadership, and organization (NACE, 2005).

Why Do an Internship?

Timothy Stanton and Kamil Ali, authors of *The Experienced Hand: A Student Manual for Making the Most of an Internship* (1987), list several reasons for doing an internship. Some of their ideas overlap with the ones we have discussed:

1. *Employment.* During a tight economy with fewer jobs available, students with internship experience stand out in the job hunt. An internship can help you extricate yourself from the "can't get a job without experience, can't get experience without a job" double bind.

2. *Take charge of your learning.* Internships are important opportunities for you to design your own learning curriculum and get away from a classroom that may be frustrating you. Decide what you want to learn, how you intend to learn it, and how you will evaluate it.

3. *Theory into practice.* An internship can add more meaning to academic study by giving you the chance to apply theories learned in class to "real-life" situations. Find out if the world as described in your sociology course really exists.

4. *Awareness through increased community involvement.* You will develop an awareness of others' needs and a greater understanding of your role and potential contributions to society.

5. *Personal growth.* Yes, you will grow from this experience. It won't transform you into a mature, responsible adult overnight, but having to solve problems in unfamiliar situations can bolster your self-confidence and show you where you need work. (Stanton & Ali, 1987, p. 4)

From the Employers' Perspective: What Do They Get Out of It?

An internship is a two-way agreement. The intern benefits and so does the employer. Most organizations have an internship or cooperative education program. As noted previously, employers get the chance to check you out during an internship experience. It is a short-term commitment for you and them. If it works out, the organization may offer you a full-time job. Their internship programs serve as a pipeline of future talent. And they save money on recruiting costs if they develop a strong internship program for students. At the same time, you are checking out the organization to see whether this will be a good match upon graduation.

Make Sure Your Experience Is Educational

The internship arrangement should be mutually beneficial for both you and the organization. It should be a positive learning experience for you, one in which you gain valuable knowledge and skills that you can transport to new work situations in the future. You need to be assertive about what you expect from this opportunity at the outset.

Consider creating a learning contract to help you outline your internship objectives. This document serves as a communication tool between you, your supervisor, the organization, and your academic institution. It can also serve as an internship agreement.

Many academic institutions use an internship agreement that is divided into three components. First, students need to complete a competence statement, which includes what you intend to learn in an anticipated learning outcomes format. The second piece is the learning strategies section, in which you describe what you are planning to do (including practical and theoretical applications). The final component describes how you and the evaluator will review and document the learning.

student profile

Deron. Deron, a management major, is looking to do an internship at a human resources consulting firm. His interests are in industrial psychology and business. A portion of Deron's internship agreement follows:

Competence Statement: knows concepts and techniques of organizational consulting at a level appropriate for a graduating senior well enough to write and evaluate client plans.

Learning Strategies: (1) will observe senior psychologists in meetings with clients, (2) will assist staff with welcoming clients and preparing for assessments, (3) will apply organizational psychology readings from course work to internship responsibilities.

Evaluation: will have supervisor read and evaluate 10- to 12-page paper at conclusion of internship. Will keep journal and make two to three entries per week.

In this example, Deron would sign the learning agreement, as would his adviser at school and his supervisor at the consulting firm. The agreement signifies a mutual understanding of Deron's commitment to the organization. Finally, before Deron starts the internship, all parties involved should agree upon the number of hours to be worked.

4.2 | What Do You Want from Your Internship?

Following the guidelines discussed previously, think about an internship that you might hold in the future. Imagine that you have secured that internship for the summer. Briefly describe a competence statement, some learning strategies, and the evaluation method. This is good practice because you will likely need some type of agreement if you plan to get credit for your experience. You should always attempt to get academic credit for an internship experience.

1. Internship site/area:

   _____

   _____

   _____

2. Competence statement (what you hope to learn):

   _____

   _____

   _____

   _____

3. Learning strategies (what you plan to do):

   _____

   _____

   _____

   _____

4. Evaluation (how you will document and evaluate your learning experience):

   _____

   _____

   _____

   _____

Exercise 4.2 should have given you some good ideas for your next internship. Keep in mind that a learning contract or agreement is strongly recommended prior to beginning your internship arrangement. Make sure all parties involved have a copy so they can refer to it if necessary.

Exploring Other Experiential Educational Opportunities

Other experiential opportunities are available to enhance your education. These include community service/service learning experiences, volunteer work, part-time work, and research exposure. Depending on your academic program, opportunities could include technical or skills training (e.g., law enforcement), apprenticeships, practicums, clinicals (e.g., nursing), and other "hands-on" experiences.

Community Service and Volunteer Work

student profile

Aruna. Aruna is a first-year international student from Mumbai, India. She is interested in the health sciences and is looking to major in Public and Community Health. Aruna wants to volunteer at the children's hospital on campus because she is considering a career in medicine. Because there is a university hospital on campus, she does not have to worry about transportation. This opportunity will allow her to do the following:

- Explore a new career option
- Get involved in an extracurricular activity
- Help other people with medical concerns

What are other potential benefits of doing community service and volunteer work? (More on this topic will be provided in a subsequent chapter of the text.) List at least three ideas regarding community service and volunteer work that you could explore.

_____

_____

_____

_____

_____

Part-Time Jobs/Work Study

student profile

Josh. Josh, a sophomore at a local community college, is interested in business and tourism management. He works 15 hours per week in the cafeteria in his residence hall. He hopes to work there throughout college. The advantages of a part-time job for Josh include the following:

- Earns extra spending money to help with tuition and college expenses
- Meets new people in the residence hall
- Develops teamwork skills with other staff members
- Has unlimited access to cafeteria-style food

What are other advantages or benefits of holding a part-time job? List all that apply. What part-time jobs have you held? What ideas about part-time jobs do you have for the future? Some colleges and universities have work study options through financial aid. Check all your options.

_____

_____

_____

_____

Research Opportunities

student profile

Eduardo. Eduardo, a Hispanic junior at a private liberal arts college, intends to study molecular biology in graduate school, so he has decided to work as a research assistant for one of his undergraduate professors. He hopes to gain the following:

- Valuable research experience in the lab and preparation for graduate studies
- A strong letter of recommendation from the professor
- Knowledge that he can apply to his classroom studies
- Academic credit and the chance to apply for a research grant

What are some other benefits of doing research work? If you were to participate in research, what might you do?

_____

_____

_____

Informational Interviewing:
Overview and Exercise

It is important to begin to talk to people in the occupations that interest you. *Informational interviewing* is basically a career term that means "chatting with someone who works in an area you find intriguing." Participating in informational interviews is an effective strategy to start networking and building contacts.

Informational interviewing is included in this chapter, Exploring Through Experience, because this strategy is an effective way to experience a variety of work opportunities that might interest you. For example, if you are interested in physical therapy, consider setting up an informational interview with a physical therapist who works in a hospital or clinic setting. Informational interviews allow you to get an up close and personal look at what a certain job or career might be like on a daily basis. It is like a sneak preview of an upcoming attraction. You get to catch a glimpse of it before you commit to making a decision about a specific career path.

Portfolio experts Satterthwaite and D'Orsi (2003) believe that informational interviewing is an effective tool to help fine tune your portfolio (to be discussed in Chapter 5). You can bring a draft copy of your portfolio (including documents and artifacts) and get invaluable feedback from the person you are interviewing. For example, you could inquire about how a certain skill (e.g., teamwork) might relate to the type of work done in a particular industry or profession.

Informational interviews can lead to other unplanned events and circumstances. For instance, a good informational interview always ends with the question: "Who else might you suggest I talk to in this interest area of _____ (fill in the blank)." Referrals lead to other contacts and meetings with influential people who could mentor you along in some helpful way.

Conducting an Informational Interview

There are no concrete right and wrong ways to conduct an informational interview. Listed below are several suggestions and questions that you might consider when doing an informational interview. Develop some of your own questions as well. Before you set up an interview, do some research on the organization, and if possible, the person you will be interviewing. You can gain valuable information from organizational Web sites, newspapers, annual reports of the organization, and information located in your career development center (e.g., alumni directories, career guides, and other related sources). Examples of questions for an informational interview include:

- How did you get interested in this occupation or line of work?
- What is your educational background? What degree or training was needed?
- What do you enjoy most about your work? What do you enjoy least?
- What are some of the challenges you face working in this industry or job?

- What current trends impact the work done here?

- How might you suggest a college student get more involved in this field?

- What role did chance events or unplanned circumstances have in your own career? (This is not a classic informational interview question, but you might be surprised at what you hear. Most people and their careers are influenced by chance circumstances—whether they want to admit it or not.)

You get the main idea. Consider other questions to add to the list. Next, you will have the chance to conduct your own informational interview.

Most students who do informational interviewing tend to really enjoy it. In fact, once they become comfortable talking to people they do not know, they learn how valuable this strategy can be for networking purposes.

Your Task

The goal is to find and meet with a professional who currently works in a field you are considering. For example, if you are thinking about accounting, you could meet with an accountant—fairly straightforward, right?

This meeting should occur in person and should not be with a family member or close friend—you cannot interview mom or dad or even your best friend. *The challenge is to meet someone new.* It may be helpful to meet with someone who is similar to you in some way (e.g., race, gender, ethnicity, age).

The Project

There are several steps to this exercise:

Step 1. Find someone to interview. Begin by asking around. For instance, a friend might know a friend who works as a teacher, a nurse, or a baker. Ask to set up an interview. Tell the person you are enrolled in a career class and want to learn more about her or his career area. Most people are eager to talk about themselves and what they do. Other sources include the Yellow Pages, the counseling/career development center, the Internet, and employer directories.

Step 2. Set up a time to meet that individual in person. If possible, visit him or her at the work site. You'll get the chance to see firsthand what the work environment is like.

Step 3. Generate a list of questions you want to ask. The questions will help to guide you through the interview. The interview should be somewhat informal so your questions and notes should serve as a tool.

Step 4. After the interview, review your notes. Also, send a thank-you note or e-mail to this person to acknowledge the time she or he spent with you.

Reminder

This should be an interesting and fun exercise. Your objective is to learn the skills of interviewing and networking so you can build your own networks in the future. Your network can lead to new and exciting opportunities!

Other Strategies for Informational Interviewing

Finally, here are suggestions to consider when doing informational interviews. We shared these tips with students in a career planning course recently, and they found them to be helpful. Several of the ideas are adapted from Satterthwaite and D'Orsi's *The Career Portfolio Workbook* (2003), the authors who suggest that informational interviews be used in conjunction with your portfolio development.

- Contact individuals in advance and be respectful of their time. Most professionals are busy people with hectic schedules.

- Seek out friends of family members to interview (e.g., a neighbor who is employed in a field that intrigues you).

- Tell the person who you are (e.g., college student) and be prepared to talk about your interests and academic pursuits. You could tell them that you are enrolled in a career planning course.

- Outline specific questions you want to ask in advance and take notes of key points. Review these notes at a later date.

- Ask if there is at least one other person you might talk to in this field or industry. (*Reminder*: this is called "networking" — one of the most effective strategies to find relevant work and career opportunities.)

- Always write a thank-you note. A handwritten note sent within 24 hours after the interview is a thoughtful touch. You want to acknowledge the time the individual spent with you. Additional information about interview correspondence will be covered more thoroughly in a later chapter.

When conducting an informational interview, be prepared for the meeting: know what questions you want to ask, be on time, and look the part.

4.4 Crafting Experiments: What If?

What would you do if you wanted to learn more about a certain major, program, or career? One approach is to think reflectively on the decision and then plan accordingly. Professor and author Herminia Ibarra (2003) encourages us to *experiment more and think less*. What does that mean exactly?

She believes that the best way to experience a new idea or career interest is to intentionally "craft experiments" to test our tentative plans. If we have a positive outcome in this short-term commitment, then we can continue to move toward a long-term decision. Although her book, *Working Identity* (2003), was written for mid-career changers, the concept of crafting experiments is applicable to everyone—including undergraduate students.

According to Ibarra, "to craft an experiment is to act in order to see where the action leads. It is to ask the most basic question: 'What if?' Experiments come in many forms: Some are unintentional, others are conducted by design, some are exploratory, others, confirmatory" (p. 95).

 follow-up questions

1. What "experiment" might you craft for yourself this semester? Identify one or two different ideas and jot down your thoughts. You might consider several ideas discussed in the chapter.

2. What other ideas or interests might you explore as an undergraduate?

3. An internship is an excellent example of a short-term commitment to do some reality testing. Write down a couple of ideas or names of organizations where you might do an internship during the next year.

Your Action Steps: Establishing a Plan

The next step is to take action on some of the options available to you. What do you need to do next in order to find an experiential education opportunity?

Exploring Internship Opportunities

Like our fictional student Mai, you are beginning to think more about doing an internship in the near future. On a separate sheet, create a detailed action plan for finding an internship opportunity. Include several steps and a timeline to complete each step. Ideas for your plan may include:

- Types of opportunities you intend to explore.
- Where you will start your search.
- What resources you will use.
- Whom you might talk to in order to get ideas and support.
- How you will initiate contact with the organization.
- A timeline to accomplish these goals.

For example, you might identify the following goal: *I plan to talk to at least four different organizations about a summer internship by the time spring break ends (mid-March).*

A second goal may be: *I will secure an internship for the summer by the last day of the semester (before finals weeks).*

To get started, record five goals here:

1. _____

   _____

   _____

2. _____

   _____

   _____

3. _____

   _____

   _____

4. _____

   _____

   _____

5. _____

   _____

   _____

Now, create an action plan that is best for you. Good luck.

Place this exercise in your portfolio.

Experience as Part of Your Complete Education

It should now be evident that experiential education is a critical piece of your academic career. You outlined numerous benefits in the previous activities. An additional advantage is that your participation in such an opportunity makes you a well-rounded student. It shows that you went outside of the "academic walls" of a classroom to enrich your educational experience.

You should definitely talk about these experiences in your interviews with prospective employers. Try to become comfortable talking about your experiences, including what you learned from your involvement. What was the value of participating in that program, internship, or activity?

Be sure to include a description of your involvement on your resume and on any graduate school applications. Employers and graduate programs want to see that you did more than just attend classes and spend countless hours in the library. A strong grade point average is important, but in many situations, your involvement in campus activities, internships, and other experiential education options is just as relevant.

Summary

Is experience the best teacher? We believe that experiential education is a critical part of one's personal and professional development. We strongly encourage all readers to get involved in some form of experiential education opportunity. It will make your school experience more fulfilling as well as help you develop skills to help you in the workplace. In this chapter, we discussed the importance of getting an internship and participating in different educational options, and we also outlined how to make the most of those opportunities.

This chapter completes the first unit, Discovering Your Authentic Self. We are now prepared to take the next step to Unit II, in which you will have the opportunity to apply this self-knowledge and your understanding of the world of work to the job search process.

In the following chapters, you will learn the nuts and bolts of resume writing, preparing letters, networking, interviewing, and other important steps in the job search process. Best of luck to you as you explore the many educational options available to you!

REFERENCES

Chatzky, J. (2003, October 27). Interns, get moving. *Time*, 162(17), 82–84.

Experience, Inc. (2004, April 5). 2004 brings a significantly brighter job outlook. Retrieved on August 7, 2005, from www.experience.com.

Ibarra, H. (2003). *Working identity: Unconventional strategies for reinventing your career.* Boston, MA: Harvard Business School Press.

Institute of International Education (2004, Nov. 15). Study abroad surging among American students. Open doors: American students studying abroad. Retrieved on August 7, 2005, from www.opendoors.iienetwork.org.

NACEWeb Press Release (2004, December 2). Internships can be key to job offer.

National Association of Colleges and Employers (2005). *Job Outlook 2005*.

Porter, E., & Winter, G. (2004, May 30). 04 graduates learned lesson in practicality. *New York Times*, p. 1.1.

Satterthwaite, F., & D'Orsi, G. (2003). *The career portfolio workbook.* New York: McGraw-Hill.

Stanton, T., & Ali, K. (1987). *The experienced hand: A student manual for making the most of an internship.* Cranston, RI: Carroll Press.

Teicher, S.A. (2005, January 11). Brief forays offer lasting lessons to U.S. students: Short, tightly focused programs allow U.S. college students exposure to worlds they might otherwise never see. *Christian Science Monitor*, p. 11.

Creating
OPPORTUNITIES

unit

II

The Chapters

This unit is an activity of imagination and ingenuity. In Chapter 5, you begin to assemble a portfolio of information, illustrations of your skills and abilities, and documents of your involvement in activities. The portfolio development builds an outstanding tool for you to use in your goal setting, networking, and job interviews.

In Chapter 6, Connecting to Employers: Job Search Correspondence and Job Applications, you will package a source of power, the written word. Through letters and e-mail, you will build a support network, develop job leads, introduce yourself to others, and build new relationships. By learning to write powerful letters, you will open more doors to job leads and opportunities.

In Chapter 7, Marketing Tools: Your Resume and References, you will weave words that capture your true self and your abilities on paper. This process will produce a catalyst for your entire job hunt. By packaging your resume with focus and character, you will propel yourself into employers' offices.

Developing Your Portfolio

SELF-MANAGED CAREER PLANNING

learning objectives

1. To learn about the purpose and use of a portfolio in today's changing marketplace

2. To discover the different types of portfolios and how to use them in different situations

3. To explore the documents included in a portfolio

4. To learn about the benefits of using a portfolio, including the concepts of branding and portfolio thinking

5. To start taking action steps toward creating your own portfolio

Don't just express yourself, invent yourself. And don't restrict yourself to off-the-shelf models.

—HENRY LOUIS GATES, JR.,

COMMENCEMENT ADDRESS, HAMILTON COLLEGE

Mai. As a sophomore, Mai is becoming more involved in her education. She is starting to get more involved in on-campus activities. In addition, she is getting valuable work experience through part-time jobs, volunteer work, and other experiences outside the classroom. Maybe you are getting more involved in your education.

More and more students are starting to put together a collection of their experiences in a tool called a *portfolio*. A portfolio is a tool to help students like Mai gather pieces of evidence that document success inside and outside the classroom. Once Mai has her portfolio together, she can use it for interviews, informational interviewing, job performance reviews, and a range of other purposes. Having such a portfolio will give you and other students the confidence to succeed and meet the goals along your journey.

In this chapter, you will learn more about a portfolio and how to create one that reflects you and your accomplishments. Portfolio development is an excellent way to learn more about yourself and to begin the process of "marketing yourself" to prospective employers.

What Is a Portfolio?

You may have heard of certain professionals who profile their work in a "portfolio." Many individuals who work in the artistic professions (e.g., artists, advertising execs, and the like) use portfolios to showcase their work to prospective clients and employers. The portfolio is a vehicle or tool used to visually display previous work projects. The documents in the portfolio serve to promote or highlight the artists' skills and creativity. Artists tend to showcase their best work in hopes of gaining future work projects with a potential client. In other words, the portfolio is a key tool to help prospect and secure gainful work.

Portfolios Are Not Just for Artists Anymore

Although artistic types used portfolios in the past, portfolio use is catching on in a wide variety of professions and occupations. In fact, anyone who intends to work should seriously consider using a portfolio. Portfolios can be relevant and useful in almost any career or occupation.

All of us have heard of using a resume to help find a job or a work opportunity. The portfolio is the resume of the future. Although you should create and use a resume in your job search, if you want to separate yourself from the competition (and you do), the portfolio is another tool to use and your ticket to success. The portfolio and, more important, the documents in your portfolio are proof of your performance—evidence of what you can contribute to a potential employer or client. The purpose of this chapter is to introduce you to portfolios and to explain why and how they are pertinent to finding work in the turbulent and ever-changing world of work.

Types of Portfolios

ortfolios serve multiple purposes. There is not one ideal type of portfolio that everyone should use. More important, there is no one right or wrong way to create a portfolio. Bostaph and Vendeland, authors of *The Employment Portfolio* (2000), contend that there are at least five types of portfolios that individuals use. They define portfolios as "vehicles by which individuals systematically display empirical evidence of their skills, training, achievements, and references" (p.1). They refer to their portfolio system as the S.T.A.R. model. The acronym stands for: S = Skills, T = Training, A = Accomplishments, and R = References. There are five portfolio types according to these authors:

- *Studio/Arts and Design Portfolio.* Artists, photographers, architects, and others use such a portfolio to display samples of their work.

- *Professional Development Portfolio.* Teaching professionals and others use this tool to assess and improve their own teaching. In the case of teachers, it may include planning and preparation materials, classroom instruction materials, and other professional development documents.

- *Instructional/Assessment Portfolio.* This format is used to document the progression of a student's work and growth over a period of time; it helps assess student performance. Documents can include samples of the student's work.

- *Career Guidance Portfolio.* This type of portfolio is used to document your own career development and career decision making. A typical career portfolio might include an introduction, a self-portrait, an education plan, a career plan, and a conclusion.

- *Employment Portfolio.* This is probably the most common type of portfolio and the one we focus on in this chapter. The employment portfolio is geared to help the user discover relevant work opportunities and secure employment. The employment portfolio can be used for all types of employment, including paid and unpaid internships. In this chapter, we outline the relevance and uses of the portfolio and give you the opportunity to start creating your own.

Why Is a Portfolio Important Now?

s we mentioned in the previous chapters, ongoing change impacts the search for meaningful work in the 21st century. We must confront countless trends and obstacles in order to be successful. Many feel a great deal of uncertainty about work and the future; students often express anxiety about planning and making career decisions at this time in

The portfolio is a key tool to help seek and secure gainful work. It is a way to separate yourself from the competition.

The attention economy is a star system. . . . If there is nothing very special about your work, no matter how hard you apply yourself you won't get noticed, and that increasingly means you won't get paid much either.

—MICHAEL GOLDHABER, *WIRED*

their lives. That said, there is reason to be positive and hopeful about the uncertainty that lies ahead (Gelatt, 1991). Although change is inevitable, we will carry our skills, experiences, and interests from one position to another. The root word of portfolio is *"port,"* which literally means, "to carry; conveying." The portfolio documents you collect will help make change and transition easier and more manageable despite the insecurity and uncertainty of the future. The portfolio allows you to carry forward your experiences and skills to a variety of new and exciting work opportunities as you move in your career. Can you think of other reasons why a portfolio might be helpful to you?

What Is Portfolio Thinking? Building Career Resilience

A recent study about portfolio use was conducted by Borgen, Amundson, and Reuter (2004) of Canada. First, these authors were convinced that portfolios were helpful to individuals who were seeking out job opportunities. Second, they hoped that individuals who used portfolios would enhance their current job situations. Third, they were interested in learning about the types of skills people learn from developing and using portfolios in their work. Here is what they found: Workers who created and used portfolios developed what they call *career resilience*. Resilience is the ability to weather the storms, to overcome obstacles in uncertain times. It is both a process and an outcome. We all have everyday stressors in life. Resilience is the ability to cope with these tensions that life presents.

The individuals in the study learned how to use their portfolios to their advantage. They began to see themselves not as permanent employees working for one employer or organization, but rather as flexible, multitalented workers who could be mobile and adaptable. They saw themselves as "portfolio workers" and they actively engaged in portfolio thinking. Perhaps more important, workers who used portfolios exhibited multiple advantages, including greater self-confidence, enhanced sense of hope and optimism, greater sense of purpose, less self-blame and guilt, and more supportive interpersonal relationships.

Portfolio use is an excellent way to help manage your own career and control your future. Overall, portfolio users feel more in control of their lives and careers. It is a proactive tool, not reactive, because there are no more guarantees when it comes to career (i.e., the days of lifelong employment with mutual loyalty between worker and organization are long gone). Study participants used their portfolios in other ways—the artifacts they collected served multiple purposes (Borgen et al., 2004). Listed below are several ways to use your portfolio.

1. Prepare resumes
2. Develop learning plans
3. Prepare for board interviews
4. Prepare for performance appraisals
5. Help create personal plans of action
6. Enhance personal marketing of skills
7. Support why one should be considered for special work projects

The old economy says, make a plan and stick to it. The new economy is so unformed, so out of the ballpark, that the rules are different: Dream wild, stick out your thumb, and climb aboard for the ride. . . . Be loose, be open to surprise, and be cool.

—HARRIET RUBIN

How might you use your portfolio? It is important for you to develop a similar approach to your own work and career in order to foster your own "career resilience." One way to develop that self-confidence and positive attitude is to begin to craft your own portfolio. The process of putting together the portfolio will likely be just as useful as the portfolio itself.

The Uniqueness of a Portfolio: Brand Yourself

Most resumes look more or less the same. Sure, the details are different and perhaps unique, but most resumes look remarkably similar. The portfolio is a way to distinguish yourself from the others. It is a tool to help you be unique and distinctive. You may have heard of the concept *branding*. Most products have a brand, or a brand message and appeal. Think about a recent commercial you watched on television. It may have involved a food product, a new car, or a cold beverage. Most likely, there was a jingle, maybe a voice-over promoting the product, and probably a variety of images that appealed to you on some level. There was a visual brand the commercial was attempting to sell you (not a big surprise, right?). This same concept of selling a product rings true for you and your portfolio—you are the product!

The defining Brand You idea: "They aren't in charge of our careers—and by extension our lives—anymore. It is up to us to fashion ourselves."

—TOM PETERS

For example, as of this writing, the band U2 is featured in a commercial with Apple Computer's new iPod digital music device. The commercial's images convey fun, relaxation, independence, and good times. U2 and Apple co-branded their products and images (Medvec, 2005). What might your "commercial" say about you? What do you want your reputation to say about who you are as an individual and worker? The portfolio is a way to demonstrate your uniqueness. The branding concept will make more sense as you get more experience in the fields that interest you, so do not worry if this idea seems somewhat unclear at this time.

The portfolio should be a reflection of you and what you have to sell to an organization or employer. Like the commercial, the images in the portfolio should be unique, creative, visually attractive, and engaging. You are the commercial or product that you are marketing to potential employers. As author and marketer Stan Stalnaker writes in his book *Hub Culture* (2002), "as an individual, your reputation is part of your personal brand—the perception and view that others have of you, the quality of your work, your ability to execute a task" (p. 22). The metaphor of *you* as a *commercial* or *brand* may or may not work for you, but you get the picture. The portfolio is a marketing tool as well as a way to provide visual evidence of your accomplishments, skills, and talents.

How Should I Start Thinking about a Portfolio?

A portfolio has a variety of purposes. The types of materials included will largely be determined by your portfolio purpose. Ask yourself: "How do I intend to use the portfolio?" It's not necessary to create a portfolio for each specific use; you can use it for multiple reasons and objectives. In the previous section, we outlined several types of portfolio use based on a study of portfolio users.

Following is a list of several other general examples of how a portfolio can be used:

- Academic purposes (e.g., application to a competitive program)
- Employment (this is the most common purpose and the one this chapter focuses on)
- Career development (e.g., showcasing highlights and accomplishments from various jobs)
- Advancement within an organization (e.g., performance evaluation or an annual review)

For purposes of this discussion, let's assume you are developing a portfolio for an internship or a first job opportunity after graduation. What might you include as documents in your collection? Satterthwaite and D'Orsi, authors of *The Career Portfolio Workbook* (2003), suggest that you start this assessment process by examining your P.E.A.K.S. They contend that your P.E.A.K.S. help determine what to include in your portfolio. So, what does P.E.A.K.S. stand for?

P = Personal characteristics. Who you are as an individual, and what personal attributes or traits define you as a person and a professional are personal characteristics. These characteristics are how you add value to a potential employer.

E = Experiences. What experiences have you had so far that helped shape you? What learning experiences have been most impactful? What mistakes have you learned from in the past?

A = Accomplishments. What are you most proud of in your life up to this point? Perhaps there is a certain goal you've reached in high school or college (or maybe in some other aspect of your life).

K = Knowledge. Knowledge refers to what you know. Have you had any special training? Did you learn something in school that is unique? One of the authors of this text recalls taking a trip to Washington, DC, during school that gave him an opportunity to learn about the American government process up close; this was both a unique experience and a chance to acquire new knowledge.

S = Skills. What special skills or talents do you possess? Perhaps you play an instrument. Perhaps you have certain skills in various technology-related fields or computer programs.

Satterthwaite and D'Orsi (2003) believe that it is vitally important to do a self-inventory of these five components. Take some time now to think about your own life by completing Exercise 5.1.

Generating Ideas for Your Portfolio

Write down several ideas for each component of the P.E.A.K.S. model. Try not to think too much about each item. Instead, jot down the items as they come to mind. Often, your first reactions are the most insightful and accurate (Gladwell, 2005).

P = Personal characteristics _____

_____

_____

E = Experiences _____

_____

_____

A = Accomplishments _____

_____

_____

K = Knowledge _____

_____

_____

S = Skills _____

_____

_____

_____

Next, briefly summarize the highlights or components to **include in your portfolio.**

_____

_____

_____

_____

_____

_____

Stanislavsky once wrote that you could play well or badly, but play truly. It is not up to you whether your performance will be brilliant—all that is under your control is your intention. It is not under your control whether your career will be brilliant—all that is under your control is your intention.

—DAVID MAMET

Your portfolio should contain evidence of leadership positions you've held and teamwork you've participated in, such as charitable or other community events.

What Documents Are Included in a Portfolio?

Now that you have a general idea about the purpose and rationale for using a portfolio, it is important to get started collecting your personal documents. Your portfolio is an evolving document; it will go and grow with you as you collect more experiences, attain new skills, and reach greater accomplishments. Start by collecting samples of your work from school, work, or activities. If you do not have some of these documents yet, don't worry. For example, you may not have a resume. In Chapter 7, you will learn how to create and use a resume. Following is a list of items to begin the portfolio collection process:

- Resume (if you have one).
- Letters of recommendation (e.g., from a teacher or supervisor). Other letters to include are letters of appreciation for some contribution you made. Also, letters of personal reference about your characteristics are sometimes included (from colleagues, friends, and other people who know you well).
- Evaluations from previous work experiences or other activities.
- Specific examples of your work (e.g., letters you wrote, papers or projects you submitted for courses). The ability to communicate in writing is the most important skill employers are looking for from new graduates. Your examples can come from part-time jobs or volunteer experiences.
- Diplomas, certificates, and other credentials (e.g., diploma from previous academic achievements, or other programs you participated in).
- Examples of *group work* you've participated in at college (e.g., something that shows strong interpersonal and teamwork skills). A group paper or project you completed for a class can serve as visual evidence that you possess this skill.
- Documents that demonstrate other *personal characteristics*, such as your attentiveness to detail, creativity, honesty and integrity, work ethic, and personality.
- Evidence of *leadership* qualities you developed through involvement in community activities or hobbies. For example, many students participate in sports and assume a leadership role on their team or within their sport. Examine possible leadership positions you have held in professional organizations, community-based initiatives, and clubs.

- Awards, prizes, or special recognition you have received.

- Any other documents you feel might be interesting and useful. Remember, there are no concrete rules about creating a portfolio. It is a tool designed to reflect you and your potential contributions to an employer.

Developing the Portfolio

Bostaph and Vendeland (2000) offer seven tips for developing your portfolio. These suggestions include:

1. Select a collaborator (someone who can help you with the process).

2. Organize your portfolio.

3. Be professional.

4. Assess the various portfolio components.

5. **Be timely in the presentation of your portfolio;** keep documents current and accurate.

6. Field-test your portfolio in actual interview situations (and informational interviews).

7. Focus on the main portfolio components.

Portfolio Organization

To begin organizing your portfolio, purchase two storage items: (1) a three-ring binder, and (2) a storage compartment or folder. Also purchase 10–15 transparent three-punch file folders. You will place your documents in these folders and insert them into the binder. Purchase high-quality, professional-looking materials that make your portfolio well-organized and easy to access.

Following is a checklist of other materials to use in your portfolio:

___ Colorful dividers for the various sections. For example, you may divide the sections by different themes: personal, academic, work, and nonwork activities (e.g., volunteer work and hobbies).

___ Tabs to label and organize the various sections.

___ Construction paper to add color (this item depends on the portfolio's purpose and use). Some industries are more receptive to creative expression and color incorporated into the portfolio. The main point is that the portfolio should be visually pleasing.

Remember: Your portfolio should be a tool that you use for multiple situations, not just that one job search after college. The portfolio has many potential uses, but it is ultimately up to you to use the tool effectively to your advantage—now and in the future. Here are several additional suggestions for creating and maintaining your portfolio:

1. Keep the portfolio organized and the materials legible.

2. Make sure the materials are easy to access. You will use the portfolio in interviews. (Your class portfolio will include other materials, such as the exercises.)

3. The portfolio must be portable. It should not be too bulky and heavy.

4. Keep the portfolio up to date. It is recommended that you display only 8–12 documents for interview purposes. This helps you focus on your main highlights and contributions. As you acquire new accomplishments and experiences, be sure to include the latest and most compelling documents.

5. Protect the portfolio. Your portfolio will last longer and look more professional if you protect the materials you plan to showcase. Protection includes using high-quality transparencies to show your documents and tabs, dividers, and paper that are durable and efficient.

Barbara Moses, Career Guru

Career Development Tips

Career management expert Barbara Moses (1999) writes about helpful tips for employees of all ages. Listed below are some career development suggestions for 20-somethings. Notice the value of developing skills using your portfolio.

1. Find a mentor, someone you can emulate and learn from.

2. Attempt to increase your experience. Do some "reality testing" by taking on short-term experiential opportunities such as internships and part-time employment.

3. Develop the skills in your portfolio.

4. Job shadow someone doing interesting work.

5. Pursue various types of education at the highest and broadest level.

6. Keep networking and expanding your "personal profile."

7. Look at opportunities in terms of what you might learn from the experience.

8. Recognize that there are no "right" or "perfect" career choices; this is a career myth.

Additional Benefits of Using a Portfolio

 ere are several additional advantages and benefits of using a portfolio for your own career development:

- *Bolsters self-confidence.* Students report that they feel more confident in interview situations when they have a portfolio they can share with prospective employers. It serves to showcase their work and add value.

- *Serves as a historical document.* Your portfolio will serve as a written text of you and your experiences over time. You can go back and review all you have achieved as you move forward in your life and career.

- *Provides evidence of your performance.* The documents in your portfolio serve as proof of your performance. Author Rich Nelles (2001) claims that the best job candidates always back up everything they claim on their resume with documentation. Nelles' research indicates that the portfolio strategy alone increases a job candidate's success rate by more than 400 percent. Not bad odds when you are trying to get that dream job!

- *Serves as a valuable self-assessment tool.* Recall that in Chapter 1 we discussed the importance of knowing yourself—your interests, skills, values, and experiences. By creating a portfolio, you inevitably learn more about who you are as an individual. You become more comfortable identifying your strengths, and, in turn, feel more at ease when sharing these attributes with others (e.g., in an interview situation).

- *Provides a tool to help you with networking and doing informational interviews.* Later in this text, we will discuss the importance of networking. The portfolio serves as a valuable tool for building your network of contacts as you share your documents with others.

student profiles

Nadira. **Putting Together a Teaching Portfolio.** Nadira is a 25-year-old nontraditional, returning student from South America. She is interested in teaching and is considering a degree in Urban Education. Nadira is currently in her third year of school. She transferred about 20 general education credits from a previous school she attended when she was 18. Her goal is to work in a metropolitan area and serve underrepresented children and families. Nadira worked as an education assistant in a local school district for four years. Furthermore, she tutored elementary age children and volunteered in her community for several years. In fact, the local community center gave her an award for "Most Dedicated Volunteer." Nadira is thinking about creating a portfolio.

- What suggestions do you have for Nadira about starting her portfolio?

- What skills do you think she possesses?

- What are Nadira's assets (e.g., traits, qualities, accomplishments)?

- What might be some of her strengths that she can showcase in her portfolio?

_____

_____

_____

_____

_____

_____

(Continued)

_____

_____

_____

_____

Tom. **Putting Together a Sales Portfolio.** Tom is a natural-born sales-man. Both his mother and father are involved in business-related fields. Tom set up his first lemonade stand when he was five (and actually made a profit by the end of the summer). He is a third-year student and is actively involved in the School of Management at his university. His long-term goal is to work as a consultant in banking and international management. Tom is fluent in French and spent two semesters in Paris last year. He is the business club vice-president and is actively involved in his fraternity (last fall he was the most successful rush chair in the Greek system and received an award). Tom is in the process of putting together a portfolio in order to explore internships for next summer.

- What advice would you give to Tom knowing what you know about portfolio development?

- What accomplishments should he showcase? What artifacts or documents should he include in his portfolio?

- Do you think knowing a second language might be valuable? If so, how might Tom find a way to include this in his portfolio?

- Because he is looking at a business career, what skills might Tom focus on as he creates his portfolio?

- What other suggestions do you have for Tom?

_____

_____

_____

_____

_____

_____

_____

_____

_____

5.2 | Develop Your Own Commercial

Imagine that you are your own "product." You have to sell yourself and your potential contributions to a potential employer or buyer. What would you sell? For example, what are some of the strengths you bring to the table? (*Hint*: Review the section in this chapter on seeing yourself as a "brand.")

On a separate sheet of paper, spend 5–10 minutes free writing and brainstorming about you as a commercial. Next, what action or step can you take to get closer to developing your product? For example, if you want to own your own business, what action can you take now to move closer to that goal?

5.3 | 30-Second Elevator Pitch

Did you know that in an interview situation, the interviewer usually sizes up the job candidate in 30 seconds or less? And he or she usually has a firm impression of the candidate within a couple of minutes of meeting the person. So, what does that mean for you? You have to make a strong first impression. It is important to develop and practice your pitch or story. If you have only 30 seconds to make a good impression, what do you say about yourself? What information do you include (or exclude)? This pitch takes practice.

On a separate sheet of paper, write a rough script for your 30-second pitch. Next, practice it on your own or in front of family members. (Practice in front of a mirror if you have some inhibitions about public speaking.) How did that feel? Were you more comfortable the more you practiced? This is a skill that takes time and practice. *Remember*: Even if you are not employed in sales, you are always selling yourself in some way.

Place these exercises in your class portfolio.

5.4   Are You a Free Agent? Autonomy in the New Economy

In Daniel Pink's popular book, *Free Agent Nation* (2001), he contends that many individuals are moving away from the traditional "employee–employer" contract where they work for a single organization. Instead, they are establishing new, independent-focused working arrangements. According to his statistics, there are at least 33 million free agents (a conservative estimate at the time). In fact, free agents may now be the largest single cluster of workers in the economy. Here is Pink's breakdown of free agents:

- 16.5 million soloists (e.g., freelancers)
- 3.5 million temps
- 13 million microbusinesses

Almost one out of every four American workers can be considered a free agent.

 follow-up questions:

1. Do you see yourself working as a free agent? Why or why not?

    _____

    _____

    _____

    _____

2. What might you see yourself doing?

    _____

    _____

    _____

3. If you had to start your own business next week, what might you do?

    _____

    _____

    _____

    _____

4. How might a free agent use a portfolio?

    _____

    _____

    _____

    _____

Include this exercise in your portfolio.

Create Your Own Portfolio

Make a plan to start or fine-tune your portfolio. If you are enrolled in a career planning course, your instructor might require you to take this next step as a class requirement. Begin by setting some short-term goals for yourself; for example:

STEP	START DATE
1. Begin collection of relevant documents	_____
2. Purchase portfolio materials	_____
3. Assemble portfolio	_____
4. Practice using portfolio with friends or family	_____
5. **Use the portfolio** in a professional setting (e.g., a part-time job, internship, or related activity)	_____

Summary

deally, you now realize the importance of creating your own portfolio. In this chapter, we discussed the rationale and purpose for using a portfolio. We then outlined the steps on how to create your own portfolio. In the rest of Unit II, we will focus on other strategies to create opportunities, including the tools to help you connect with employers—job applications, resumes, and references.

REFERENCES

Borgen, W.A., Amundson, N.E., & Reuter, J. (2004). Using portfolios to enhance career resilience. *Journal of Employment Counseling, 41*(2), 50–60.

Bostaph, C., & Vendeland, R. (2000). *The employment portfolio.* Upper Saddle River, NJ: Prentice Hall.

Gelatt, H.B. (1991). *Creative decision making: Using positive uncertainty.* Menlo Park, CA: Crisp Publications.

Gladwell, M. (2005). *Blink: The power of thinking without thinking.* New York: Little, Brown.

Medvec, J. (2005, February 14). You, too, could learn a lot from U2. *Star Tribune,* p. D8.

Moses, B. (1999). *The good news about careers: How you'll be working in the next decade.* Toronto, Canada: Stoddart.

Nelles, R. (2001). *Proof of performance: How to build a career portfolio to land a great new job.* Manassas Park, VA: Impact Publishers.

Peters, T. (1999). *Reinventing work: The brand you 50.* New York: Alfred A. Knopf.

Pink, D. (2001). *Free agent nation: How America's new independent workers are transforming the way we live.* New York: Warner.

Satterthwaite, F., & D'Orsi, G. (2003). *The career portfolio workbook.* New York: McGraw-Hill.

Stalnaker, S. (2002). *Hub culture: The next wave of urban consumers.* New York: John Wiley & Sons.

Williams, A. G. (2001). *Creating your career portfolio* (2nd ed.). Upper Saddle River, NJ: Prentice Hall.

Author's Note: A special thank-you to Carmen Croonquist, Director of Career Services, University of Wisconsin–River Falls, for her insightful suggestions and feedback on this chapter.

Connecting to Employers

JOB SEARCH CORRESPONDENCE AND JOB APPLICATIONS

learning objectives

1. To understand how to use various letters in the job search process

2. To learn the key elements to include in each type of job search letter

3. To understand the purpose, use, and limitations of job applications

4. To examine difficult questions and learn how to answer them

chapter

6

Experience is not what happens to you. It is what you do with what happens to you.

—ALDOUS HUXLEY

student profile

Mai. Mai found a posting for an internship at her campus career center. The posting was placed by a company that manages organ donations in the state. The firm is seeking a college student to work full-time over the summer on accounting projects that include the monthly close process, budgets, operations analysis, and fixed-asset accounting. The posting asks that applicants submit their resume with a cover letter within two weeks.

"This is exactly what I need right now," Mai thinks. "I've taken the first two courses in my accounting major. Now, I want to do some actual accounting work, not more reading about accounting work. Better yet, this company is on the edge of campus and I can walk to work.

"I need to make some adjustments to my resume to line it up better with the job description. But I want to make sure my cover letter also helps me stand out from other candidates. I've got to do some work on that," Mai decides.

Writing is not speaking. When you speak, you can see and hear whether the other person understands you. If you notice that your message isn't clear, you can restate it or ask the other person to tell you what she didn't understand. You may have several opportunities to make sure your message is understood.

When you write, however, you have to get the message correct the first time. You may not have a second chance to correct miscommunication.

The letters you write during your job hunt are some of the most important letters you will ever write. Likewise, job applications also communicate either positive or negative messages to potential employers. By writing captivating, clear, well-thought-out letters and completing neat and clear job applications, your chances in the job search increase immeasurably. Spend time on your job search letter writing, and it will pay off.

Types of Letters for the Job Search

A letter is more than simply words on paper. It conveys sounds, ideas, feelings. It captivates or it bores. It inspires and energizes action or it is a major turnoff. A letter is really part of you. What do you want it to say about you?

Because you will write a variety of letters during your job search, we will look at seven major types:

1. Cover letter
2. Thank-you letter
3. Network letter
4. Acceptance letter
5. Job offer rejection letter
6. Response to a rejection letter
7. Resignation letter

Using all seven letter types, as necessary, during your job search attests to your professionalism and says something (hopefully positive) about your communication abilities. Be energized when you write them! They are not to be "slapped on" or "shot out." They are very important if your job search is to be a success.

Guidelines and Tips

Before beginning to write your letters, think about the format to use and the style to exhibit. Format is the general plan, or organization and arrangement, of the letter. Style is your unique mode of expressing your thoughts on paper. Because the style paints an image of your personality, it is an important part of your letter writing.

Here are some basic guidelines for writing letters:

1. *Write original letters.* The key to originality is innovation and showing your personality in a way that differentiates you from other job hunters. An original letter personalizes your job hunt and reaches out to the employer in your unique way.

Write original letters to personalize your job search. The key to originality is showing your personality.

2. *Address your letter to a specific person.* With thank-you letters, this is obvious. But when you answer some job postings or if you are mailing out resumes to target companies, initially you may not have the name of a person to address your correspondence to. Telephone the organization and ask for the name, spelling, job title, and mailing address. Don't rely on directories or other printed matter because they become out of date quickly.

3. *Don't use sexist language in your greeting or in the body of the letter.* "Gentlemen," "Madame," and "Dear Sir" are all sexist and horribly out of date and may offend the reader. In your salutation, use the first name, or find out the person's courtesy title (Mr., Ms., Mrs.).

4. *Keep the letter to a maximum of one page.* This usually means several short paragraphs. You must write clear, complete, grammatically correct sentences that are concise and to the point. Your reader doesn't have the time to read a tome. Make sure the content is rich, engaging, and makes the reader want to meet you.

5. *Check language, grammar, spelling, and abbreviations.* Don't use convoluted expressions such as "Enclosed herewith, please find my resume." Use positive expressions and avoid negative words. Spelling, grammar, word usage, and sentence structure are crucial. Check all of these areas yourself, but also have someone else

proofread your letter. Remember, word processing spell checkers check most spelling but not improper word usage, so use the checker but also proofread fiercely.

6. *Tone down the use of "I."* So many cover letter writers use the word "I" to start almost every sentence. Thin these after your first draft. At most, every other sentence can start with an "I."

7. *Word process most of your letters.* Cover letters, network letters, acceptance letters, rejection letters, and resignation letters should be word processed. Thank-you letters can be handwritten.

8. *Use the same stationery you use for your resume.* Use high-quality, 20-pound bond paper with matching envelopes in conservative colors (ivory, off-white, buff, tan, or gray). If you are applying for a position in such highly creative areas as the arts, advertising, or design, you may be freer with your color choices. Good linen texture adds a quality touch, but avoid parchments and onion-skin papers.

Parts of a Letter

emember the basic parts of a letter:

1. Personal identification
2. Date
3. Inside address
4. Salutation
5. Opening paragraph
6. Body paragraphs
7. Closing paragraph
8. Complimentary closing
9. Signature
10. Typed name
11. Enclosures
12. "c:" or copy

These parts are used in most job search letters; a thank-you letter need not follow this format as rigidly. A brief explanation of each part follows.

Personal identification. Put your name, mailing address, telephone number(s), and e-mail address at the top of your letter as a letterhead.

Date. A date helps both you and the addressee keep your information in order.

Inside address. Include the addressee's name, along with his courtesy and job titles, company, and mailing address.

Salutation. The salutation is your greeting to the person to whom you are writing. Generally, you will use "Dear Mr." or "Dear Ms." followed by the last name. If you know the person on a first-name basis, you may use the first name.

Paragraphs. Write a minimum of three paragraphs and no more than five. Keep the paragraphs relatively short and to the point. Let's examine the function of the different paragraphs:

- *Opening paragraph.* Use your opening paragraph to explain why you are writing. Be specific; for example, "In response to the advertisement for the Radiologic Technologist position placed in the February 9 edition of the *Des Moines Register*, I have enclosed my resume for your review."

- *Body paragraphs.* Follow the opening paragraph with one or two short to medium paragraphs. Each paragraph should contain relevant information depending on the type of letter you are writing. If desired, use bullets to differentiate specific points.

- *Closing paragraph.* Recap some of the information from the prior paragraphs if needed. Detail how the employer can get in touch with you by including your phone number, e-mail address, or both.

In the following sections, we will discuss the specifics for each paragraph as it relates to the type of job correspondence you are writing.

Complimentary closing. You will close, generally, with "sincerely," "yours truly," or a similar closing.

Signature. Make your signature legible.

Typed name. Typing your name is standard protocol.

Enclosures. Not all letters have enclosures, but if you are sending your resume or other papers, your letter should include this line.

"C:" or copy. In other words, you are mailing copies of the letter to another party or parties.

Types of Job Search Correspondence

n this section, we will discuss the types of job search correspondence and provide examples of each.

Cover Letter

Cover letters are usually the most important piece of correspondence in your job search process. Your cover letter may be the first glimpse an employer has of you, so it must be a compelling indication of your professionalism, your abilities, and your style.

Writing a compelling letter takes effort. You need to find something interesting to say about the organization and yourself in order to stand out from the pack. Depending on the job, it is estimated that your chance of gaining interviews from resume "mail-outs" to companies is about 3 percent. For advertised positions it is higher, but you are still playing the numbers game. Highlight some of your best strengths that fit the employer's needs in order to stand out.

Take heart, however. Most cover letters are extremely boring. If you can write a letter that draws the reader in and interests her in you, your chance for an interview increases dramatically. Of course, you need to have the qualifications and ability to do the job, but a successful cover letter can lead the way for the employer to discover that you do.

Messages and value to convey in a cover letter. *In the space below, list three messages you want to convey to the reader of your cover letter. Following each message, indicate why it is important for success in your job search. Following these responses, write about the overall value you bring to an employer in a way that makes her want to hire you.*

1. Message: _____

   Reason this is important for your job search: _____

   _____

2. Message: _____

   Reason this is important for your job search: _____

   _____

3. Message: _____

   Reason this is important for your job search: _____

   _____

   The value I bring to an employer is . . . _____

   _____

Like the messages you developed, you must communicate the value you can bring to an organization when you write a cover letter. Be sure to incorporate the critical value you bring!

Step-by-Step Cover Letter

Your cover letter should include the following parts:

Opening paragraph. Explain how you found out about the position and what interests you about it. You might also indicate what interests you about the company, especially if there has been some positive news about the organization recently. Start drawing the reader in at this point with an interesting opening.

Body paragraphs. Highlight key aspects of your background and qualifications. Skills, work experience, academic credentials and achievements, and any relevant special training should go in these paragraphs. You may have one or two paragraphs in this section.

Closing paragraph. Reiterate your interest in the position and your desire for an interview. Detail how the employer can get in touch with you, whether by phone, e-mail, or both.

Figure 6.1 shows a sample cover letter.

figure **6.1** *Sample cover letter.*

MAI NGUYEN

153 9th Street South   E-mail: mnguyen@hotmail.com   Home Phone: (612) 555-8892
Minneapolis, MN 55444   Cell Phone: (404) 555-7124

January 23, 20XX

Ms. Beth McComb
Manager of Financial Operations
Life Promises, Inc.
955 Zander Road East
Dana City, MN 55114

Dear Ms. McComb:

I am interested in applying for the Accounting Internship position that was posted on-line through the University of Minnesota's Career Center. My resume is enclosed for your review.

Currently, I am pursuing a degree in business at the University of Minnesota with a major in accounting. I am in my junior year and would like to obtain a high-quality internship for the summer to build on my current level of work experience. Your internship looks like an ideal opportunity for me at this time.

My background includes business experience in office and retail settings. Through those experiences, I have developed strong customer service, organizational, and attention-to-detail skills that fit the requirements of your position. I also have a variety of leadership and community involvement experience that fits with Life Promise's philosophy of helping people. My computer skills include extensive use of Microsoft Excel, Access, and Word.

I would greatly appreciate the opportunity to meet with you to discuss this internship and find out more about this opportunity. Please feel free to contact me by phone or e-mail. Thank you for considering my application.

Sincerely,

Mai Nguyen

Mai Nguyen

Enclosure

Find a job or internship posting that interests you. Write a sample cover letter for the position, using the suggestions from this section. Before you write the letter, respond to the questions below. Your responses will help you target your letter and make it more effective.

1. How did you find out about the position?

   _____

   _____

2. What is your interest in the position and organization?

   _____

   _____

3. What are your qualifications for the position?

   _____

   _____

   _____

4. List your relevant education and work experience:

   _____

   _____

   _____

   _____

5. Reiterate your interest about the position:

   _____

   _____

6. List your contact information and make sure it is easily found on the letter:

   _____

   _____

   _____

   _____

After you complete the letter, evaluate it according to the items listed above. Are they reflected in your letter?

Place this exercise and your sample letter in your portfolio.

Thank-You Letter

Whether you've had an informational interview, a networking meeting, or an actual job interview, you must send the other person a thank-you letter. Of course, there are other reasons beyond common courtesy to send a thank-you.

For job interviews, follow-up thank-you letters reemphasize your interest in the position and the company. Follow-up thank-you letters also give you the opportunity to reiterate your qualifications and supply additional information if needed.

What if you've had a job interview but the position no longer interests you? Thank-you letters are still important because you never know what the future may hold for you with that employer. The employer is now part of your network and your paths may cross again, be it for another position or if you end up in the same industry.

After networking meetings and informational interviews, send a thank-you letter (see Figure 6.2). These people helped you and usually are interested in your progress. They may also have the ability to hire you for jobs at some time. Send them a thank-you to convey your gratitude, professionalism, and interest.

Step-by-Step Thank-You Letter

Although there is no set way of writing thank-you letters, consider the following tips:

- *Handwritten or word processed?* Either handwritten or word processed thank-you letters are acceptable. If sending a handwritten letter, write clearly and legibly. If you are supplying a significant amount of additional information, you may want to word process your thank you.

- *Send thank-you letters to all interviewers.* Make sure you get the correct spelling of names, addresses, and titles for all of these people.

- *Reference the meeting.* People are busy! Help them recall you faster by combining your thank-you statement with the context of the meeting in the letter's first paragraph; for example: "Thank you for the opportunity to interview for the Science Instructor position last Wednesday."

- *State your continued interest and enthusiasm.* For job interviews, if you are still interested in the position and organization, clearly state your interest; for example, "After interviewing for this position, I am very excited about the opportunity to work for Mill City Manufacturing." If you are less interested in the position, you need not emphasize this.

- *Emphasize your fit.* Again, if you are still interested, emphasize your fit with the position and organization; for example, "I believe that there is a good match between my qualifications, the position, and the environment of your company."

- *Clearly state your thank you.* Usually, this is done in both the opening paragraph and the final paragraph.

- *Give contact information.* Be sure to include your phone number, mailing address, and e-mail address. The organization may need to contact you one way or another concerning job status. Your network contacts may want to know how to contact you too.

figure **6.2** *Sample thank-you letter.*

MAI NGUYEN

153 9th Street South
Minneapolis, MN 55444

E-mail: mnguyen@hotmail.com

Home Phone: (612) 555-8892
Cell Phone: (404) 555-7124

February 3, 20XX

Ms. Beth McComb
Manager of Financial Operations
Life Promises, Inc.
955 Zander Road East
Dana City, MN 55114

Dear Ms. McComb:

I want to thank you again for giving me the opportunity to interview for the Accounting Internship position. I really appreciate the time you spent with me and enjoyed meeting you and your staff.

After interviewing for this position, I am even more excited about this opportunity. This internship would be a great learning experience for me, and I think I can make a strong contribution to the company. The positive work environment at Life Promises ideally matches the kind of work setting I am seeking. I hope you feel my background, skills, and interests match what you are looking for in an intern.

As you mentioned, I will wait until next week to hear from you about your decision. Please feel free to contact me if you have any additional questions about my background and interests. I look forward to hearing from you and hope I have the opportunity to work with you through this internship.

Sincerely,

Mai Nguyen

Mai Nguyen

According to a survey by *The Career Exposure Network* (2004), 82 percent of employers and recruiters stated that sending a thank-you note is a critical follow-up step after the interview. It indicates a certain level of professionalism and demonstrates that the candidate is serious about the job opportunity.

Interestingly, 81 percent of employers and recruiters said that e-mail is the preferred method of receiving a follow-up from a candidate. Whichever way you go, e-mail or hard copy, it's important to send thank-you notes after your interviews!

Source: CareerExposure News & Resources, *Employers and recruiters still expect thanks after interviews* (April 29, 2004). Available at www.careerexposure.com/resources/resources_521.jsp.

Network Letter

Network letters help enlist friends, business associates, and acquaintances in your job hunt. Because network letters are more formal than a simple phone call, they send a stronger message about your determined attitude in the job search process. Keep these ideas in mind if you decide to send network letters:

- Contact friends and associates to ask for advice and ideas. If you are contacting someone you don't know, reference the contact person or information source in your letter.
- Don't judge the value of any one person. That is one of the beauties of networking! You know many people want to help you, but you don't exactly know who will be the best resource. Get the word out about your search through your letter.

Figure 6.3 shows a sample network letter.

personal **THINK PIECE**

Three messages for a job search network letter. *In the space below, list three messages you want to convey to the reader of your network letter. Following each message, indicate why it is important for success in your job search.*

1. Message: _____

   Reason this is important for your job search: _____

   _____

2. Message: _____

   Reason this is important for your job search: _____

   _____

3. Message: _____

   Reason this is important for your job search: _____

   _____

figure **6.3**   *Sample network letter.*

MAI NGUYEN

153 9th Street South   E-mail: mnguyen@hotmail.com   Home Phone: (612) 555-8892
Minneapolis, MN 55444   Cell Phone: (404) 555-7124

March 17, 20XX

Ms. Veronica Arp
Selesky & Slipkay, LLP
776 Kristina Street
Summer, MN 55111

Dear Ms. Arp:

I am currently working on my bachelor's degree at the University of Minnesota, with a major in accounting. I am very interested in speaking with you about employment opportunities at Selesky & Slipkay, LLP.

Through my studies at the university and my work experiences, I developed a strong range of skills and knowledge for a career in public accounting. I enjoy the challenge of working with clients and applying accounting concepts and fundamentals on audit engagements.

My work experience, extracurricular activities, and community involvement enabled me to develop my strong detail orientation, and problem-solving and organizational skills. I also developed excellent communication skills through these experiences. I believe that these skills especially suit a career in public accounting.

Enclosed is my resume for your reference. I would enjoy speaking with you further about opportunities with your firm. I can be reached at the phone number or e-mail shown above.

Sincerely,

Mai Nguyen

Mai Nguyen

Enclosure

Acceptance Letter

One of the most fulfilling and exciting letters you will write is an acceptance letter for a job offer. As with all of your job search correspondence, this letter should convey your professionalism, intelligence, and enthusiasm to the employer and continue the positive relationship developed during the interview process.

In addition, an acceptance letter is your opportunity to confirm your understanding of a job offer. Sometimes, confusion can occur during the excitement of the job offer and acceptance period. An acceptance letter helps you clarify and verify details of the offer. It also provides written proof of the offer terms and is especially useful if a verbal agreement differs from the organization's standard policies (e.g., you could take vacation time during the first three months of employment).

Following are some general points to remember when writing an acceptance letter:

- Begin with a short opening paragraph that expresses your enthusiasm for joining the firm and thanks them for the job.
- In the second paragraph, spell out the agreed-upon terms of employment.
- If necessary, include a sentence to correct misunderstandings that may have occurred during the offer or negotiation process.
- In the closing paragraph, restate your excitement about joining the company.

Figure 6.4 shows a sample acceptance letter.

Letter Rejecting a Job Offer

Sometimes it is necessary to reject a job offer. It may be that the job is not right, that it doesn't meet your requirements, or that you have just accepted another offer. Whatever the case, take the time to thank the employer for the offer.

When rejecting an offer, handle the situation diplomatically. It's a small world, and your paths may cross again concerning future opportunities. Express your appreciation for the offer; then, indicate that you won't be able to accept it. It isn't necessary to provide a reason or to expound on any reason you do provide.

Consider these points when writing a letter of rejection:

- The first paragraph should express thanks for the job offer and may include your rejection of the offer.
- The second paragraph can include additional thanks to other individuals at the company who were helpful to you during the employment process.
- In the third and final paragraph, restate your appreciation for the offer.

Figure 6.5 shows a sample letter rejecting a job offer.

figure **6.4** *Sample acceptance letter.*

MAI NGUYEN

153 9th Street South   E-mail: mnguyen@hotmail.com   Home Phone: (612) 555-8892
Minneapolis, MN 55444   Cell Phone: (404) 555-7124

April 20, 20XX

Ms. Veronica Arp
Selesky & Slipkay, LLP
776 Kristina Street
Summer, MN 55111

Dear Veronica:

Thank you for all the help you gave me during the interview process for the Accountant
Associate position with Selesky & Slipkay, LLP. I feel this is a great opportunity and I'm
excited to become part of your team.

At this time, I would like to formally accept your offer of employment. As we discussed,
the terms of employment are:

- Report to work on Thursday, June 1, 20XX, at 8:00 a.m.

- Salary is $40,000 annually.

- Vacation: 2 weeks after 1 year, 3 weeks after 3 years, 4 weeks after 5 years.

- Benefits plan including medical, dental, long-term disability, life insurance, and 401(k)
  retirement plan per the materials you sent to me.

If there are any discrepancies in my understanding, please call or e-mail me. Thanks again
for this great opportunity. I'm looking forward to joining the organization on June 1.

Sincerely,

Mai Nguyen

Mai Nguyen

figure **6.5** *Sample job offer rejection letter.*

MAI NGUYEN

153 9th Street South
Minneapolis, MN 55444

E-mail: mnguyen@hotmail.com

Home Phone: (612) 555-8892
Cell Phone: (404) 555-7124

April 25, 20XX

Ms. Cynthia LaMarche
LaMarche Communications, Inc.
753 Kubesh Street
Madison, WI 50333

Dear Ms. LaMarche:

Thank you for your Assistant Accountant job offer. I am very flattered that you are interested in employing me in your organization; however, I regret to inform you that I will be unable to accept your offer.

I am very impressed with LaMarche Communications. Everyone treated me extremely well during the interview process, and I'm sure this would be a great team to work with. My decision to turn down your job offer was a difficult one, and I hope you will consider me for future opportunities.

I wish you and your company continued success. If I can be of any help to you in the future, please let me know.

Best regards,

Mai Nguyen

Mai Nguyen

Letter Responding to Rejection

On the other end of the spectrum is the letter you may write in response to a rejection of your job candidacy. Most likely, you will not write this letter every time you are rejected for a job, but in cases where you really wanted the job, it is a good idea to do so. As we've said before, it's a small world and your paths may cross again concerning future opportunities.

In your letter, make your disappointment clear but not overwhelming. Positively express your appreciation concerning the people and the process. Clearly state your continued interest in working for the organization and express your interest in future opportunities.

Here are some main points to include:

- The first paragraph should express thanks for the interview process.
- The second paragraph can include your disappointment as well as additional thanks to other individuals at the company who were helpful to you during the employment process. Emphasize your continued belief in your fit with the organization.
- In the third and final paragraph, restate your interest (if this is still the case) in the organization and leave open future opportunities.

Figure 6.6 shows a sample letter responding to a rejection of your job candidacy.

Resignation Letter

Resigning from a position can be emotional—joyful, sorrowful, or some of each—but it still must be handled skillfully and professionally.

Writing a resignation letter is your opportunity to leave the company on a good note, no matter the circumstances. Your employer provided you with a job and an income, so it's fitting that you show your appreciation.

Remember: don't burn bridges; build and reinforce them. You never know when you may be back asking for help or a job in the future.

Figure 6.7 shows a sample resignation letter.

E-mail Letters

Use of e-mail in the job search process is standard procedure today. Organizations regularly accept resumes through e-mail with, the e-mail message itself serving as the cover letter.

Use some caution when using e-mail during the job search process, however. Here are some tips:

- For job openings, only use e-mail if the company recommends doing so.
- Consider the e-mail as a cover letter and write it appropriately. Do not dash off an e-mail as though you are responding to a friend. Take the professional approach and write your e-mail as you would a regular cover letter.

figure **6.6** | *Sample letter responding to rejection.*

MAI NGUYEN

153 9th Street South
Minneapolis, MN 55444

E-mail: mnguyen@hotmail.com

Home Phone: (612) 555-8892
Cell Phone: (404) 555-7124

April 19, 20XX

Mr. James Andrew
Anndow Products, Inc.
4949 Baboo Road
Nadeen Prairie, MN 55670

Dear Mr. Andrew:

Thanks again for all your assistance during the interview process for the Accountant
position with Anndow Products. I really appreciate the time you took out of your
schedule to assist me.

Although I am disappointed in not being selected for the position, I want you to know
that I remain very interested in opportunities with Anndow Products. I especially
enjoyed meeting you and all of the members of your team. Anndow Products is an
exciting place to build a career.

I want to reemphasize my interest in your company and hope you will keep me in mind
concerning other positions that fit my skills and abilities. Thanks again, and I hope we
can speak in the future.

Sincerely,

Mai Nguyen

Mai Nguyen

figure **6.7** *Sample resignation letter.*

MAI NGUYEN

153 9th Street South   E-mail: mnguyen@hotmail.com   Home Phone: (612) 555-8892
Minneapolis, MN 55444   Cell Phone: (404) 555-7124

April 30, 20XX

Seung Yung Han
President
Rosen International
5844 Shinners Road
Tarrah, MN 55336

Dear Seung Yung:

It is with regret that I submit my resignation as Accounting Clerk. I have accepted the position of Accountant Associate with Selesky & Slipkay, LLP beginning June 1. My resignation is effective four weeks from today.

It has been a pleasure to be associated with this organization and its people. I have enjoyed working with you, and you have contributed immensely to my professional and personal growth. I will always be grateful for all that you have done for me.

I wish you continued success and success for Rosen International. I'm sure our paths will continue to cross in the future.

Sincerely,

Mai Nguyen

Mai Nguyen

- For networking, use e-mail primarily with friends and associates or when a friend or associate has "opened the door" for you with people you are meeting for the first time.
- Develop your e-mail along the same lines as a regular networking letter.
- For thank-you letters, be professional and sincere and develop your e-mail as you would a regular thank-you letter.
- We don't recommend using e-mail for accepting or rejecting offers. These are usually best handled by phone with your letter as a follow-up.
- Responding to rejection letters should not be done by e-mail. Again, a phone call or letter is preferred.
- Never use e-mail for resignation letters!

Use caution when using e-mail during the job search process. If you do use e-mail, compose your correspondence as carefully as you would a regular letter.

Final Tips on Letter Content

Here are a wide variety of issues and tips to be aware of as you write your letters:

- *Active voice.* Build each sentence or idea around a specific active verb.
- *Short sentences.* Long, rambling sentences are hard to read and difficult to understand.
- *Short paragraphs.* Paragraphs in job-hunting letters are usually shorter than in literary writing. Ideally, each paragraph should deal with only one general subject.
- *One page.* More than one page is an immediate turnoff.
- *Short, simple words.* Use conversational words.
- *Don't editorialize.* Use facts and support each statement with an example.
- *"I" sentences.* Limit the use of "I" to start sentences. Make sure you talk about what you can offer the employer more than "what *I* want."
- *Redundancy.* Eliminate redundant word usage.
- *Correct word usage.* The words in the following chart are often misused. If you use any of these words in your letter, make sure you use the correct one.

Advice/advise	Continually/continuous	Flammable/inflammable	Loose/lose
Affect/effect	Council/counsel/consul	Foreword/forward	Meantime/meanwhile
Allude/refer	Different from/different than	Fortuitous/fortunate	People/persons
Allusion/illusion	Discreet/discrete	Good/well	Predominant/predominate
Alright/all right	Disinterested/uninterested	Hopefully	Principal/principle
Alternate/alternative	Economic/economical	I/me/myself	Regardless/irregardless
Among/between	Eminent/imminent	Imply/infer	Shall/will
Ante-/anti-	Enthuse	Insure/ensure/assure	Stationary/stationery
Bi-/semi-	Etc.	Its/it's	That/which
Can/may	Farther/further	Lay/lie	Was/were
Capital/capitol	Fewer/less	Lend/loan	Which/who
Chose/choose/chosen	Firstly/secondly	Like/as	Who/whom
Complement/compliment			

- *Transitions.* Each sentence in each paragraph should flow smoothly and logically after the sentence before. Good use of transitional words is your key.

- *Readability.* The letter should be enjoyable to read.

The "Look" of Your Letter

Here are some final tips on letter writing concerning paper, fonts, graphics, and other aesthetic concerns:

- *Paper and ink.* Use standard 20-pound, 8½-by-11-inch paper. Your letter needs to be as sharp and legible as possible. This means black ink on white, light gray, or off-white paper.

- *Graphics, lines, and shading.* Avoid graphics, lines, and shading.

- *Fonts.* A 12-point font size is ideal, but 10-point and 11-point fonts are also acceptable. Choose a distinct, clear font, such as Times New Roman, Helvetica, or Arial.

- *Abbreviations.* In general, avoid abbreviations except for state names and street type (St., Blvd., Ave., etc.).

Job Applications: Purpose and Limitations

Job applications are a necessary part of the employment process. These forms have sections on personal information, education, work experience, salary history, position desired, skills and qualifications, accomplishments, references, eligibility for employment in the United States, veteran status, criminal convictions, and other information.

Job applications also show your legal rights and the company's legal rights concerning misrepresentation or omission of information on the application, termination of employment, and discrimination laws. Job applications also have an accompanying affirmative action information form concerning your ethnic background.

Usually, you will fill out a job application before you interview for a job. For professional positions in business, education, law, medicine, and the arts, a job application may be an after-the-fact element of the job interview—completed after the interview takes place.

Don't take job application forms lightly! Filling them out well attests to your neatness, thoroughness, attention to detail, and professionalism. For some positions, they are the initial screening mechanism for candidates. In some situations, the job application may take the place of a resume. Therefore, it should be treated as an important component of your job search process.

The basic factual information about your education, training, and experience is especially important. It is not unheard of for one candidate to receive the job offer over another candidate for having a neater application or for having stated some critical piece of information that the other candidate did not.

Your honesty is most important. Many organizations will terminate your employment if any information is false, sometimes even in situations where you made an honest mistake. Be careful when filling out these forms!

Here are some basic tips to follow when filling out job applications:

1. Read and follow the directions on the application.

2. Complete the form in black ink or use a typewriter.

3. Have your basic information already assembled including details concerning your education, work history, references, and so forth.

4. Tell the truth. Remember, lying on an application is usually grounds for termination—even after years of employment. Also, don't exaggerate your abilities.

5. Spell and use words correctly.

6. Use abbreviations with care. If the reader doesn't know your abbreviations, don't use them.

7. Answer questions completely. Fill in every blank. Unanswered questions are typically viewed negatively—as though you are hiding something or are careless. If a question does not apply, write "N/A" (not applicable).

8. Don't write "see resume" on the application. This translates into the message "I am lazy," plus it requires extra work for the employer to reference your resume.

9. Choose an appropriate job title for the position desired. Do not write "anything" under position desired. Give this answer some focus, such as "Entry Level Accounting" or "Data Entry" or "Human Resources Assistant."

10. Write "Open" or "Negotiable" for salary wanted. Negotiation concerning salary comes later during the offer stage.

11. Sign and date the application with your formal name. Do not use nicknames, and do include your middle name or initial.

12. Attach your resume. Your resume can highlight your skills and abilities better than a job application can.

Figure 6.8 shows a sample job application.

| *figure* | **6.8** | *Sample job application.* |

This application is effective for 120 days from the date you complete it. If you are still available for employment after that time, you must reapply. Failure to fully complete this application may result in non-consideration.

_____ is an Equal Opportunity Employer. All applicants and employees are considered for employment, development, advancement, and earnings based upon their skills, performance, and potential without regard to race, color, religion, sex, national origin, age, disability, veteran status, sexual orientation, or any other condition or characteristic protected by law. You are not required to give information to any inquiries prohibited by law.

_____ will make reasonable accommodations to applicants and employees with disabilities to enable them to participate in the hiring process and to perform the essential functions of the job where the accommodation does not pose an undue hardship for the company.

Background Verification Notice

I understand that the information I provide in this application must be complete and accurate to the best of my knowledge. I realize that falsification and/or incomplete information may jeopardize my employment now or in the future. _____ or its agents may seek to verify this information and may make inquiries by securing a consumer investigative report concerning my criminal convictions, employment experience, education, and motor vehicle record (if applicable). I understand that I have a right to obtain, upon written request to _____ within a reasonable time after making this application, a complete and accurate disclosure of the investigation conducted in connection with any consumer investigative report on me requested by _____. I authorize the release of information relating to these areas of inquiry.

Signature: _____ Date: _____

Please print in ink.

Personal Data

Name	Social Security Number	Home Phone
Address (Street, City, State, Zip Code)		
Position Desired*	Date Available	Willing to travel? ☐ Yes ☐ No	Relocate? ☐ Yes ☐ No
Are you authorized to work in the U.S.? ☐ Yes ☐ No	If No, Visa Type and Number		
Have you been convicted of a crime?** ☐ Yes ☐ No If Yes, please detail–Offense and Disposition	How long ago?	City, State	

Source

How were you referred? ☐ Employment Agency/Firm ☐ Employee Referral ☐ Internet ☐ Newspaper ☐ Other Source
Please Identify – Name of Newspaper, Employment Agency, or Other Source or Person

*Any application containing indefinite responses such as "Any available position" will not be considered.

**Previous convictions of a crime do not necessarily exclude an applicant from consideration for employment. All circumstances will be considered, including age at time of offense, seriousness and nature of violation, and rehabilitation.

figure **6.8** *Continued*

U.S. Military Service

Branch	Final Rank

Service Schools or Special Experience related to job for which you are applying?

Education

	SCHOOL NAME	CITY, STATE	MAJOR COURSE OF STUDY	YEARS	DEGREE OR CERTIFICATE RECEIVED
High School					
College(s)					
Graduate					
Other					

Employment   Please list all employers beginning with your present employer.

Firm Name	Address		Phone	Dates From	To
Position Held	Base Salary Beginning	Ending	Supervisor Name Title		
Reason for leaving					
Firm Name	Address		Phone	Dates From	To
Position Held	Base Salary Beginning	Ending	Supervisor Name Title		
Reason for leaving					
Firm Name	Address		Phone	Dates From	To
Position Held	Base Salary Beginning	Ending	Supervisor Name Title		
Reason for leaving					
Firm Name	Address		Phone	Dates From	To
Position Held	Base Salary Beginning	Ending	Supervisor Name Title		
Reason for leaving					

Referrals

Is there anyone you would refer:		
For what type of position:	What is the best way to contact them:	
Mailing Address		
Home Phone	E-mail	Other

Remember that employers sometimes use job applications to quickly find out whether you have specific skills or training that are required for the job. Companies design job applications for easy, quick reference in finding out those key skills. This is why it is critical to fill applications out efficiently and thoroughly. Just because key information is on your resume doesn't mean it will be noticed by the employer. Make sure it is also shown on the job application so all bases are covered.

Obtain a job application from an employer of interest and complete it, noting the various categories the application includes.

General Information and Suggestions for Completing the Application

Equal Opportunity hiring statement/background verification policy/hiring policy. This is employer information for you to read, sign, and date.

Name/address/phone/e-mail/social security number. Use your full legal name and address.

Position(s) applying for. Indicate the position in line with your skills and experience.

Work hours/availability/start date. State "open" if you can work any shift or start anytime.

Education. Complete thoroughly and highlight particularly relevant education and course work.

Employment history. List both paid and unpaid employment, including military service and self-employment. Use action statements in the "Duties" section. Avoid negative statements in the "Reason for Leaving" section. If you were fired, write "Laid off" or "Terminated." It is permissible to check "No" for "May we contact this employer" for current employers.

U.S military service. Complete if you have served in the military. Indicate any special training, education, or skills that are relevant for the position.

Other skills. Include any relevant skills, memberships, presentations, languages, publications, or other pertinent information.

Training and certifications. List relevant training and certifications and time frames for each.

References. Do not include family or other relatives.

Criminal record/convictions. Be honest. Employers do hire applicants with criminal records. Concisely state the incident and add a statement about how you have turned things around to a positive direction.

Signature and date. Read, sign, and date the application. Take note of the information here concerning accuracy, false information, disclosure of information by third parties, and physical examinations.

Place your sample application in your portfolio.

We need to emphasize the importance of completing the job application neatly with accurate and honest information. As with interviewing, be honest but don't be stupid. Make sure the message you communicate through job applications is a positive one that emphasizes your strengths and abilities and defuses your weaknesses and "baggage."

Problems? *In the left-hand column below, list several weaknesses or problems in your background that an employer might be concerned about. In the right-hand column, write a positive phrase that you could use on a job application to reduce an employer's fears about the issue.*

Problem/Weakness   **Stated Positively on Job Application**

1. _____   _____

2. _____   _____

3. _____   _____

4. _____   _____

Unattractive areas can be explained in an interview. Practice explaining these areas! If you need to, script these areas so they are easier to get through during your interviews.

Difficult Questions on Applications

Stay positive! There are few flawless job applicants, and the same can be said for organizations. Recognizing that you are not the only one who has to handle difficult situations may help. The secret is to turn adverse situations into positive learning experiences.

Most biased questions have been eliminated from employer applications due to provisions of the Civil Rights Act (1964) and the Americans with Disabilities Act (1991). Under these Acts, it is illegal to discriminate against any employee because of sex, age, race, national origin, ethnic group, religion, color, family status, or physical or mental conditions.

Your task is to write thoughtful responses that sell you as a strong candidate. Your goal in completing a job application is to get a job interview and a job offer. Below are a few areas that cause difficulties for many applicants.

Gaps in employment. Look for ways to explain these gaps in positive terms. If you attended school, stayed home to raise a family, volunteered at the library, spent a year traveling the world, or had some other significant life experience, mention it as long as it is positive. Other not-so-positive reasons can cause problems. Criminal convictions are one such area.

Criminal record. Openness and honesty is usually the best policy here. Employers hire people who have made mistakes and are ready to return to society in a productive way. Locate these employers! Often, you can get help from your parole officer, a school, or a state placement adviser. On the application, discuss training you received during your incarceration and how that has moved you in a positive direction.

Attendance and absences. Although it is inappropriate to ask questions concerning medical problems, employers may ask questions about your attendance. Employers want to know how dependable you are. If you're absent a lot, for whatever reasons, you may be screened out of the hiring process. Poor attendance may indicate problems with health, accidents, attitude, or work performance. If you have a poor attendance record without any positive way to explain it, you may just have to confess and promise to do better.

Unemployment compensation. Questions concerning unemployment compensation have disappeared from most job applications. If you have received unemployment compensation, you must respond "yes." You may explain if there is room on the application, but watch how you word your explanation.

Worker's compensation. An employer may not inquire into an applicant's worker's compensation history before making a conditional offer of employment. After making a conditional job offer, an employer may inquire about a person's worker's compensation history in a medical inquiry or examination that is required of all applicants in the same job category. Top employers will not have this question on their job applications. If you see this on an application, ignore it.

Reason for leaving past employer. It is very important to answer this question well and positively. Obviously, you shouldn't write "Couldn't get along with the grumpy old boss," "Personality conflict," or "Standing made my legs hurt." Give a positive reason for leaving. Do not make negative statements about your employer. If you were fired, write "Laid off" or "Terminated."

Reason for leaving current employer. Respond to this question as if it read, "Why do you want to leave your current job or employer?" Think of your reasons, and write a response that is positive and also explains the value you bring to an employer. Viable reasons may include the following:

- Seeking full-time, permanent employment
- Need part-time work while attending college
- Desire employment in my field of training
- Advancement opportunities
- More energizing responsibilities
- Higher salary

Your answer should be one an employer can understand and accept.

Position wanted. Always choose a position and level that is compatible with your work experience and education. If you don't have management experience, don't write "Manager." You won't be selected for an interview. A better choice is to write "Management Trainee" or "Entry-Level Management."

Don't write "anything." Employers need to know what you want. It helps them meet their needs and your needs. Naming a position also helps you focus more specifically on an area and be more direct in the interview.

Work schedule. If there are certain days, hours, or holidays that you cannot work, be sure to apply for positions with schedules that meet your needs. Honestly indicate the days or shifts you can work.

Book and Internet Correspondence Resources

ome of the better books on job search correspondence include the following:

- *Cover Letters for Dummies*, Joyce Lain Kennedy
- *Cover Letters That Knock 'Em Dead*, Martin Yate
- *201 Dynamite Job Search Letters*, Drs. Ron and Caryl Krannich
- *175 High Impact Cover Letters*, Richard Beatty

Web sites that have good information on job search correspondence include the following:

- Campus Career Center: www.campuscareercenter.com
- Career Builder Network: www.careerbuilder.com
- College Grad Network: www.collegegrad.com
- Monster.com: www.monster.com
- Quintessential Careers: www.quintcareers.com
- Student Central: www.studentcentral.com

Summary

Your job search correspondence is absolutely critical to your success in job hunting. Not only does it help you uncover opportunities and connect with others, but it also gives you exposure, one of the keys to developing job leads and keeping people informed of your status. As we've continually stated, your correspondence lends credibility to your professionalism, your determination, and your ability to build relationships. All of these elements will enable you to succeed in your process. Continue to positively push your correspondence and uncover the best opportunities for yourself!

Remember, job applications include a variety of tricky questions. Follow the suggestions in this chapter so you aren't tripped up in the process. Continue to take a positive approach and portray yourself as a capable candidate. This will open doors and prevent others from shutting during your job search.

Marketing Tools

YOUR RESUME AND REFERENCES

chapter

7

I can accept failure, but I can't accept not trying.

—MICHAEL JORDAN

Mai. Mai is excited as she thinks about writing her resume. "I really need to get my resume done. It's time for me to get going on my internship search. Oh, I nearly forgot, the study abroad and scholarship committees need one too! I hope I write my resume the right way!"

Mai's predicament is one that most job seekers worry about. That is, they want to write the resume the "right way." Clearly, there are important aspects to consider when writing a resume, but there is not one absolutely correct way. The most important thing is for you to write your resume in a way that best portrays your skills, abilities, and knowledge for employers.

A well-written resume won't get you a job—on its own it never does—but it will open doors to interviews and give you the confidence you need in those interviews. A well-written resume that shows your key skills, abilities, and knowledge increases the likelihood that you will secure interview opportunities in the career directions you desire. With its companion document—a focused cover letter—your resume is the key correspondence tool used in your job search.

Remember, your resume is not a static item. It is a living, ongoing document that you use to catalog relevant experiences for presentation to interested parties. Plan on revising your resume frequently, whether or not you are actively seeking new employment. Frequent revisions keep you focused on your career development and help you evaluate your status and progress.

Resume Introduction

In this chapter, you will examine the elements of resume writing. Your goals, education, work experience, and personal background combine to direct you toward one resume or another. Traditionally, chronological resumes—the ones that cover your background in historical sequence from past to present—are used by most people. But if you are making a career change, the chronological format may not be appropriate. Instead, a functional resume may be more suitable. The major resume forms are explained later in this chapter.

Besides choosing a format, you will make other choices concerning your resume, including:

1. Type of information
2. Presentation order
3. Headings
4. Amount of white space
5. Font and size of print

6. Paper color and type

7. Overall layout

After completing this chapter, you will be able to develop a resume that highlights your key strengths and links you to your targeted employers and jobs.

Where Are You Going?

Before putting your resume together, give some serious thought to your long-term career plans. Do not be lulled into thinking your resume is a dull, dry restatement of your work and education history. Raise your level of thinking and realize that your resume is a living, ongoing, working document about you and your career path.

For these and other reasons, it is wise to create your resume yourself rather than relying on a resume writing service. Who better than you can really perfect your resume? You know yourself best and can bring to your resume your character and direction. Even more important, you continue to look within yourself and examine what you want to do and what you have to offer employers. During the process, you learn to identify with the product and how to market that product—you!

personal **THINK PIECE**

The themes of your resume. *In the space below, list three major themes you want your resume to tell the reader. List each theme, then indicate why you want that message to be sent to the reader.*

1. Major theme: _____

   Reason for sending this message to the reader: _____

   _____

2. Major theme: _____

   Reason for sending this message to the reader: _____

   _____

3. Major theme: _____

   Reason for sending this message to the reader: _____

   _____

What Is a Resume?

A resume is a marketing piece, an advertisement, a brochure. It is a tool to open doors to career possibilities and interviews. From that point on, it serves as a point of discussion concerning your background, qualifications, and fit with the job at hand.

A resume is not the clinching item for obtaining a job offer. Rather, it is an opening item for discussing employment opportunities, a reference item during informational interviews, and a general communication tool about you to others.

The Three C's of Resumes

Clear, concise, and corresponding: these are the three C's of resumes. All resumes, regardless of format, must have these three elements to be effective.

Clear

First, your resume needs to be completely clear to the reader, neatly outlining your work and education background, skills, knowledge, abilities, interests, and objectives in easily understood language. Make it easy for your reader! Remember, someone screening candidate resumes for a job usually has many resumes to read. If the reader has to struggle to understand your resume, she may instead choose to look at the other candidates' resumes. A resume that is difficult to understand is destined for the "no" pile.

Concise

We all receive product brochures in the mail. Those brochures usually do not detail each product feature; rather, they highlight the product's most important features in general terms. Your resume (your brochure), which is about you (the product), should be written in a similar manner. It should highlight those critical aspects about you in a way that elevates the interest of people in the hiring loop.

Before putting together your resume, give serious thought to your long-term career plans.

Your resume is like a brochure, giving the reader an initial indication of product features but not all of the specifics. It is meant to draw the reader in, to encourage the reader to ask more questions, to pique the reader's interest in your capabilities. Write your resume concisely so the reader can quickly move through it with increasing interest in you.

Corresponding

Write your resume for your future job, not for your past job(s). When first writing or revising their resume, most people describe only what they did on their jobs. They fall into the trap of describing job duties and fail to illustrate skills and accomplishments. The resume reads like a dry textbook and fails to link the person to his desired future career.

Writing your resume with an idea of where you are headed with your career is critically important. Research information about your new career using books, Web sites, and, most important, informational interviews with people in that line of work. When you begin writing your resume, you can focus it in the direction of your future career using the information obtained through your research.

That makes sense not only from the standpoint of developing interview opportunities, but also from a psychological viewpoint. How can you get excited about your job search with a resume that restates what you did in a job or jobs that you are no longer interested in? Link your resume to your future, increasing your energy and optimism at the same time.

In addition, know your reader and the job you are addressing. What may be appropriate terminology for one particular job may not suit the next job. Multiple versions of your resume with different wording may work best for your job search.

Who Should Get Your Resume?

As with networking, almost anyone is a candidate to receive your resume. Do not view your resume as merely an information piece to connect with existing job opportunities. Certainly that is its most frequent use, but you should view your resume more broadly—it is an information document for any and all readers. Use it as such! Give your resume to those people with whom you have informational interviews. Give your resume to family, friends, acquaintances, really anyone in your network. Encourage them to send it along to other people who can help you. Remember that it is an advertising tool.

Types of Resumes

The age-old resume question is, "Should I make my resume a chronological one or a functional one?" As with most choices in life, the answer is "It depends." Both styles have their places in the job hunt. Both styles have advantages and disadvantages depending on the type of job you seek. Following is a review of the pros and cons of each.

Chronological Resume

The chronological resume can actually be labeled the "reverse chronological" resume because your education and work experience is listed in reverse chronological order. Typically, the chronological resume is best for a high school or college graduate who is entering the formal job market for the first time or for someone who is changing jobs within a career field. It is the most common form of resume in use today and is the most familiar to employers.

PROS

- Easier for the reader to follow and has a logical sequence
- Emphasizes work and education accomplishments in specific situations
- Highlights other important activities and interests
- Excellent for pursuing positions within current field at the same or a higher level of responsibility

CONS

- Limiting to someone who is changing careers
- May fail to highlight the most relevant work skills for the job or career now being pursued
- May bury prior, most relevant work experience at the expense of the chronological sequence
- May overly emphasize "job hopping" (to your disadvantage)
- May emphasize time gaps if you have little or no work experience

Figure 7.1 shows a sample chronological resume for a recent college graduate.

Functional Resume

The functional resume focuses on skills, abilities, and experiences, but not in the context of specific jobs. Details on previous jobs held may be entirely omitted or given only the briefest listing. These resumes may be best for someone with very limited work history, someone reentering the workforce after a significant absence, someone with a significant work history that is not relevant to the current job objective, or someone changing careers.

PROS

- Organizes and summarizes experiences along specific skills or functions
- Clearly focuses on accomplishments
- Allows de-emphasis of less relevant work experience
- Can shift focus from aspects of background that can hurt employment chances (long periods out of the workforce, job hopping, and so forth)

CONS

- Arouses suspicion among employers because of what it doesn't show
- Does not tell employers how recently skills were used
- Does not tell employers the context of the skills and which jobs are linked to them
- Not a good style for someone remaining in her field
- Hard to follow relative to employment history

Figure 7.2 shows a sample functional resume.

figure **7.1** *Example of a chronological resume.*

JACOB THOMAS

4593 Willow Lane
Minneapolis, MN 55455

(612) 555-4553
e-mail: jthomas@tc.umn.edu

Education	UNIVERSITY OF MINNESOTA	Minneapolis, MN

Bachelor of Science in Business
Graduation: May 2007 Major: Finance
Cumulative GPA: 3.6

Experience	THE PILLSBURY COMPANY	Minneapolis, MN

Finance Intern

- Assisted controller in meeting reporting needs and corporate goals through collection of data and generation of reports.
- Performed audits and financial analyses on a wide range of projects.
- Developed key performance measures spreadsheet for internal analysis.

June 2006 – present

GENERAL PRODUCTS, INC.   Minneapolis, MN

Accounting Clerk

- Verified accuracy of financial reports and troubleshot problem areas.
- Generated various financial reports, including daily, weekly, and monthly sales, expense reimbursements, and sales' commissions detail.
- Assisted with month-end closing.

April 2005 – May 2006

SPORTS UNLIMITED   Minneapolis, MN

Sales Associate

- Assisted customers with product recommendations and selection.
- Arranged products for attractive merchandise display.
- Completed daily, monthly, and annual inventory.
- Named Sales Associate of the Month, December 2003.

March 2004 – April 2005

Computers
- Experience on IBM and Mac PCs
- Skilled with Microsoft Excel, Word, PowerPoint, Windows

Honors
- 3M Leadership Scholarship
- Phi Theta Kappa Honor Society
- Carlson School and College of Liberal Arts Dean's List

Activities
- Investment Club and Finance Association—President
- Excel Leadership Development Program
- Red Cross Volunteer
- Intramural Basketball

References   Available upon request

figure **7.2** *Example of a functional resume.*

Angela Pierce

1186 SUMMIT DRIVE, ST. PAUL, MN 55113   (651) 555-4458   •   E-MAIL: APIERCE@AOL.COM

SUMMARY

- Excellent problem-solving skills and desire to increase efficiency of the organization
- Strong communication skills developed in customer service settings
- Demonstrated leadership and interpersonal skills in work and extracurricular activities

SKILLS

Problem Solving

Developed and used spreadsheet to analyze inventories and made recommendations for optimal inventories levels. Assisted customers with product and service concerns in a satisfactory and timely manner. Developed and conducted new member orientation for sorority.

Accounting

Completed fixed-asset schedules and booked depreciation for current year. Responsible for various monthly general ledger accounts including accuracy and month-end reconciliation. Assisted with compilation of year-end financial statements.

Leadership

Trained and managed a work staff. Assigned duties to employees and monitored work. Served as vice-president of a student association and developed mentorship program. Developed and coordinated various sorority activities.

Communication

Supervised, trained, and interacted with coworkers and customers. Conducted presentations to orient new sorority members on annual basis. Communicated with a wide diversity of people through volunteer work. Speak foreign language fluently.

WORK HISTORY

Genuine Products, Inc., Plymouth, MN	*Summer 2006*
University of Minnesota, Minneapolis, MN	*April 2005 – June 2006*
McDonald's, Minneapolis, MN	*June 2004 – August 2005*

EDUCATION

University of Minnesota, Minneapolis	Major: Accounting
Bachelor of Science in Business	Expected graduation: May 2006
	Cumulative GPA: 3.4

ACTIVITIES

- Student Association for Accounting
- U. S. Olympic Festival Volunteer
- Loaves and Fishes Volunteer
- Intramural Basketball and Volleyball

LANGUAGES

- Write and speak fluent Spanish

References available upon request.

figure **7.3**

Strengths of specific resume formats.

CAREER STATUS	CHRONOLOGICAL	FUNCTIONAL
New graduate (high school)	●	
New graduate (college)	●	
Returning to workforce		●
Changing jobs (same career)	●	
Changing industries (same career)	●	
Changing careers	■	●
Gaps in employment history	■	■
No previous work experience	■	●
Significant job hopping		■
Several jobs; little growth	■	■
Highlight specific areas		●

■ *If written smartly and carefully, the chronological form may work.*

■ *Be able to explain what happened during these periods.*

Which Resume for Which Situation?

Figure 7.3 may help you determine the most suitable style of resume. A word of caution, however: everyone's situation is unique. The following recommendations should be taken as general recommendations only. Your particular situation determines the resume style to use. Remember, write the best resume both in content and format that will get you to your future.

Preparing Your Resume

 ou should focus on two major areas when preparing your resume: content appeal and visual appeal. Both of these areas are examined next.

Content Appeal

Content appeal refers to what your resume says, including not only your narratives but also the categories you choose to show on the resume. The most common general categories include the following:

Heading. This contains basic information about you, including:

- *Name.* Use your legal first and last name. A middle name or middle initial is optional. Your name should be in a larger type size than anything else shown on the resume.

- *Address.* If you are a student away from your permanent address, include your local address.
- *Phone.* Use your home or cellular phone number.
- *E-mail.* Include this because it is an efficient way for employers to contact you about job opportunities.

Job objective. Including a job objective is optional. Experts disagree as to whether an objective should be included. A good general rule is that if you are targeting your resume to a specific position, include a job objective. If you do not have a specific job targeted, leave the objective off. If you are posting your resume on a Web site, try to write an objective that fits a career family or job title for which employment opportunities are available. Examples include the following:

- Computer-aided drafting and design, specializing in mechanical design
- Medical records technician position working for a hospital or medical clinic
- Sales position with an organization dedicated to quality customer service
- Entry-level accounting position that uses current technical skills and allows for future growth
- Technical writing position focusing on computer and scientific issues

Education. Whether your education or experience section comes next depends on your career status. If your education background is less relevant than your work experience, list your education later. If your education is what is required by the employer and your relevant work experience is light, list your education first.

The amount of detail you use here depends on the length of time you have been out of school—the longer the time, the less detail. If you are a recent graduate, your education may be one of your biggest selling points, thereby requiring a somewhat larger section.

Items to include are the following:

- *Schools.* List schools attended and their locations (city and state is sufficient). If you've attained a college degree, omit high school attended.
- *Degree.* Show the degree you received and when. If you're currently working on a degree, show the expected date of graduation. This is the only time you can show future information on your resume.
- *Major.* Show your major field of study as long as it is relevant to the position you're applying for.
- *GPA.* Include your grade point average if it is significantly strong (3.0 or above).
- *Honors.* Show honors or scholarships if they are significant or relevant to your field.
- *Course work.* List if relevant and you are a recent graduate.
- *Study abroad.* List the school, city, country, and time frame.

Experience. Typically, this section is composed of paid work experience, but may also include significant unpaid work experience or activities. Your experience section must highlight those skills, accomplishments, and responsibilities relative to your job objective. Weave the relevant things you've done with the direction you want to pursue. In other words, prioritize the key activities that will get you to your future job.

Tips for this section include the following:

- List the organization name, your title, dates, city, and state.
- Bold either the organization name or your title, whichever would be most attractive to future employers.
- Describe current activities in present tense; past activities in past tense.
- Use action words to begin your sentences (refer to the list provided later in this chapter).
- Use strong, results-oriented terms when writing your descriptions.
- Use terminology that reflects the skills and abilities needed in the job or career you desire.
- Stress the skills, accomplishments, and activities that fit your future job.
- Quantify your accomplishments.
- Use reverse chronological order.

If you use a functional resume format, develop categories to illustrate your experience. These categories may be organized according to your transferable skills or your career field-specific skills. Transferable skill categories include supervisory, management, administrative, problem solving, creativity, analyzing, organizing, researching, and quantitative. Career field-specific skill categories include advertising, accounting, teaching, writing, training, research, computers, selling, counseling, finance, and marketing.

7.1 | Cataloging Your Skills and Achievements

To get your arms around your skills, list your jobs, volunteer experience, achievements, extracurricular activities, and other experiences before creating your resume. Use the following exercise to begin your catalog.

On a sheet of paper, list the headings shown on the chart below. In the first column, list a variety of activities you've been involved in, including jobs, volunteer experience, achievements, and extracurricular activities. Fill out the chart with special emphasis on the skills you used in each situation and relevant achievements or results. The directions that follow should guide you.

Activity (1). An activity is a particular situation you will transfer to your resume. Work, volunteer experience, and extracurricular school activities typically make up the bulk of your items here. These are also the key ingredients, along with your education, that will inevitably be asked about most in a job interview. You must know these situations thoroughly to have a successful job interview!

Activity (1)	Organization (2)	Period of Time (3)	Duties (4)	Skills Used (5)	Achievements or Results (6)
Cashier	Wal-Mart	6/03–4/05	Checked out customer purchases	Accuracy Attention to detail Communication	Employee of Mo.—Aug. 2004

Organization (2). Obviously, this is where the activity occurred. For jobs and volunteer experience, be ready to list the city and state where the activity occurred. For this worksheet, however, merely list the organization for eventual transfer to your resume.

Time Period (3). This is the time period when the activity took place. If you are still doing the activity, show the current date as "present"; for example, 1/02-present.

Duties (4). Most people devote the greatest amount of energy to this section. Unless you are looking for another job that ties directly into the duties you have already, don't overly indulge when describing your duties. Today, organizations hire people for their skills, not their past job duties. For now, simply list a few of the duties you had in the activity.

Skills Used (5). This is probably the most critical portion of your resume. Whether you are seeking a job similar to ones you've had in the past or an entirely new one, spend most of your time describing the skills used in prior experiences. List them briefly on this worksheet, but be prepared to expand on them in your resume. Even more important, be prepared to discuss them at length in an interview.

Be honest about your skills and don't exaggerate. Remember, anything on your resume is fair game for a question during an interview. If you list a skill that you really didn't use much or don't possess, you can fall flat during an interview if questioned about it.

Achievements or Results (6). List your positive achievements or results from the activity. Quantifiable results that show your abilities and give you credit are best. Don't be shy about strong achievements, awards, or results. You need to convey your best qualities on the resume and during the interview.

Action-oriented accomplishment statements communicate the value you bring to an employer. Use these statements generously. Consider the following examples:

- Increased productivity and quality . . .
- Improved service . . .
- Developed lesson plans . . .
- Created database system . . .
- Streamlined operations . . .
- Reduced cost of . . .
- Increased sales . . .
- Implemented a new program in . . .
- Improved communication and information flow by . . .
- Coordinated marketing plans through . . .

Statements that are specific and illustrate past successes increase your chances of being selected for an interview! (See Figure 7.4 for a list of action words to enhance your narratives.)

Other. Items in this section are important because they may reflect key transferable skills that employers look for. This section may include the following:

- *Computer skills.* If you are in the technology field, list these in a separate category.
- *Foreign language skills.* Indicate level of fluency.
- *Memberships in professional or community organizations.* Indicate positions held and dates.
- *Volunteer activities.* Indicate positions held and dates.
- *Honors and awards.* If you are a recent graduate, you may make this a separate section.
- *Licenses or certifications.* Indicate how current.
- *Publications you've written.* Indicate name, date of publication, and publisher.
- *Conferences where you've made presentations.* Indicate name and date of conference, and subject of presentation.

---

figure **7.4** *List of action words for writing narratives.*

Accomplished	Clarified	Developed	Fashioned	Invented	Programmed	Scheduled
Achieved	Classified	Devised	Focused	Investigated	Projected	Schooled
Acted	Coached	Diagnosed	Forecasted	Launched	Promoted	Screened
Adapted	Collected	Directed	Formulated	Lectured	Provided	Set
Addressed	Compiled	Dispatched	Founded	Led	Publicized	Skilled
Administered	Completed	Distinguished	Generated	Maintained	Published	Solidified
Advanced	Composed	Diversified	Guided	Managed	Purchased	Solved
Advised	Computed	Drafted	Headed up	Marketed	Recommended	Specified
Allocated	Conceptualized	Edited	Identified	Mediated	Reconciled	Stimulated
Analyzed	Conducted	Educated	Illustrated	Moderated	Recorded	Streamlined
Appraised	Consolidated	Eliminated	Implemented	Monitored	Recruited	Strengthened
Approved	Contained	Enabled	Improved	Motivated	Reduced	Summarized
Arranged	Contracted	Encouraged	Increased	Negotiated	Referred	Supervised
Assembled	Contributed	Engineered	Indoctrinated	Operated	Regulated	Surveyed
Assigned	Controlled	Enlisted	Influenced	Organized	Rehabilitated	Systemized
Assisted	Coordinated	Established	Informed	Originated	Remodeled	Tabulated
Attained	Corresponded	Evaluated	Initiated	Overhauled	Repaired	Taught
Audited	Counseled	Examined	Innovated	Oversaw	Represented	Trained
Authored	Created	Executed	Inspected	Performed	Researched	Translated
Automated	Critiqued	Expanded	Installed	Persuaded	Restored	Traveled
Balanced	Cut	Expedited	Instituted	Planned	Restructured	Trimmed
Budgeted	Decreased	Explained	Instructed	Prepared	Retrieved	Upgraded
Built	Delegated	Extracted	Integrated	Presented	Reversed	Validated
Calculated	Demonstrated	Fabricated	Interpreted	Prioritized	Reviewed	Worked
Cataloged	Designated	Facilitated	Interviewed	Processed	Revitalized	Wrote
Chaired	Designed	Familiarized	Introduced	Produced	Saved	

The amount of detail in this section is typically less than that in the experience section. However, if your experience with one of these areas is significant, add more detail or move the activity to the experience section.

Interests. This section is optional. If you do include it, indicate a few interests that may separate you from other candidates or may be good conversation items in an interview (e.g., skydiving, photography, dog trainer, etc.).

References. A reference line is optional. If used, it should be listed as only one line: "References available upon request."

Visual Appeal

Your resume must look professional in every way—in its format, printing, and paper. Here are some thoughts on the visual look of your resume.

Bullets or paragraphs? Should you format your resume using bullets or paragraphs? The answer, like the resume types, is "It depends." As with types of resumes, bullet and paragraph formats each have pros and cons. Following is a review of each type as well as a combination of the two.

PARAGRAPH STYLE

- *Pro #1:* You can put more information on a page.
- *Pro #2:* Some experiences lend themselves best to this style.
- *Con #1:* It can be difficult for the reader to identify individual achievements and skills.
- *Con #2:* Resume reviewers may be turned off by its "book-look" and prefer a bullet style for a quicker read.

BULLET STYLE

- *Pro #1:* Easier for you to portray individual skills, accomplishments, and activities.
- *Pro #2:* Less wordy look may be more inviting for readers who are in a hurry to read resumes.
- *Con #1:* Uses more space because each bullet starts on a new line.
- *Con #2:* May not give the level of detail to sufficiently describe an experience.

Both paragraphs and bullets. This can be a very effective way of showing your resume, but carefully construct it so it does not have a cluttered or overly busy look.

Printing. Laser-printed resumes are the norm and look the best. Be fore-warned that inkjet printers have a tendency to "bleed" ink on the printed copy. Laser-printed resumes generally have a crisp look and don't bleed.

Paper. High-quality paper can be obtained at copying centers and printing shops. You might consider having a copy center copy your resume from a hard copy you supply. This generally results in an excellent final copy for distribution. Consider the following tips:

- Use paper that is heavier than laser printer paper. Ask for suggestions from your copy center.
- Colors should be limited to white, off-white, light gray, or other moderate colors, unless you are in the arts or advertising industries, where creativity is more critical. There you can be more creative in color and style.
- Select matching envelopes and stationery for printing cover letters and mailing your resume.

Stylistic tips. Following are some suggestions to help your resume look its best:

- Use white space appropriately. Do not write the resume like a page in a novel.
- Use at least 3/4-inch margins on the top, bottom, and sides.
- Keep sentences to the point, using a minimum of articles (e.g., *a*, *the*).
- Thoroughly edit all unnecessary words.
- Write clearly, positively, and concisely.
- Write to your specific target audience in the industry or career you desire.
- Primarily include relevant information and skills that fit your job objective.
- Use strong action words to draw in the reader.
- Give examples to highlight activities and responsibilities.

student profile

Mai. **Mai's Resume.** Mai spent a weekend constructing the first draft of her resume. She found it took a lot more time than she anticipated. "I can't believe how hard it was to put my resume together," she told a friend. "Will you please read through it and check for errors?"

Her friend gladly did so and noticed one spelling error, a slightly different font size on one line, and an extra line space between two major sections.

"I can't believe it. I read and checked this over 10 times. Oh, what a process to go through! There must be an easier way!"

Mai's frustrations are the same most job seekers have when completing their resume. It takes a lot of work and patience to make the final resume perfect. Even then, the resume should be frequently revised as one's experiences evolve.

Figure 7.5 (page 188) shows Mai's resume after she corrected the problems her friend uncovered. As you read through the resume, consider these questions and write your answers in the space provided:

- What is your initial impression of the attractiveness of the resume?

_____

_____

(Continued)

(Continued)

- Did Mai use action-oriented wording to describe her experiences?

  _____

  _____

- Did Mai effectively indicate her accomplishments?

  _____

  _____

- Did Mai exhibit any particular themes or characteristics about herself?

  _____

  _____

- What general career direction do you think Mai might pursue based on her experiences?

  _____

  _____

Should You Tailor Your Resume to a Specific Position?

Absolutely! You, of course, are qualified for a wide range of jobs. The more education and training you obtain, the wider the range grows. As you search for and uncover job opportunities, revise your resume to best fit the job in question. That will best position you to get interviews.

Be absolutely sure you are capable in all of the areas you mention. Do not overly exaggerate your skills and abilities. For example, if you worked with computers in your job as a graphic designer, it's not a good idea to tailor your resume to a computer programmer position. Granted, you used computers at work but not in the same context as a programmer. Exaggerating on your resume and during the interview may mean big trouble. You may get the job and be expected to perform at the level you contended you could. Being fired would be the next reason for a new job search.

At the same time, clearly promote what you can do. So many jobs today require so many of the same transferable skills, you owe it to yourself to explore them. For example, the world of business has so many overlapping areas in product (or service) management and product (or service) development. What about the accounting and finance fields and their overlap? How about the computer field, with its range from computer programming to network administration to systems analysis to Web design (which can overlap advertising). Explore various options that fit your skill set.

figure **7.5** *Mai's resume*

MAI NGUYEN

153 9th Street South Minneapolis, MN 55444	E-mail: mnguyen@hotmail.com	Home Phone: (612) 555-8892 Cell Phone: (404) 555-7124

OBJECTIVE Entry-level accounting position that uses current technical skills and allows for future growth

EDUCATION University of Minnesota   Minneapolis, MN
Bachelor of Science in Business   *Expected graduation: May 2008*
Major: Accounting
Cumulative GPA: 3.34

EXPERIENCE **Certified Accounting Professionals, Inc.**   St. Paul, MN
Administrative Support   *June 2005–present*

- Gaining knowledge about business practices while assisting accountants with administrative details
- Providing customer service and information through receptionist duties including answering phones, mailing out information about the firm's services, and checking clients in for meetings
- Organizing meeting schedules and communicating meeting details to staff accountants and clients
- Scheduling appointments for staff accountants

Jeannette   Bloomington, MN
Sales Associate   *January 2004–June 2005*

- Helped customers with product selection and recommendations through personalized service
- Conducted in-store demonstrations of new fragrances
- Created attractive store displays for seasonal merchandise
- Top-ranked sales associate for spring quarter 2005
- Achieved highest level of new credit applications for spring and summer quarters 2005

LEADERSHIP **Knight Residence Hall**, Student Representative—Facilities   *Spring 2005–present*

- Head equipment replacement initiative including purchase of new furniture and disposal of obsolete chairs, tables, and miscellaneous equipment
- Negotiate with vendors concerning purchase of new equipment

Selig Drug Initiative, Volunteer   *Spring 2005–present*

- Conduct presentations to student athletes concerning hazards of drug use
- Promote health awareness activities to students

Stewart Ethics-in-Leadership Club, Activities Chair   *Spring 2004–Fall 2005*

- Enlisted and coordinated guest speakers for monthly presentations on ethics
- Coordinated catering and created decorations for annual dinner

COMMUNITY SERVICE **Como Zoo**

- Volunteer for 2005 Zoo Boo Halloween Event

Kids on the Block

- Performed puppet plays for elementary students about alcohol, drugs, and disabilities

AWARDS Dean's List (Fall 2005)
University of Minnesota Advantage Scholarship
Kraft Foods North America Scholarship

7.2 | Your Resume

We discussed a variety of topics on resumes so far. Now it's time to put your resume together. Select a chronological or functional resume format and put your resume together using that format. For this exercise, follow these guidelines:

1. Include a job objective.

2. Refer to Exercise 7.1 on cataloging, to your job search portfolio from Chapter 5, and to other exercises in previous chapters to help write your background.

3. Refer to the Preparing Your Resume section earlier in this chapter.

After you finish your resume draft, ask yourself whether it speaks to the job objective you set for yourself. Revise it as necessary. Also ask yourself whether your resume "draws" the reader in to ask more questions about you. Finally, give the resume a good look and ask yourself whether it looks good.

You may want to repeat this exercise for the other type of resume. Compare the resumes for the message each sends, and then select the resume that fits you and your career direction best.

File this resume in your portfolio.

Field-Test the Resume

Have some friends read your resume, and then ask for constructive feedback. Ask them to describe your background from reading the resume. If their descriptions are fuzzy, revise the resume to make it clearer. Also, have people in the career field you are interested in review your resume.

Review your resume to ensure it is perfect. Here are some key questions for you to use:

_____ 1. Does the resume look neat and attractive at a first glance?

_____ 2. Did you honestly represent yourself?

_____ 3. Is the resume free of spelling and grammatical errors?

_____ 4. If you wrote an objective, is it relevant to the position you desire?

_____ 5. Is the content relevant to the position you are applying for?

_____ 6. Did you use the appropriate tense for past and present experiences?

_____ 7. Did you use action-oriented words?

_____ 8. Did you include results and accomplishments?

_____ 9. Did you write your experiences with rich content?

_____ 10. Does the resume attractively portray you?

_____ 11. Does the resume sell your abilities?

_____ 12. Will an employer be interested in giving you a job interview?

E-Resumes for Online Distribution

The resumes discussed to this point are "formatted" and used for hard copy distribution to employers (direct mail, job fairs, at the interview) and for general networking. This section discusses how to convert your resume from a hard copy format to an e-resume format.

There are several reasons for converting your resume to an electronic-friendly version. First, a resume sent as an e-mail attachment may be displayed inconsistently from computer to computer. The resume that looked perfect on your computer may look disjointed on someone else's, including an employer's.

Second, employers post job opportunities on their Web sites and independent job posting Web sites. Independent job posting Web sites also allow you to post your resume in a database that employers search for candidates. Again, your perfect-looking resume may look very imperfect on those sites.

It is important that you prepare your resume so its content is not garbled and formatted poorly when transmitted electronically. The various available formats are discussed next.

Text Format

This format is not visually appealing because it strips all formatting that makes your resume attractive. However, the reason for a text format is to make your resume compatible with employers' keyword-searchable databases. You want your resume to have a high "hit rate" with the employers' keywords, thus increasing the likelihood of a job interview. A text resume is compatible with all computer programs and will display itself accurately. You can use a text format resume for:

- Posting on job boards (Web sites)
- Pasting pieces into your profile on job boards
- Pasting into the body of an e-mail to employers in addition to attaching your formatted resume

Convert your resume to an electronic-friendly format so that you can post and e-mail your resume without it becoming garbled.

The best way to make a text version is by using your regular word processed resume and making the following adjustments:

- If developed with a resume wizard or template, retype the resume as a basic word processed document.

- Convert bolded items to all capitals.
- Convert bullets to dashes or asterisks.
- Use an easy-to-read font.
- Space the resume to a maximum of 80 characters per line.
- Double-space between each work experience or other major narratives.
- Save your resume as a .txt file.

After proofreading, e-mail it to yourself and review it for layout. Make any necessary final adjustments. Although the text format resume is the least visually appealing, a well-developed one will effectively connect with employers' keyword databases.

Rich Text Format

The rich text format resume is easily created in most word processing programs merely by saving the resume as a rich text file (.rtf). The rich text file version will look the same as your formatted word processed version. Generally speaking, the formatting and attractive visual presentation created in the original document remains in the rich text resume, although more complex formatting (such as columns or tables) may not. It's best to test the rich text resume by sending it to a few friends to see how the formatting looks on their end.

Rich text is an excellent choice as an e-resume attachment because it is compatible across all platforms and word processing programs. It's also far less vulnerable to viruses than Word documents. In terms of attachments, it's the best choice when you can't determine what file type the employer prefers. Paste the text version into the body of the e-mail message to which the rich text resume is attached.

Other Options

PDF files and HTML formats are other available options. PDF files usually cannot be scanned for keywords, and special software is required to make them. HTML formats require Web-design knowledge. At the end of the chapter, there's a list of sources that are helpful in constructing these formats.

Using Keywords to Increase Your Opportunities

It is estimated that 80 percent of employers use keyword databases to evaluate candidates. In order to increase your interview chances, prepare your resume in a way that includes keywords and phrases that are of particular interest to each employer. To increase the chance that an employer's software identifies you as a good job candidate:

- Use action words and skill words
- Use key terminology related to the job
- Use key terminology related to the employer's industry
- Highlight relevant accomplishments that are closely related to the job

A good technique is to make a "Summary of Qualifications" section that includes some keywords. It is important to include keywords throughout your resume; an appropriate amount is 25–35 keywords. For example,

- Analyzed <u>new product proposals</u> and conducted <u>internal rate of return analysis</u>.
- Managed <u>customer database</u> and <u>upgraded sales tracking system</u>.
- Coordinated <u>marketing campaigns</u> and <u>special events</u>.
- Performed <u>cross-functional</u> coordination of new facility construction.
- Oversaw <u>merchandise procurement, negotiated terms with vendors, and coordinated distribution of product</u>.

Figure 7.6 shows an example of an e-resume. Use keywords, and your chance of being selected for an interview increases!

Final Resume Tips

 lthough there is no perfect way to write a resume, there are some key things to keep in mind. We call these the *absolute musts* of resumes:

- Write your resume to your job objective and relevant job description!
- Write interesting narratives that are clear and rich and draw the reader in. Use action words to highlight relevant duties, activities, abilities, and accomplishments. Use relevant terminology from the field in which you are job hunting.
- Be honest! Anything on your resume is subject to questions during interviews. If you can't discuss the item, don't include it.
- Eliminate spelling and grammatical errors. Some employers receive thousands of resumes per month! These employers look for ways to weed some out, and a spelling or grammatical error could put you in the discard pile.
- Eliminate pronouns. Traditional resumes do not have pronouns. Pronouns also take up valuable space that is better served using the rich content of your skills and abilities.
- Account for all time periods since high school, including those during which you were not employed.
- Use your legal name (the one on your driver's license and legal documents).
- Do not include personal information: health, marital status, gender, race, religious preference, and age are all no-nos. There is a qualifier here, however. If you've worked or been a volunteer in a church or religious setting, it is okay to put that on the resume. What you don't include is your religious preference (e.g., "Religious preference: Catholic").
- Avoid computerized resume templates. Companies recognize the "canned" nature of these resumes immediately. Such resumes send a wrong message about you—namely, that you are taking the easy way out to produce your resume. This can hurt or eliminate your candidacy for a job. Also, templates are often difficult to change if you want to alter the format.

figure **7.6** | *Sample e-resume.*

Mai Nguyen

153 9th Street South, Minneapolis, MN 55444 * (612) 555-8892 * mnguyen@hotmail.com

EDUCATION

University of Minnesota, Minneapolis, MN
Bachelor of Science in Business
Major: Accounting
Cumulative GPA: 3.34
Expected graduation: May 2008

EXPERIENCE

Certified Accounting Professionals, Inc., St. Paul, MN, Administrative Support, June 2005 - present
* Gaining knowledge about business practices while assisting accountants with administrative details
* Providing customer service and information through receptionist duties including answering phones, mailing out information about the firm's services, and checking clients in for meetings
* Organizing meeting schedules and communicating meeting details to staff accountants and clients
* Scheduling appointments for staff accountants

Jeannette, Bloomington, MN, Sales Associate, January 2004 - June 2005
Served customers by providing personalized retail experience
* Helped customers with product selection and recommendations
* Conducted in-store demonstrations of new fragrances
* Created attractive store displays for seasonal merchandise
* Top-ranked sales associate for spring quarter 2005
* Achieved highest level of new credit applications for spring and summer quarters 2005

LEADERSHIP

Knight Residence Hall, Student Representative, Facilities, Spring 2005 - present
* Head equipment replacement initiative including purchase of new furniture and disposal of obsolete chairs, tables, and miscellaneous equipment
* Negotiate with vendors concerning purchase of new equipment

Selig Drug Initiative, Volunteer, Spring 2005 - present
* Conduct presentations to student athletes concerning hazards of drug use
* Promote health awareness activities to students

Stewart Ethics-in-Leadership Club, Activities Chair, Spring 2004 - Fall 2005
* Enlisted and coordinated guest speakers for monthly presentations on ethics
* Coordinated catering and created decorations for annual dinner

COMMUNITY SERVICE

Como Zoo
* Volunteer for 2005 Zoo Boo Halloween Event

Kids on the Block
* Performed puppet plays for elementary students about alcohol, drugs, and disabilities

AWARDS

Dean's List (Fall 2005)
University of Minnesota Advantage Scholarship
Kraft Foods North America Scholarship

Book and Internet Resource Resources

The following books have sample resumes for your review:

- *Get the Interview Every Time: Fortune 500 Hiring Professionals' Tips for Writing Winning Resumes and Cover Letters*, Brenda Greene
- *The Complete Idiot's Guide to the Perfect Resume*, Susan Ireland
- *Job Hunting for Dummies*, Max Messmer
- *Resumes for Dummies*, Joyce Lain Kennedy
- *The Perfect Resume*, Thomas Jackson
- *Resumes That Knock 'Em Dead*, Martin Yate

The following Web sites have some of the best resume tips:

- Career Builder Network: www.careerbuilder.com
- Career Magazine: www.careermag.com
- Career Web: www.careerweb.com
- College Grad Job Hunter: www.collegegrad.com
- Monster.com: www.monster.com
- Student Central: www.studentcentral.com

Resume Glitches
The Humorous Side

Robert Half International, the executive recruiting firm and parent company of Accountemps, reports finding the following statements on resumes. Make sure your word usage is better than that shown here:

- "Objection: To utilize my skills in sales."
- "Served as an assistant sore manager."
- "Reason for leaving last job: Pushed aside so vice president's girlfriend could steal my job."
- "Work history: Bum. Abandoned belongings and led nomadic lifestyle."
- "My salary requirement is $34 per year."
- "I'll starve without a job, but don't feel you have to give me one."

Please don't let these kinds of resume glitches happen to you! Have a friend review your resume.

References

In the past, employers placed a great deal of emphasis on references for job candidates. The messages sent by former employers, community associates, and others who knew the candidate frequently determined the job offer.

Today, things are less cut and dried. Some employers continue to place great weight on reference checks. Others may only make reference checks as a formality to the job offer—in other words, only a bad reference will prevent the job offer from going to you. Some employers may ask for references but not call them, feeling that no candidate will list someone who will give him a bad reference.

As a job seeker, however, you need to have a number of references regardless of the policy on checking them. Your references should be people who will promote your candidacy. In this section, we will examine best steps for managing your references.

Whom to Use as a Reference

Choose people (nonrelatives) who know your work habits, accomplishments, community activities, academic abilities, or character well. Enlist references from people you trust, those who will maintain confidentiality and will give an honest, good reference about you. This group could include the following:

- Former supervisors
- Former work peers
- Business associates
- Former or current associates from community activities
- Former or current teachers and instructors
- Others who know your abilities

The first three reference types can attest to your work habits and may be able to discuss your personality and ability to get along with others. The last three types can discuss a variety of areas, including work habits, academic abilities, personality, and character.

What about asking current supervisors or coworkers to be your references? It depends on the situation. If you are a graduating student and have a campus job that ends upon graduation, you may have supervisors or others serve as a reference. In other cases, though, having supervisors and coworkers as references is very risky. Both have a vested interest in you staying in your job. Only in unique situations do we recommend including them as references.

Also, friends and family members should not be asked to be references. Employers view them as being biased, of course, so the employer may not value what they have to say about you. More distant relatives might be included as a reference if they know you from a work, school, or activities context.

Top Five Rules of References

1. Ask permission from each person you want as a reference.

2. Be sure the person will give a positive reference about you.

3. Thank your references for their help and send them a thank-you note after they grant you permission.

4. Keep your references informed of your job search progress.

5. Stay in touch with references during the times you are **not** looking for employment. If you connect with your references only when you are in a job search, this sends a negative message that you are simply "using" them.

Limitations of References

Good references are not a replacement for your qualifications for a job. References can only support your candidacy for a job; they cannot get you a job by themselves. You must approach your job search from two directions: (a) I have the ability to get this job done, and (b) my references can back up my work habits, abilities, and character. Your job search will fail if you believe your references will get you a job by themselves.

Preparing Your List of References

A standard format for references is shown in Figure 7.7 (see p. 201). Complete Exercise 7.4, and then compile your initial list of references and **file it in your portfolio.**

Who Knows What You Can Do?

When we think of references for employment purposes, most of us start with people we know. We then assume that these people can comment on our skills, knowledge, and work habits. For this exercise, however, you will reverse the process and look at your skills, knowledge, and work habits first.

1. In Part A below, brainstorm three possible references.

2. In Part B, list three jobs and some of the key skills, knowledge, and work habits that are important qualifications in these jobs.

3. In Part C, list people you know who can best describe your abilities in these areas.

4. Are the people on each list in Part C the same? Are these lists the same as your initial list in Part A? If not, does it make sense to have a flexible list of references based on the particular job in question?

Part A

REFERENCES

1. _____
2. _____
3. _____

Part B

Job #1: **KEY SKILLS, ABILITIES, AND WORK HABITS**

1. _____
2. _____
3. _____
4. _____
5. _____

Job #2: **KEY SKILLS, ABILITIES, AND WORK HABITS**

1. _____
2. _____
3. _____
4. _____
5. _____

Job #3: **KEY SKILLS, ABILITIES, AND WORK HABITS**

1. _____
2. _____
3. _____
4. _____
5. _____

Part C

BEST REFERENCES FOR JOB #1

1. _____
2. _____
3. _____

BEST REFERENCES FOR JOB #2

1. _____
2. _____
3. _____

BEST REFERENCES FOR JOB #3

1. _____
2. _____
3. _____

figure **7.7** *Standard format for references.*

Phil Johnson
Co-owner
Wilson Exteriors
994 Willow Drive
St. Paul, MN 51155
(651) 555-9897
pjohnson@wilsonexteriors.com

Sara Richards
Accountant
McCoy Computers
1142 Irving Drive
Minneapolis, MN 53101
(612) 555-2231
rich@mccoy.org

Nadine Lilly
Sales Representative
Minnesota Technology, Inc.
794 River Lane
Minneapolis, MN 53113
lill@minntech.com

A Word on Past Employers

You may have had a job situation that ended badly. Bad chemistry with a supervisor or coworkers, uninspiring or boring work, a layoff, or a firing are all examples of work situations gone bad. Warning signals go up if you do not list a past employer or a past supervisor as a reference. Usually, you have little to worry about. Organizations are wary of legal action if they give a bad reference about former employees, so most now only verify a former employee's dates of employment and salary.

If you are worried that a former employer may give a bad reference, contact the company. Notify both your former supervisor and the human resources department that a reference check may be in the works and that you hope there won't be any problems on their end. It is highly unlikely that someone will hurt your chances for new employment if you follow that procedure.

Letters of Recommendation

Some positions require you to submit a letter of recommendation. In other cases, consider sending copies of recommendation letters with your resume or application. Still other times, it might be worthwhile to bring copies of recommendation letters and give them to your interviewer.

Whatever the situation, here are some simple guidelines when obtaining recommendation letters:

- Request letters from people who know your work habits from previous employment or community involvement. Copies of your resume or work samples can help them write about your work skills and work ethic.

- Request letters from people who know of your education or training. Copies of your transcript and any training certificates can help them write about your abilities and overall intelligence.

- Give some guidelines to the letter writer. Have the writer focus on your performance, ability to work with others, personality, and other key areas of interest for the employer.

- Give the writer some information about the job or jobs you are pursuing. Providing a job description helps the writer frame the content of the letter better and focus on skills required by the position.

Summary

In this chapter, you learned about the various types of resumes, including their purposes. The pros and cons of each type were detailed. This chapter helped you catalog your skills and abilities in order to write an effective resume. We recommended tailoring your resume to specific positions. Stylistic and visual appeal tips were offered. We recommended field testing your resume. Finally, you learned how to develop your resume for online distribution.

You also learned about the uses of references and recommendation letters. The proper use of each will help you position yourself well and achieve success in your job search.

USING THE JOB DESCRIPTION TO POSITION YOUR RESUME

It is usually necessary to make adjustments to your basic resume when you apply for specific jobs. By making these adjustments, you can more closely link your resume to the job requirements and increase your probability of obtaining a job interview.

The key to making these adjustments is to closely read the job description. By analyzing the job description, you can identify the key skills and knowledge the employer wants from a candidate for a particular job. In this exercise, we describe how to make these adjustments and test your ability to do so.

Find a job posting for a position in a career field you are interested in. Sources for postings include job posting Web sites, employer-specific Web sites, newspapers, and your campus career center. In the space below, list the key skills, knowledge, and traits highlighted in the job description.

Job: _____

Key skills desired: _____

_____

_____

_____

Knowledge desired: _____

_____

_____

_____

Traits: _____

_____

_____

_____

Key questions to answer about this job description:

- What keywords should you include in your resume that are targeted toward this job?

- What action words are important to include?

- How should you change your basic resume to apply for this job?

Your resume must still be an honest reflection of your work and nonwork activities, but it is clear that one resume does not fit all job opportunities. That is why you should tailor it to the job you have targeted. Doing so increases the employer's interest in interviewing you.

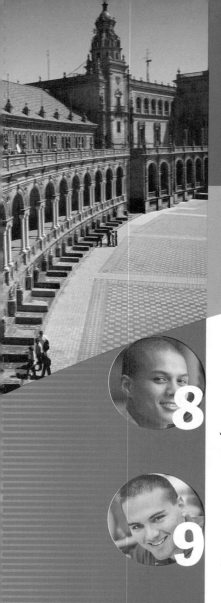

Selling
YOUR TALENTS

Planning and executing the step-by-step job hunting process are the goals of Unit III, Selling Your Talents. Conducting a well-thought-out and coordinated job search takes strong planning and strong execution. By focusing your search, you will achieve those objectives, resulting in a satisfying job search.

The Chapters

n Chapter 8, Networking and Job Sourcing: Grow Your Possibilities, you learn the secrets of marketing your way into employers' offices for interviews. You learn about the importance of networking and how to network effectively during your job search. Marketing yourself through your networking activities enables you to tap the hidden job market. To supplement the networking activities, you will need to access publicized job openings. Key job sources are highlighted, with special emphasis given to those sources most helpful for students.

There are costs and risks to a program of action, but they are far less than the long range risks and costs of a comfortable inaction.

—JOHN F. KENNEDY

In Chapter 9, Interviewing: Achieve Job Search Results, you learn the steps to effective interviewing. After working hard to get the interview, you must now convince the employer that you can do the job well and should be hired. This chapter teaches you the keys to discussing your job qualifications and your fit with the job and organization.

Networking and Job Sourcing

GROW YOUR POSSIBILITIES

chapter

8

It's choice, not chance, that determines your destiny.

—JEAN NIDETCH

student profile

Mai. Mai feels a little hesitant as she walks to the campus career center. On-campus interviews start next week and she wants to check in with her career counselor. She thinks to herself, "I've done some good preparation for the whole process. I've read about the organizations and their internship descriptions. I've gone over my experiences and I'm ready to talk about them and how they fit the employers' needs. And my resume must have been good because I've been selected for several interviews. But I feel that something is missing."

She tells her counselor about her preparation and her concerns. The counselor says, "You've done some excellent preparation. Have you also talked to anyone who works full-time in the accounting industry? They could give you some good insight about what the work is really like and they may know something about the employers you're interviewing with." Mai responds sheepishly, "That's what's missing! I need to do that before next week."

Conducting networking meetings, whether they are informational interviews or networking for employment, is crucial in the job search process. The insight and the information you can obtain from these meetings make what you've read about come alive, increasing your confidence in the interview room. It may also uncover job opportunities—most jobs are filled through networking, not through newspaper ads, executive search firms, college career offices, and the Internet. Surprising?

This section teaches you how to develop a strong networking plan to get the job search results you desire.

Networking: An Overview

Networking is something you should be doing on a continuous basis! During job searches, your networking should increase, but this increase should be in addition to using your existing base of network contacts. One of the most critical mistakes people make is that they stop networking when they *aren't* looking for a job.

So, what is this thing called networking? One of the best definitions comes from a university student who said, "Networking is creating and maintaining relationships with people who have the potential to assist you now and in the future."

What a simple and great definition! At the heart of these relationships is the exchange of information. When you consider the career aspect of networking, added to this exchange of information are advice and referrals that can help you manage your career.

Most people have a network of at least 200 personal contacts, all of whom have a like number of contacts. As you start networking, be absolutely sure you access your network's networks! It's amazing how fast you can create connections to people who can help you with your job search.

Let's take a look at the major groups to focus on during your networking:

- Family and friends
- Professional associates
- Community members
- Prior employers and associates
- Other business associates
- School associates
- Potential employers

Each category is discussed in greater depth in the following sections.

Family and Friends

Your family and friends are usually the people who want to help you the most. That's great, but they may be unable to directly help you get a job because they may not be able to hire you. However, they do know many people who have direct control over hiring or access to job opportunities.

One of the biggest mistakes made by job searchers is failing to ask this "circle" of associates for help. Yet the people this group knows are usually the ones with whom you will make your most effective connections.

Figure 8.1 illustrates your networking "circles." Many job searchers mistakenly limit their networking to those people in the outer circle—the

figure **8.1**

Your networking circles.

COLD CALLS AND COLD CONTACTS

PEOPLE YOUR FAMILY AND FRIENDS KNOW

FRIENDS AND RELATIVES

YOU

"cold calls" or "cold contacts." Frequently, these are people the searcher does not know, but who have access or knowledge about job opportunities. The drawback is that the job searcher does not have an established relationship with the person being contacted. Because it is difficult to establish your credibility quickly with this group, the results are usually minimal and often disheartening.

A second mistake is limiting yourself to asking friends and relatives if they know about job openings—focusing on the circle closest to you. Usually the answer is "No, but I'll look into it," without satisfactory results.

The key to achieving good networking results is to focus on the second circle, the people your friends and relatives know, and get to their networks. This is usually where you will have your best results. You "get to" this group by asking your friends and relatives if there is anyone they know that you should speak to about opportunities. Your friends and relatives can open the door to these people, who may have the power to hire or provide job leads. This word-of-mouth advertising is one of the most effective ways to uncover opportunities because it is so personal. Make sure you ask your strongest support group for their help in this way.

Professional Associates

Doctors, lawyers, dentists, clergy, accountants, bankers, real estate agents, insurance agents, stockbrokers, financial planners, and essentially anyone you have a professional relationship with fall into this category.

Due to the nature of the professional/business relationship, these people should be a prime networking focus. Approaching them is a low-risk proposition because you are their client. Now it's time to ask them for their help.

Community Members

People you know from religious, social, community, recreational, or political organizations fall into this category. The common interests you have with others in these groups makes them easy to approach. Now you can ask them for career and job search help.

Prior Employers and Associates

Prior bosses, peers, subordinates, department heads, and other employer personnel you've interacted with in the past are in this group. These individuals know you in a work context and understand many of your work habits and abilities. They can provide fresh insights about opportunities for you.

Other Business Associates

Clients, customers, vendors, buyers, sales representatives, and others you've connected with in a business context make up this category. Your relationships with these people are through work, so it makes sense to ask for their assistance concerning work issues. Current coworkers may also be approached if your goals need not be kept confidential.

Networking is "creating and maintaining relationships with people who have the potential to assist you now and in the future." This includes your instructors and advisors.

School Associates

Instructors, administrators, and fellow students fall into this group. Usually, you became acquainted with these people during your years of preparing for employment. Talk to them!

Potential Employers

This list will grow based on your discussions with the other groups' members. For now, think of employers of interest and a contact person if you know one. An ideal way to build this list is by attending career fairs, discussed in the next section.

Building Your Network

Besides building your network through discussions with your current contacts, there are various other avenues you may consider. These opportunities are often easier to find than you think. Following are several networking possibilities that may be helpful.

Professional Organizations

You should be able to identify several professional organizations that are linked to your career interests. These organizations hold periodic meetings and conferences that are ideal situations to meet new people and expand your network. Many organizations have low-cost student memberships that entitle you to many of the same benefits as a full professional membership. You can meet professionals in the field, learn from them, and possibly uncover internship or job opportunities, including job postings that the general public cannot access.

Alumni Associations

Most colleges have alumni associations that are accessible to current students. Like professional associations, they conduct periodic meetings and events where students can participate. Some alumni associations also provide students access to individual alumni for networking or mentoring purposes. These are great opportunities for students to learn from others who have the shared experience of attending the same college. Frequently, alumni volunteer to serve as mentors to students and want to assist them with their careers.

Employment or Career Fairs

Besides serving as great opportunities to find jobs, employment fairs are excellent networking avenues. These fairs may be held either on-campus for students or off-campus for both students and the general public. Even if you are not looking for a job in the immediate future, they are great ways to connect with employers for your future job search.

Student Clubs

Student clubs specifically affiliated with a career area or college major are best for career networking. Getting involved in a student organization is an excellent way to expand your network. Becoming an officer or active member is even better. Such participation helps you meet other students, college staff and faculty, and in many cases, employers. Frequently, an emphasis is placed on professional development, and clubs will host guest speakers to talk about their industry or career field.

Student Networking Groups

In some larger cities, you may find citywide student networking groups. Like student clubs, they may emphasize professional development and enlist employers and individuals to speak about career topics.

8.1 Network Contact List

Keeping your network organized is an important part of networking effectively. Try to develop a system that works easily for you. A variety of methods are effective, including:

1. Collecting business cards and filing them in a Rolodex
2. Assembling contact information in a planner or personal desk assistant
3. Designing a spreadsheet that allows you to add comments and sort by category

In this exercise, you are to start organizing your list, including action item categories. This will help you to store information about each person and the interactions you have had with each one. A sample spreadsheet might include the following column heads:

Name/Title	Date	Topic	Action	Reconnect
Address				
Phone				
E-mail				

Your ultimate objective is to develop your list and begin to contact those people for help in your job or career search. Don't judge or evaluate the contacts as to their usefulness or helpfulness at this point. Set a goal of 50 names for your initial set of contacts and continue to add to the list over time as your connection meetings take place.

Add your network contact list to your portfolio.

Contacting Contacts

ow that you have a network contact list, the exciting part begins. It's time to start contacting your network. Are you ready? Excited? Nervous? Let's get to it.

Networking Etiquette

It is absolutely critical that you exhibit excellent etiquette and professionalism when you connect with your contacts. Granted, with your friends you may be a bit more casual, but being too casual with them has its drawbacks too. Your conversations may wander off the topic, leaving you frustrated and without obtaining the help you need. With people who know you less well, your manners and professionalism must be impeccable. Here are some key tips:

1. *Think professionally.* Regardless of the "level" of the person you are meeting, he or she is a professional in the field. Get into the professional mode and orient your discussion in that manner. In fact, it's important you begin to think of yourself as a professional. Begin to divest yourself of the label "just a student" and that will increase your desire to meet people in your field of interest.

2. *Dress nicely.* Although jeans are the common student "uniform," shy away from them during your networking activities. Business casual is the better standard to use—it gives you a more professional image and puts you in a more professional mood during your meeting. In some meetings, business professional may be the necessary level of dress. Evaluate the situation beforehand and dress accordingly.

3. *Introduce yourself well.* Know what you will say in your introduction, even if it is just, "I'm Blake Johnson and I am currently a student at the University of Minnesota studying engineering."

4. *Be focused during your conversations.* Although small talk is important to establish rapport, don't wander off the topic too much. If you are job hunting, say it! If you are interested in finding out more about career paths, say it!

5. *Ask well-thought-out questions.*
   - Inquire: "Do you know anyone who . . . ?"
   - Pyramid: "Do you know others in your field who . . . ?"
   - Spot opportunities: "It sounds as if some of my abilities would fit those roles in your organization."
   - Volunteer: "Can I help you with what you need?"

6. *Use key contacts sparingly.* Don't wear out your welcome.

7. *Be prepared to offer help.* Networking is always a two-way street.

8. *Keep in touch.* Keep your network informed of your progress and of the help they've been.

9. *Give your resume to your contacts if appropriate.*

10. *Send a thank-you note.* Always send a thank-you to the person, either a handwritten note or an e-mail. This is an absolutely critical part of networking and portrays a positive, courteous image of you.

Ask for What You Need

Asking for what you want and need is a critical part of the job hunt process. In truth, however, most of us don't know how to ask for things. Surprised? Well, how many times have you *not* received what you have asked for? For most of us, the answer is "many times." The problem usually lies in the process and mechanics of asking.

Anthony Robbins, renowned motivational speaker and author of *Unlimited Power* (2000), provides us with insight on the correct mechanics of asking:

1. *Ask specifically.* Messages may often be mixed up and unclear. If you ask for "more money" and receive a quarter, then you have received what you asked for. In order to get what you want, you must know the details: who, what, when, how, and why.

2. *Ask a person who can help you.* How many times have you asked and not received because the person you asked could not give you what you wanted? If the person doesn't have what you want, you are wasting valuable time and resources—yours and theirs. Find someone who has what you want; then talk to that person.

3. *Create value for the person you are asking.* When you ask someone for something, there needs to be a reason for the person to give you what you want. Create value for the person and he or she will help!

4. *Believe fervently in what you are asking for.* Belief is contagious. If you believe strongly in what you are asking for, it is likely that another will believe in it as well. But if you halfheartedly believe it, it is likely that few will believe in you. Your belief must inspire others to act.

5. *Ask until you get what you want.* How many times do you have to ask? How many people do you have to ask? The answer is "until you get what you want." Asking until you receive doesn't mean that you ask only one person. It may mean asking many people or altering your method of asking. It may mean reevaluating what you want or creating new value. Evaluate your results, adjust your presentation, and try again until you get what you want. (pp. 218–220)

Other Networking Tips

ollowing are some final thoughts to help your networking efforts.

- *Prepare for every meeting.* Follow the steps in Chapter 4 on informational interviews.

- *Meet as many people as you can.* Network as part of your natural conversation with people if appropriate.

- *Don't let your network languish.* Keep your networking active even when you are not job hunting.

- *Don't limit your network too narrowly.* Anyone can be a source of help and information.

- *Don't focus on networking only as job hunting.* You're also looking for information.

- *Understand the two-way street of networking.* Networking works best when it is a give-and-take relationship, one where you think about what you can do for the other person as much as about what the other person can do for you.

By taking the time to prepare yourself well and following networking etiquette, you will obtain important job search information and leads. Successful networking requires time and energy. Don't shrug it off as something that is easy to do—don't "wing it." Invest in the effort and it will pay off for you.

Phone calls often are your initial contact when networking. Exhibit professionalism and coordinate a smooth flow of information and questions.

Making Phone Contacts

Whether you are networking for job leads or setting up informational interviews, you must have excellent phone etiquette and a plan. Phone calls are often your initial contact point when networking. Exhibit professionalism and coordinate a smooth flow of information and questions. The impression you make is a lasting one, so prepare well. Here are your preparation points and some tips.

PREPARATION

- Get yourself organized for the phone call.

- Script or outline your conversation. Plan what you want to say so that you will sound prepared.

- Have writing materials and a calendar handy to note comments and book appointments.

- Keep your resume in view to help you articulate your skills and career objectives.

THE CONVERSATION

- *Be positive!* Think positive thoughts about your abilities and the person you will be speaking with.

- *Establish rapport immediately.* Your opening comments and voice tone set the mood of the conversation. Your voice portrays your attitude. Be alert, pleasant, positive, natural, and expressive.

- *Identify yourself immediately; then state the purpose of your call.* For example, you might say, "Good morning, Mr. Chan. This is Maria Wilson. I'm calling to find out about career opportunities with the Dayton Company. May I take a few minutes of your time?" If you've been referred by a mutual acquaintance, state that too.

- *Ask the person whether this is a good time to talk.* If it is not, ask when you could call back.
- *Ask your questions in a positive, inquiring manner.*
- *Be ready to talk about your background, abilities, skills, and goals.*
- *Be ready to talk about what you are looking for.*

- *Listen well.*
- *Use the contact's name often.* In a direct conversation, listeners typically hear astutely only the first several words said immediately after hearing their name.
- *Show that you are listening intently by being engaged in what the person has to say.* Respond appropriately and positively to his remarks.
- *Close with a friendly ending.* Thank the person for her help and ask whether she knows of any other person you should talk to. Offer to be of help if the person ever needs your assistance.

> *Your ability to succeed in selling yourself doesn't depend on what happened in your past, but on how you see your future. Convince yourself that you will be successful and you'll convince others as well.*
>
> —DOROTHY LEEDS,
> *MARKETING YOURSELF*

THE FOLLOW-UP

- Record the call and any notes in your portfolio.
- Write a thank-you note or letter.
- Complete all follow-up tasks. If your contact recommended that you call someone else, make the phone call as soon as possible.
- Keep in touch and update the contact as you deem fit.

Update Your Network Contact List

Whenever you have a network contact meeting or conversation, update your network list to help you remember important information and follow-up tasks as you progress in your search. Additionally, your notes will help you in future network meetings and might pay off in job opportunities as you present yourself as a qualified, capable future employee.

Job Search Sources

There are a wide range of job sources beyond your personal network. Here are some key ones for you to consider.

College Career Development Center

Your college career development center should be an integral part of your job search. Many career centers coordinate employer job opportunities including job postings and on-campus interviewing. These centers are also a prime source for internships. Register with your center and make full use of its services including job and internship leads.

Employer Web Sites

Employer Web sites typically include full-time job opportunities and may list internship opportunities. In most cases, applications are done online through the Web site. A good strategy is to identify the companies or organizations you would like to work for and check the Web sites for opportunities.

Internet Sites

Some employers post job and internship opportunities using large employment Web sites. Application for these jobs is done through the particular Web site. This route can be a helpful supplement for your search, but make sure the site is well-known and reputable. Some of the major sites that we recommend include:

- www.monster.com
- www.quintcareers.com
- www.careerbuilder.com
- www.careerjournal.com
- www.collegegrad.com
- www.hotjobs.com
- www.wetfeet.com
- www.vault.com
- www.careermag.com
- www.studentcentral.com
- www.campuscareercenter.com
- www.internweb.com
- www.internjobs.com
- www.rsinternships.com
- www.collegejobboard.com

Career or Employment Fairs

This is an excellent source for students and nonstudents alike. Be sure to take full advantage of these events for full-time, part-time, and internship opportunities. Some of these occur on campus and others will be found elsewhere in the community.

Newspapers

Daily newspapers list job ads including full-time and part-time opportunities. Internship postings are less common, but you may find a few of them. Those jobs advertised in newspapers are heavily weighted toward candidates with at least several years of full-time work experience.

Temporary Employment Companies

These are good job sources to get some work experience during your student years. Also, many organizations use temporary employment companies in order to hire for full-time openings. These organizations "check out" the temporary worker and then offer a full-time position if the person is a good performer.

Trade Papers, Magazines, and Journals

Employers post job opportunities in periodicals related to their industry. For example, engineering jobs are posted in engineering journals or trade papers. Even more than daily newspapers, these postings are heavily weighted toward candidates with several years of experience in the particular field.

Employment Agencies

These agencies typically serve experienced workers better than college students. Be sure to thoroughly read anything you sign should you decide to enlist one of these agencies in your search.

Professional Organizations

Employers frequently post job opportunities with professional organizations. Usually, these opportunities best suit workers who have job experience and may not be the best source for college students looking for full-time, part-time, or internship opportunities.

Unsolicited Direct Contact with Employers

This cold-calling technique through phone calls, e-mail, letters, or showing up at the workplace is not a particularly effective method of job searching. Cold phone calls or e-mails are unprofessional. Likewise, showing up and asking to talk with someone about opportunities is intimidating and off-putting. Letters with a resume attached are usually ignored. We discourage you from using these methods that only waste your time and energy.

Summary

In this chapter, we examined the key aspects of networking. Networking is one of the most powerful ways to obtain information about employment, careers, and job leads. It should be one of the most used tools in your job search. Pursue networking throughout your job search, and keep your networking activities going even when you are not looking for employment.

REFERENCES

Leeds, D. (1992). *Marketing yourself: The ultimate job seekers guide.* New York: Berkley Publishing Group.

Robbins, A. (2000). *Unlimited power.* New York: Fireside Books.

Interviewing

ACHIEVE JOB SEARCH RESULTS

chapter

9

They always say time changes things, but you actually have to change them yourself.

—ANDY WARHOL

Mai. Mai was very diligent about her career planning during the first two and a half years of college. She took a wide variety of classes. She met frequently with her academic advisor for help with course planning. She used the career center extensively, meeting with a career counselor to discuss options and develop a career plan, and she took part in various career workshops. She was involved in two student organizations on campus, the Student Accounting Association and the International Student Club. She volunteered in the community with the local food shelf and with Big Brothers/Big Sisters.

But Mai was nervous. It was the start of the spring semester and on-campus interviewing was about to begin. She signed up for several interviews for internships in the accounting field. "Despite all of my career exploration and planning, I'm a little scared. These interviews will be different from any interviews I had for my high school jobs. I hope I've prepared enough."

Interviewing may be the most nerve-wracking part of the job search. Sweaty hands, dry mouth, and a worried look are some of the signs of an anxious job candidate. An inability to articulate thoughts, unclear speech, and confused dialogue are signs of communication breaking down.

You needn't be a victim of an interviewing downfall. In this chapter, we will help you prepare for interviews so that you can convince the interviewer to hire you. Clearly, the interview is the most important part of the job search process. By focusing on what you have to offer an organization, you will reduce your nervousness and present yourself as the ideal candidate for the job.

The Ten Principles of Interviewing

 These principles will help you get into the right frame of mind as you conduct your interviews.

1. *Tell the truth.* Honesty is the best policy.
2. *Be yourself.* Relax and forget all the things you're supposed to do. If you've prepared well and have the qualifications for the job, you can go on automatic pilot.
3. *Speak well of others.* This includes former employers, bosses, coworkers, and company products and services.
4. *Maintain good eye contact.* But don't "lock on" and stare.
5. *Ask appropriate questions.* Focus on the job itself, the company, and the employer's expectations. Refrain from asking about pay, benefits,

and unions in the early stages. These come into play later if you get a job offer.

6. *Don't overly press the employer about your standing compared to other candidates.* This puts the employer on the defensive and hurts your chances.

7. *Don't be intimidating in your interviewing style.* Employers want employees who can work together. The message that intimidation sends goes against that goal.

8. *Don't act bored.* You're at the interview because you're interested in the position, so show consistent interest.

9. *Find out the next step in the process.* Ask about when a hiring decision will be made, what the next step in the process is, and when you will hear about your status.

10. *Close with a smile, a handshake, and a thank-you.* Be positive and professional.

Types of Interviews

Interviews come in all varieties. Initial interviews may be completed by the human resources representative or directly by the hiring manager. Interviews may be done by one person, a group, or a committee—by telephone or through video conferencing. We will look at several basic types you may encounter.

The Basic Interview

In this type of interview, the interviewer asks the candidate specific questions about his or her abilities, skills, and background. Questions focus on the candidate's ability to fulfill the key duties of the job. Usually, the interviewer asks the candidate to expand on or clarify some of the information contained in the candidate's resume. The interviewer usually takes notes as an aid in making a decision on the job seeker's candidacy. After the interviewer completes his or her questions, the candidate usually is given an opportunity to ask questions about the job, organization, and work environment. Most interviews follow this format.

Tips for the basic interview include:

1. Know your background and career goals thoroughly.

2. Be able to expand on items in your resume.

3. Focus on the question that is asked; don't go off on tangents with your answers.

4. Use specific examples to illustrate your skills and abilities.

5. Don't rush through answers; give thorough and complete answers.

6. Get plenty of rest the night before the interview.

7. Relax yourself and engage the interviewer through high-quality answers and self-presentation.

The Telephone Interview

A telephone interview is sometimes used for an initial screening of candidates. It is also frequently used for candidates who live beyond driving distance to the employer, and it may be used as a way to determine whether the company will pay to bring the candidate in for a face-to-face interview.

As in most interviews, employers typically focus on your interest in the job and the information shown on your resume. For candidates, phone interviews have both advantages and disadvantages compared to in-person interviews. Advantages include the following:

- You usually feel more relaxed.
- You can easily refer to your resume.
- You can interview from home or another comfortable setting.
- You can easily take notes.

Disadvantages include the following:

- You may feel too relaxed and lose the adrenaline push of an in-person interview.
- You usually feel less connected to your interviewer(s).
- The interview seems "flatter," without the energy and life of an in-person interview.
- It's usually harder to engage the interviewer.

Following are some tips for conducting these interviews:

1. Dress just as you would for an in-person interview. This helps you get into a professional mood.
2. Have a copy of the same resume the interviewer has for reference.
3. Have paper, pens, and pencils ready for notes.
4. Be ready for the basic interview questions: Why are you interested in this job? What is your background? What are your future goals?
5. Have a professional voice mail message on your telephone. Do not have cutesy stories, music, or other gimmicks on the message.

The Group Interview

A group interview consists of two or more people asking you questions. There may be a primary interviewer, each interviewer may ask the same number of questions, or each may ask questions related to her work area. Group interviews are frequently used in situations where a hiring committee was established to help identify the best candidates. In these situations, the committee typically has a set list of questions to ask each candidate. Tips for group interviews include the following:

1. Speak to and make eye contact with the person asking the question. You can vary the eye contact toward other group members at times, but primarily speak to the person who asked the question.

2. Focus on answering the questions, not on the additional sets of eyes focused on you.

3. Bring extra copies of your resume in case some of the group members don't have a copy.

In a group interview, two or more individuals will ask you questions. Bring extra copies of your resume in case some group members don't have a copy.

Interviews During a Meal

Sometimes interviews are done over a meal with one or more interviewers. Here are a few key guidelines:

1. Stay in your "interview mode" throughout. You are there mainly to be interviewed, not to eat.

2. Pay close attention to your table manners.

3. Order something easy to eat. Don't order messy sandwiches, pasta, or other hard-to-eat foods.

4. Don't order alcohol, even if your interviewer does.

5. Don't get off track. Follow the interviewer's lead concerning the topic area, but realize that this is valuable time for you to discuss your qualifications.

Serial Interviews

Serial interviews may or may not be planned. This type of interview occurs when someone interviewing you feels that someone else in the company may be interested in what you have to offer. In some cases, the company may want a variety of people to interview you to look at your abilities.

Tips for these interviews include the following:

1. Speak of the specific abilities you can offer the organization. Don't worry too much if some interviewers vary from the initial position you were interviewed for. Tell them which position you were initially brought in for, but then tell them it was determined that others should interview you too. Give a solid overall picture of what you can do and where your interests lie.

2. Realize that people at different levels have different interests. Tell them why you're there, but also try to tie into their interests by asking questions and speaking about your abilities.

3. Be flexible. You may feel you are being shuffled around—you are! Make the best of it. Look at it as a way of exploring some additional opportunities.

4. Bring extra resumes.

The Interview Process: Goals and Concerns

oth you and the interviewer have goals and concerns during the interview process:

YOU

- Present yourself well
- Demonstrate the value that you will bring to the job and company
- Examine your fit with the job and company
- Attain appropriate job offer

INTERVIEWER

- Represent the company and position well
- Find the best possible candidate
- Maintain credibility through a good selection of candidates

As the interviewee, you should demonstrate why you are suited to the position and organization by supporting your contention with examples of skills, abilities, and accomplishments. It all starts with research—first, research about the company and job, and second, research about you and your fit to the job.

Preparation: The Path to Interviewing Well

here are two sides of the interviewing coin on which to base your preparation. The first side is the job and the organization. The second side is you.

The job and organization preparation requires that you do some homework. This is relatively less taxing than preparation about yourself because all you have to do is research information about the job and organization.

Preparation One: Research the Job and Organization

The first part of your interview preparation concerns the job you are interviewing for and the organization you are interviewing with. You should know a great deal about both in order to interview effectively and receive a job offer.

What You Need to Know

1. *Job description.* If responding to a newspaper ad or an online posting, you already have the job description, but if the interview came by word of mouth, contact the company for a description. If there is no description available, research the position using the library and online sources discussed later. Don't walk into the interview without some concrete knowledge of the position being offered.

2. *Description of the organization.* Find out about the organization's main products or services. Also, research the organization's size, goals, geographic location(s), sales revenue, profitability, stock price, main competitors, direction over the last two or three years, and outlook.

3. *Management style and company philosophy.* Examine the organization's mission statement, structure, and values.

4. *Organization culture.* Discover the environment and culture of the organization.

5. *Wage/salary range.* Examine industry or geographic salary surveys.

Where to Find Information

Information resources can be broken down into a few major categories: online sources, organization sources, library sources, college placement offices, and people. Each area is described next.

Web sites. Web sites are becoming the most comprehensive information source about organizations. Most large and medium-sized organizations have Web sites with extensive information, including annual reports. This will provide much of your company information.

Other useful sites include the following:

- Investor Relations Information Network: www.irin.com
- Web100—Big Business on the Web: www.metamoney.com/w100
- Hoover's Online: www.hoovers.com
- Wall Street Journal Online: www.wsj.com
- Fortune 500: www.fortune.com
- *Occupational Outlook Handbook:* www.stats.bls.gov/

Organization sources. Call the organization you're interested in and ask them to send you information. Ask for information about the organization in general and about specific job opportunities. Better yet, if you know someone inside the organization, have that person get information for you.

Library sources. Your library has many information sources for researching organizations and careers. Many libraries now have separate career planning areas with books, videos, computers, and databases. Some of the most valuable sources of information include the following:

- Trade and business periodicals, including *Forbes, Business Week, Fortune, Working Woman, U.S. News and World Report,* and many more
- Trade and business directories, including *Standard and Poor's, Value Line, Dun & Bradstreet, Encyclopedia of Associations, Thomas Register of Manufacturers,* and *Corporate Report Factbook*
- Key newspapers, including the *Wall Street Journal,* the *New York Times,* regional papers, and local papers
- *Occupational Outlook Handbook*
- *Dictionary of Occupational Titles*
- *U.S. Government Manual*

Career development centers. Most colleges have career development centers. Like libraries, they have a lot of information on careers and organizations. Most of these offices also have Web sites. Check with the office in advance to see whether you can use their services, because some colleges restrict use to current students and alumni.

People. Your network and their contacts are often the most overlooked resource in career planning. As discussed in Chapter 8, talk to people in your network about careers, jobs, companies, and industries. Obtain the information you need and ask for their advice.

Preparation Two: You

The second part of your preparation is an area about which you are the expert: *you!* Take the attitude into every interview that you are there as the expert about you and will explain to the interviewer all about you. No one else can do it as well. It is up to you to convey the key qualities that will make the employer more interested in you as a potential employee. This is usually harder work than your organization and job research is, but it is even more critical for a successful job search. The remainder of this chapter discusses the most important preparation you can undertake: preparing to answer (and ask) interview questions.

Developing Your Answers to Interview Questions

 e prepared to answer questions with positive, honest, and example-laden responses. To best portray your abilities, prepare carefully. This is the other half of the "research coin."

Following is a series of questions for you to consider when preparing for most interviews. Each specific job will usually have more narrowly focused questions related to the job itself, but the following questions are quite common modern interviewing practices.

"Tell me about yourself." Probably the most common of all interview questions, this is often asked at the beginning. Due to its nature and place as a "kickoff" question, it is a time for you to score points for yourself. Take the initiative with the question and give an overview of yourself, your abilities, your direction, and why you are interested in the company and the job. This is your time to draw the interviewer in and get her interested in what you can do for the organization. Here are some tips:

1. *Take about one minute to answer this question.* If you have an unusually compelling story, go a bit longer.

2. *Use a chronological approach, starting with your oldest information and bringing the interviewer to the present (and future).*

3. *Cover the major relevant pieces of your background.*

   - *Early history.* Warm up the interviewer by briefly telling her where you're from and what your interests are.

   - *Education.* Describe your high school, college, and relevant training for the job. Highlight your career interests and how they developed.

   - *Work background.* Discuss your work background and transitions, especially those positions most relevant to your current career interests, with some focus on responsibilities and accomplishments.

   - *Job and career goals.* Tell the interviewer why you are interested in the job and company and where you see your career heading in the future. Describe your career goals, your interest areas, and how they developed.

   - *Value that you bring to the position.* Especially highlight what you can do for the company.

4. *Highlight your resume, but expand it.* Describe the "whys" of the career actions you took, including the reasons for the career you've chosen, the education or training you have accomplished, and your goals.

Exercise 9.1 offers you an opportunity to develop a script for the question "Tell me about yourself."

Use the space below to outline your "Tell me about yourself" script.

1. "Tell me about yourself": Introduction

_____

_____

_____

_____

2. Relevant background and goals:

_____

_____

_____

_____

3. Education and training:

_____

_____

_____

_____

4. Work background:

_____

_____

_____

_____

5. Job and career goals:

_____

_____

_____

_____

6. Value you bring:

_____

_____

_____

_____

File this information in your portfolio for future use.

"Why do you want to leave your current job?" You should be honest and straightforward, and, most important, positive in response to this question. Make sure you highlight the positive draw of the job you are looking for, not the negatives of your current job. Say some positive things about your current job, especially those that highlight things you've learned and growth you've experienced.

If you lost your job because of downsizing, restructuring, or changes in company direction, explain this concisely and positively. We are in an era of these major changes with organizations, and your interviewer will understand.

If you were fired, carefully script your answer because this incident is a very sensitive area for you when interviewing. Your entire interview could be affected by this prior incident. Tell the truth, but frame it positively. Most times a firing may take place when your job performance is below standard. The causes of weak performance often are due to a mismatch in what you or the employer thought the job was about and your skills and abilities. Frame your answer in those terms.

"What qualifies you for this job?" Reading the job description in advance of the interview will help you prepare for this question. Relate the duties of the job to your skills and abilities, and give examples to highlight those skills and abilities. This question should be in the front of your mind as you enter the interview. Be ready to attack it and score points on it.

"What are your major strengths and weaknesses?" This question, one of the classic all-time interview questions, is actually being used less and less by interviewers. Why? Because it is a question that may or may not get at the heart of the matter: your ability to do the job you are interviewing for.

Nevertheless, prepare for it, if only because it helps you catalog some of your major selling points and gives you more confidence going into the interview. Exercise 9.2 offers you an opportunity to develop scripts for your major strengths and weaknesses.

As you work through this exercise, keep in mind that you need to focus on those skills that are most relevant to the job you're interviewing for. Certainly, many skills you have are transferable to a variety of jobs. Definitely work through those and talk about them in the interview. But be very sure you identify two or three critical skills and abilities and talk about them as your strengths.

Major Strengths

Strength #1: _____

Where/when shown: _____

_____

_____

Specific situations and examples: _____

_____

_____

Strength #2: _____

Where/when shown: _____

_____

_____

Specific situations and examples: _____

_____

_____

Strength #3: _____

Where/when shown: _____

_____

_____

Specific situations and examples: _____

_____

_____

File this in your portfolio.

As you next work through your weaknesses, keep in mind our maxim to "be honest, but don't be stupid." Each of us has weaknesses. Honestly talk about your weaknesses in the interview, but don't dwell on them. Concisely state the weaknesses and, most importantly, tell the interviewer how you are currently working to improve them. Offering this information will convey your motivation and initiative—a critical work ability in the current world of work—to the interviewer.

Major Weaknesses

Weakness #1: _____

Where/when shown: _____

_____

_____

How you compensate for it: _____

_____

_____

How you're improving it: _____

_____

_____

Weakness #2: _____

Where/when shown: _____

_____

_____

How you compensate for it: _____

_____

_____

How you're improving it: _____

_____

_____

Weakness #3: _____

Where/when shown: _____

_____

_____

How you compensate for it: _____

_____

_____

How you're improving it: _____

_____

_____

File this in your portfolio.

"What major skills can you bring to this job?" This closely links to the qualifications question, and you should have answers ready from your preparation. Again, line up your skills and abilities with those needed to perform well on the job. As always, highlight with examples.

"What are the areas you will need to work on most to do this job well?" Through your research and job search, you should be examining and interviewing for jobs that fit your skills and abilities. Therefore, you presumably can tackle the core duties of most jobs you interview for. There probably are some areas you will need to improve to really do the job well. Focus on those during this question. And don't forget, getting used to a new organization and new coworkers could be areas to discuss.

"What do you know about our company? This job? Our industry?" You should have covered this with your prior research. If you weren't able to find much information (which can occur with small or private companies), say so and ask the interviewer for more information.

"What have you learned from prior jobs that will help you succeed in this one?" Again, don't drift too far from the job you are interviewing for. During your preparation, honestly ask yourself questions about what experience is transferable from prior jobs. Firmly link these areas to the new job.

"What have you learned through your education that will make you successful?" Select some relevant pieces from your education and training that will make you successful. Make sure they relate to technical knowledge in performing the job and general skills or relationship building (e.g., work well with others and teamwork).

"Where do you see yourself in three to five years?" Good employers want good employees who will grow and be able to offer more to the company over the long run. Examine career paths in your field and opportunities with the companies you are interviewing with. Lay out how you see these years developing for you, and your career, with this employer.

General Employment Interview Questions

Although it is impossible to provide a comprehensive list of the most commonly asked interview questions, it is

As the interviewee, you will need to demonstrate why you are suited to the position and organization, giving examples of your skills and accomplishments.

important to have some understanding of typical questions. Here is a sampler of important interview questions:

YOUR GOALS

- What are your short-term work goals?
- What are your long-term work goals?
- Why did you choose this career? Where will it lead you?
- What other types of positions interest you?
- Why did you choose this field?

EDUCATION/TRAINING

- What was the best thing you learned in school?
- Do you have plans for additional training or education?
- What was your favorite school subject? Your least favorite?
- If you could change one thing about your education or training, what would that be?

THE JOB/ORGANIZATION

- What qualifies you for this job?
- Why do you want to work for us?
- What do you find most attractive about this position? Least attractive?
- What salary range are you expecting?
- What kind of people do you like to work with?
- In what kind of an environment do you work best?
- What are you looking for in a job?
- Do you like to work independently or as part of a team? Why?
- How do you plan to stay up to date in your field?
- Would you relocate?
- Are you open to traveling in this job?

TRAITS AND VALUES

- What are your most important values?
- What is the most important lesson you've learned in life?
- Describe your personality.
- What one characteristic best describes you?
- How do you motivate people?
- What motivates you?
- How do you handle criticism?
- Describe a situation where you were in a leadership role.

PREVIOUS EXPERIENCE OR EMPLOYMENT

- What did you particularly like about your past jobs?
- What qualities in a supervisor are most important to you?

- Describe your best boss and your worst.
- Describe your best job and your worst.
- If I talked to your last employer, what would I hear about you?
- How did you get along with your last supervisor?
- What did you think of your last employer? How would you evaluate the firm?
- Why did you leave your last job?
- What did you like best about your last job?
- What did you like least about your last job?
- Do you feel you have good communication skills? Why?
- Which communication skills are your best? Which are your weakest?
- What role do you typically play when you are in a group activity?
- Can you describe for me a group situation you thought did not work out well?

CHALLENGES, STRENGTHS, AND WEAKNESSES

- Describe the most difficult situation you have been in and how you handled it.
- What has been your greatest accomplishment?
- What have you learned from your mistakes?
- What three things do you want me to know about you?
- Are there any questions you wish I had asked you?

Keep in mind that these are just examples of questions. Continue to examine your major skills, knowledge, and direction in order to answer interview questions well. That will be the best preparation about the "you" side of the preparation coin.

Behavioral-Based Questions: Future Performance Can Be Predicted from Past Performance

Behavioral-based questions are typically the most important interview questions, and most good interviewers use them. Most likely, how well you answer these questions will determine how well the interviewer views your job candidacy.

Behavioral-based interview questions assume that past performance is a good indicator of future performance. Interviewers therefore ask questions about skills and abilities associated with the job in question. They attempt to get at the behaviors you exhibited in past situations that you are also likely to face on this job. The candidate who can best describe how he dealt with those situations in the past will most likely get the job offer.

Behavioral-based questions frequently start with "Tell me about a time when . . ." Common areas interviewers examine include the following:

- Teamwork skills
- Communication skills
- Leadership skills
- Planning skills
- Analytical skills
- Motivational skills
- Conflict management skills
- Interpersonal skills

- Technical knowledge
- Creativity
- Adaptability
- Customer service
- Dealing with change
- Dealing with unstructured situations
- Management of people
- Management of processes

One of the best ways to answer behavioral-based questions is to do all of the following:

1. Discuss the situation you faced

2. Describe the actions you took

3. Detail the results of your actions

Using the space below, choose an area from the preceding list (or another area appropriate to your job interests), formulate a question that gets at your skills and abilities, and script an answer to the question.

1. "Tell me about a time when:" _____

_____

_____

2. Situation: _____

_____

_____

_____

_____

_____

3. Actions: _____

_____

_____

_____

_____

_____

4. Results: _____

_____

_____

_____

_____

_____

File this in your portfolio.

Structuring your answers as discussed above makes it easier to describe your abilities and easier for the interviewer to follow your story. Making it easy for the interviewer to follow your explanations is one of the most critical aspects of interviewing well. Remember, it's not the candidate with the best qualifications, education, or skills who necessarily gets the job offer. It is usually the candidate who best communicates her qualifications, education, and skills who gets the job offer!

Negative Questions

Unlike many of the positive behavioral-based questions, negatively phrased questions are ones that require more preparation. These questions usually focus on difficult work-related or other situations. They may take the form of:

- "Tell me about the last time you made a mistake at work."
- "Tell me about a time when you had a problem with a coworker."
- "Describe the last teamwork situation you were in that was difficult."
- "Have you ever had a boss you didn't like?"
- "What is a difficult work environment for you?"

An interviewer asking these kinds of questions usually is interested in learning how you handle problem occurrences. In the heat of an interview, these questions can throw you off your game. Here are some suggestions for responding successfully:

- Think about problem situations from your past.
- Develop scripts like those you have for the positive behavioral-based questions.
- Prepare for these questions at least as well as for any other question.
- Get through your answer concisely but without giving the feeling you are avoiding the question.
- State the situation, what happened, how you limited damage, and what you learned.
- Use examples that are not your worst mistakes, worst workplace occurrences, or worst boss situations.

Use the space below to script an answer for a negative question.

Question: _____

_____

1. Situation: _____

_____

_____

_____

_____

2. Actions: _____

_____

_____

_____

_____

3. Results: _____

_____

_____

_____

_____

_____

File this in your portfolio.

Responses to Inappropriate and Illegal Questions

How would you respond to these questions?

- "Are you married or single?"
- "Do you plan to have children?"
- "When and where were you born?"
- "Have you been hospitalized in the last five years?"
- "Have you ever been charged with a crime?"
- "What country are you from?"
- "What church do you attend?"
- "What is your ethnic background?"

These questions range from inappropriate to illegal if asked in job interviews. Due to federal equal employment laws, questions relating to marital status, religious preference, ethnic background, age, and race are clearly illegal for employment purposes. Other questions, including ones about health status, financial status, criminal background, and children, border on illegal depending on the job in question. Most human resource professionals know which questions are illegal and cannot be asked in an interview. Nevertheless, some interviewers may not have such knowledge. Being asked any of these questions places you in a difficult position because you are interested in working for the company and do not want to give a bad impression.

If faced with these questions, you need to know how to deal with them. Following are some suggestions for addressing these situations:

- Ask, "How is this relevant to the job?" or "Why do you ask that question?"
- Say, "I don't think that is relevant to the job requirements."
- Answer the question. If your instinct tells you it was asked in a non-threatening manner or not as the basis for hiring, this may be your best response. Remember, however, you are under no obligation to answer illegal questions.
- Contact the Equal Employment Opportunity Commission and report the incident.

You need to consider what message is communicated by a company when one of its representatives asks illegal questions. Is it simply a slip-up? Does the interviewer lack the knowledge of what constitutes an illegal question? Does it illustrate poorly qualified representatives, and if so, does this indicate that other employees are poorly qualified? Or, at worst, does it show a discriminatory bias in hiring?

The bottom line on illegal questions is to get through them and then consider the incident during your decision-making process.

A Special Case: Case Interviews

Case interviews increased in popularity among interviewers in recent years. They are most often used in the business and education industries. For positions in consulting, case interviews are the primary interview type. Other industries and functional areas are starting to use cases during interviews, including investment banking, sales, and marketing. Preparing for this type of interview takes special attention.

Types of Case Interviews

Strategy cases. Strategy cases involve some form of business problem. The case outlines a business situation, and the interviewer asks the interviewee to develop a business recommendation to address the situation.

Investment cases. Investment cases are found in the investment industry. The case outlines an investment situation, and the interviewer asks the interviewee to provide a rate of return or profitability analysis of the situation.

Individual client cases. Individual client cases are typically used in interviews for education jobs. A case outlines a student or client with particular issues, and the interviewer asks the interviewee to develop an educational, counseling, or development plan for the student.

Wild card cases. Wild card or "brain teaser" cases are used less now than in the past. These cases usually present a one-sentence question about an obscure issue; for example, "Estimate the number of bicycles in China" or "How many ping-pong balls fit in a 747?" Like all other case interviews, the interviewer is examining the logic and problem-solving process of the interviewee.

Doing Well on Case Interviews

Case interviews can be unsettling if you don't prepare for them. People may freeze up so much they are unable to do even simple math. Nevertheless, proper preparation can help you focus and do well in these interviews. Compared to regular interviews, case interviews help you to focus on a specific issue or problem. This prevents your mind from wondering what the next question will be.

Following are some preparation tips for case interviews:

Read about case interviews. There are a number of books and Web sites that can help you. See the suggestions at the end of this chapter for sources.

Practice many case interviews. Visit your campus career center and practice a case interview with a counselor. Ask your career center if they have additional resources about case interviews. Continue your preparation by having friends conduct case interviews with you.

Understand how you are being evaluated. Case interviews are much less about "getting the right answer" than showing your problem-solving skills, analytical abilities, and logic. Interviewers are focusing on your thinking processes and ability to work toward a recommendation. "Getting it right" is secondary to your ability to come up with a *good* recommendation.

Key Areas of Concentration During Case Interviews

Realize it is of utmost importance to steadily work toward a recommendation or solution. Here are our tips to do this in a manner that will impress the interviewer:

1. Read or listen to the case carefully.

2. Ask the interviewer questions to clarify the facts in the case.

3. Ask the interviewer questions about other issues related to the case (e.g., competitors, product, marketplace, client presenting a problem, organization or client background, organization resources, customers, employees, management, etc.).

4. Highlight key issues for consideration in developing your solution.

5. Begin to develop an easily understood hypothesis that moves you toward your recommendation.

6. Ask the interviewer if the hypothesis is reasonable given the economic climate or the client's issues.

7. Work toward your recommendation by continuing to ask the interviewer questions about the situation.

8. Frequently summarize your developing recommendation relative to the identified issues.

9. Continue to clarify issues with the interviewer.

10. Finalize your recommendation, including likely outcomes and risks.

You have been hired by a producer of deli meats to investigate their recent decline in market share. The client wants an action plan to reverse the trend.

Details

The firm produces packages of sliced deli meats at all price levels (generic, mid-level, and premium). The market share loss is primarily in the premium category. The brand is relatively well-known.

The higher-priced premium products carry a higher profit margin. Competitors maintained their price levels during the company's recent loss in market share. The products are sold in grocery stores and delis. Grocers maintained the same placement of the product on their shelves during the decline period.

The company continued the same advertising and marketing campaigns as before the drop in market share. The three other major competitors did not make any noticeable changes in their promotional efforts during the period, and all four companies use the same distribution channels. Each of the competitors has about 20 percent of the market and the client has 40 percent. The market is growing moderately in all three price point categories.

The profile of customers buying the premium deli meats has not changed, but a survey of customers indicates there is more variability in product quality than that of the competition. Some customers changed to the competition due to this difference.

In the space below, write up your process for working toward a recommendation. Then, describe your recommendation and its potential results and effects.

Nervousness: Getting a Grip

Face it, most people are nervous going into an interview. Having us tell you not to be nervous simply does not work. However, we can recommend a number of ideas to reduce your nervousness:

- *Be prepared!* Above all else, strong preparation is the best remedy for nervousness. Know what you want to tell the interviewer about yourself, and know about the company and job.
- *Don't be rushed the day of the interview.* Get yourself organized and dressed well in advance. Allow plenty of travel time so you arrive at least 15 minutes early.
- *Embrace the interview!* Interviewing is exchanging information with another person. Be positive and exhibit confidence in your voice and your mannerisms.
- *Get a good night's sleep!*

Your Competitive Edge: The Value You Bring to the Organization

What is it about you that will make the employer want to hire you compared to other candidates? How do you go about setting yourself apart from the rest of the pack?

These are key questions you must have answers for if you are to get the job offers you want. Of course, you also need the skills and knowledge required to perform the job. But are there other things such as your work style, work attitude, or work personality that will make the interviewer start looking at you as the top candidate? Give some serious thought to this and how to portray these qualities in the job interview.

You need a nice "package" about yourself that sets you apart. Areas you may wish to consider as part of your package include the following:

- Proven track record of getting results
- Ability to work well in difficult settings
- Ability to persuade other people of your viewpoint
- Proven technical abilities in similar jobs
- Ability to work with a wide range of people
- Ability to manage processes well
- Ability to manage people well
- Desire to use past experience and develop further in this new job

Give some serious thought to two or three major themes that set you apart from the pack, but always remember, they must firmly link with the ability to perform successfully in the job you're interviewing for.

Questions You Should Ask
in the Interview

The pressure is taken off of you (sort of) when the interviewer asks whether you have any questions. This is still a time for you to be "on." You can continue to score points in the interview by asking engaging questions that show the depth of your knowledge about the company, position, and industry. This is still a critical time in the interview, and you should continue to connect with the interviewer. The purposes of your questions are threefold:

- To nail down the specifics about the job
- To exhibit your knowledge and insight about the company, job, and industry
- To obtain information that will help you make a decision on a job offer

Write out a list of questions to take to the interview so you don't forget any important ones. Here are some sample questions that are valuable to ask:

JOB

- Why is this job open?
- What is the work environment like?
- Could you break out the activities in this job and tell me how much time I would spend on each one?
- What is a typical day like on this job?
- Who would I be working with primarily?
- What other departments would I be working with?
- What is your management style? (Ask this question of your potential supervisor.)
- How do you see this job changing in the next few years?
- What training do you provide to support an employee in this job?
- How will my work performance be measured?
- Given my skills, how do you view my fit with this job?
- What is the career path associated with this job?

COMPANY

- What is the company culture like?
- What major challenges does the company face in the next three years?
- How does the company view its employees and their roles?
- What is the overall management style?
- What is the organizational structure?
- How does the department this job is in fit within the company?
- What long-term training and education does the company support for its employees?

- Would you expand on the company's mission statement? (Ask this question only if you have located and read the mission statement.)
- Would you describe your experience with the company?
- What do you think the company's greatest strengths and weaknesses are?
- What are the major challenges from competitors, and how is the company addressing them?
- How is the company addressing major industry trends?

Checklist and Miscellaneous Preparation

When you make arrangements for the interview, ask some questions about the interview procedure including:

- Who will conduct the interview?
- How many interviews will there be?
- How long will the interview(s) last?
- Request directions to the workplace and parking information.
- Have a job description sent to you in advance.
- Request that other information about the company be sent to you in advance.

9.6 Interview Preparation Checklist

Each time you get ready for an interview, you should follow a variety of steps in order to perform well. Use the checklist below to make sure you haven't forgotten anything. Grade each item A through F, reflecting how successful you've been at accomplishing each step.

_____ 1. Research the company and job.

_____ 2. Conduct your self-assessment (skills, knowledge, goals, and accomplishments).

_____ 3. Assess the value you bring: your competitive edge.

_____ 4. Prepare the questions you will ask.

_____ 5. Dress professionally. (Check grooming and attire immediately before interview.)

_____ 6. **Pack your portfolio.** (Include extra resumes, letters of recommendation, training certificates, work samples if appropriate, references list, and so forth.)

_____ 7. Rehearse your handshake and greeting.

_____ 8. Obtain details about the interview in advance (where, when, number of interviews and interviewers, who will do interview(s), length of interview(s), directions to workplace, parking, etc.).

_____ 9. Arrive 15 minutes early for the interview.

_____ 10. Tell your story to the interviewer.

_____ 11. Ask for the job—if you want it!

_____ 12. Send thank-you notes promptly.

your turn . . .

Dressing for Interviews

Here are a few questions about interviewing dress for you to consider. Answer them with what you know now.

1. What is the "typical" style of dress in your industry of choice?

   _____

   _____

2. What is appropriate interview dress in your industry of choice?

   _____

   _____

3. Would your future supervisor dress dramatically differently from her subordinates? How?

   _____

   _____

The Interview Wardrobe

Dressing for interviews is trickier than it was years ago. In recent years, organizations have moved toward more casual dress at work. Now, some organizations are swinging back to more formal dress, while others remain more casual.

For job interviews, dress within the norms of the industry. For a business position, this means a business suit. For other environments, more casual wear might be appropriate. For example, if you're interviewing for an accounting position with a large company, a suit is in order, but if you're interviewing for a position as a dental hygienist, nice casual is in order. An interview for an automotive technician position might require even more casual attire. Before your interview, attempt to get an idea of what "normal" attire is for the organization and job.

Regardless of the industry norm, a clean, professional appearance is necessary in all cases. In this section, we will detail a professional wardrobe for the job searcher.

Men's Professional Interview Wardrobe

Suits

First impressions are critical and your suit is the most noticeable part of your wardrobe. Take the care and time necessary to buy one that fits you and your needs, keeping in mind the following tips:

- Choose a wool or quality wool blend suit in a solid color. Black, charcoal, navy, and gray are your best color choices.

First impressions are critical. Take the care and time to find clothing that suits you and the interviewing situation.

- Select a plain single-breasted style without fancy buttons, stitching, or other decorations.
- Be sure the suit fits properly. Have your suit fitted by a professional tailor.

Shirts and Ties

The white, long-sleeved dress shirt is still the best business shirt to wear for interviews. Here are some additional tips:

- Go with cotton or cotton/polyester for the best look.
- Make sure your shirt is ironed well, especially an all-cotton shirt.
- Your shirt should not be too roomy or too tight.
- Always wear an undershirt.

Your tie is an important part of your attire and can give your look some color. Here are some tips:

- Choose a quality silk or silk look-alike tie.
- Coordinate texture, pattern, and color with your shirt and suit.
- Bow ties are not appropriate for interviews.
- Stay away from club or group insignias.
- The tip of your tie should touch the top of your belt buckle.

Shoes and Socks

An appropriate look in shoes is also important. Here's what to look for:

- Wear black or cordovan if it matches your suit.
- Shoes should always be darker than your suit.
- Polish your shoes.
- Wear solid black or dark blue over-the-calf dress socks (never white).

Accessories

Small items can send a big message to others. To complete your good impression, follow these tips:

- Choose a black or navy leather belt with a small traditional buckle.
- Wear a tasteful watch.
- Keep rings to a minimum.
- Earrings, beads, chains, or fancy buckles should not be worn.
- No piercings!

Women's Professional Interview Wardrobe

The Business Suit

Buy a good-quality skirted suit with jacket or a similar pants suit. Don't be too trendy unless you are interviewing in the fashion or advertising industries. Neutral colors work best. Black, navy, gray, tan, taupe, bone, and brown are the safest colors. Wool, wool blends, and cotton are the most suitable materials.

Your skirt should be a comfortable length, straight or slightly flared, preferably to the knee. Skirt lengths are important and should not be too long or too short. If you find yourself tugging at your skirt while sitting, it's too short.

Blouses

Cotton, linen, and silk are the best fibers and will give you the best look. White is always the safest and looks professional, but don't be afraid to use other colors. Be sure, however, to have a sales consultant help you pull your look together.

Shoes and Hosiery

Buy sensible low-heeled pumps, with quiet soles and heels (no open toes or spike heels). Neutral colors are again the safest: black, navy, taupe, burgundy, or brown. Shoes should be polished, clean, and in good repair. Wear skin-colored pantyhose.

Purse

Use your own judgment as to whether you need to carry a purse. A simply designed bag in dark brown or black leather is the best choice.

Jewelry

When it comes to jewelry, keep it simple: less is better. Jewelry should be functional or give you presence.

Hair, Makeup, and Grooming

Your hair should be styled to convey a professional image, and your makeup should be subtle and understated. Use lipstick that blends in, not stands out. Use perfume very sparingly if at all. No piercings other than for one earring per ear.

Casual Dress for Job Interviews

If you are applying for a job in a skilled trade, your attire may need adjustments. Use common sense in the selection of your attire, and dress in a fashion similar to the work environment. For example, an interview for an auto repair position does not require a suit.

Portfolio: What You May Need

Black, dark brown, or leather covered are the best choices for your portfolio. Take the time to collect the necessary items to make this accessory work for you. Include the key items you assembled in Chapter 5, plus additional materials, including:

- Resume
- Reference list
- College transcript (if you are a current or recently graduated student)
- Recommendation letters
- Appropriate samples from work experiences, activities, community involvement, and other experiences
- Work performance reviews (if confidentiality is not an issue)
- Awards
- Relevant activity samples
- Writing samples

Practice Demonstrating Your Portfolio

Practice presenting your portfolio before your interviews. Have friends ask you typical interview questions and demonstrate your portfolio to them. Ask them for constructive feedback on how well you demonstrated the portfolio. Make changes as necessary.

Use your portfolio to illustrate your skills and abilities. Outstanding examples of your work provide an employer with concrete evidence of your capabilities.

Self-Evaluation: Assess Your Performance

As soon as practical, review what happened during the interview. Make a quick set of notes and add to them as the day progresses. Consider the following as you initially review the interview:

- What was my overall impression of the interview?
- What did I do well?
- What areas do I need to improve?
- What specific questions were a problem?
- What did I learn from this interview?

Figure 9.1 is a sample evaluation sheet you may model, or you may design your own. In any event, complete a form like this for each interview you have. Use these sheets to track your interviews and help you make improvements for future interviews.

Develop a Plan for Improvement

Most of your interview probably went well if you did your preparation in advance. Of course, there are always areas to improve, so continue on with your self-evaluation. Focus on the key areas that did not go so well or where you did well but would like to do better. About your areas for improvement, consider these questions:

- Are these improvements really necessary for me to make?
- Does each improvement take me closer to my goal of obtaining the job I want?
- Will I commit to making these improvements?
- Have I set reasonable time frames for these improvements?

Make sure that you hold yourself to the time frames set for your improvements. Not only will you get better through your improvements, you'll feel better about yourself and your interviewing abilities.

Figure 9.2 is a sample of an improvement form you may use, or you may create your own. As you have additional interviews, complete an evaluation for each one or develop a sheet that summarizes your plans for continued improvement.

Reassess Your Interest in the Position and the Organization

Rarely is your view of a job situation the same after an interview as it was before the interview. You are usually more or less interested in the job based on the new information you have obtained. At this point, evaluate how you view the position. Asking the following questions should help:

- How well do I understand all aspects of the position?
- Has my interest in this position changed compared to before the interview?
- Am I still interested in pursuing this position?

| *figure* **9.1** | *Interview evaluation.* |

ORGANIZATION: _____

NAME OF INTERVIEWER(S): _____

POSITION INTERVIEWED FOR: _____

DATE OF INTERVIEW: _____

Rate yourself on your interview performance in each area:

E = EXCELLENT   **G** = GOOD   **F** = FAIR   **B** = BELOW AVERAGE   **P** = POOR

AREA ASSESSED

First Impression: Handshake, greeting, eye contact, expression   (E) (G) (F) (B) (P)

Poise and Confidence: Calm, little nervousness, focused
demeanor, positive answers expressed with enthusiasm and
confidence   (E) (G) (F) (B) (P)

Preparation for Interview: Readiness to discuss abilities, fit
an understanding of the organization and the job   (E) (G) (F) (B) (P)

Communication Skills: Able to articulate answers well and in
an interesting fashion   (E) (G) (F) (B) (P)

Strengths and Weaknesses: Able to illustrate strengths and
explain weaknesses   (E) (G) (F) (B) (P)

Qualifications and Abilities: Able to illustrate skills and abilities
required to perform the job   (E) (G) (F) (B) (P)

Interest in Job and Organization: Exhibited strong interest in
the job and organization   (E) (G) (F) (B) (P)

Questions: Asked well-thought-out questions about the job and
organization   (E) (G) (F) (B) (P)

Appearance: Professional appearance for the industry   (E) (G) (F) (B) (P)

Overall Evaluation: (E) (G) (F) (B) (P)

figure **9.2** Interview improvement summary.

Interview and Date: _____

Area for Improvement: _____

_____

Action(s): _____

_____

_____

Time Frame: _____

Interview and Date: _____

Area for Improvement: _____

_____

Action(s): _____

_____

_____

Time Frame: _____

Interview and Date: _____

Area for Improvement: _____

_____

Action(s): _____

_____

_____

Time Frame: _____

You must like your job to perform it well. Evaluating your interest in the job after the interview increases the possibility of accepting a job you'll like. Don't forget to evaluate whether this is really a job you can perform well in.

You also need to evaluate the organization. Again, after an interview, your view of the organization may change for the better or worse. Here are some questions to consider:

- Do the organization's mission and values fit mine?
- Are these the kind of people I would like to work for?
- Does the organization's culture fit me?
- Is this a company I would like to work for?

As with your assessment of the position, finding an organization you like increases the chance you will perform well in your work. Finding the right environment for you is important and will bring you greater happiness on the job.

Follow Up with the Organization

Following up with the organization is a critical component of your job search success. If you are legitimately interested in the job after the interview, you need to positively send the clear message that you want the job. Following are the things to do:

Send a Thank-You Letter

Amazingly enough, over half of all candidates interviewed for jobs do not take the time to send thank-you letters. Not only is it important from a job search perspective, it is also a common courtesy. Even if you don't want the job, send a thank-you letter. Show your professionalism.

Job offers are won or lost based on whether a candidate sent a thank-you letter. In an "even race" for a job, if one candidate sends a thank-you and the other doesn't, guess who gets the job offer? Obviously, the person who sent the note. Don't let yourself fall victim to laxness with thank-you letters.

Follow Up with a Phone Call or E-mail

Before you leave the interview, make sure you know what the next step is in the process and when you will hear from the organization again. If the employer does not contact you within the time frame set, call or e-mail them the day after they were to contact you.

Some other reasons for contacting the employer include the following:

- Set or confirm another meeting time
- Provide additional information

- Update the employer on new developments (such as another job offer)
- Withdraw your name from consideration

Tips concerning contacting the employer:

- Never become a nuisance.
- Respect the employer's time frames.
- Know why you're calling. Think through and script or outline what you want to say if necessary.
- Be positive, friendly, and to the point.

Do not contact employers to "wear them down" for a job offer. That kind of strategy may backfire on you. Be professional and you will portray yourself well to your potential employer.

The Typical Job Offer Process

hen a job offer is made, the hard work starts all over again. Here are a few suggestions to help you get through the process successfully:

1. *Get the offer in writing.* This is especially critical if negotiations are to follow. Do not negotiate without a written offer from the organization.

2. *Review the offer.* Make sure it includes all relevant details discussed up to this point. Contact the employer for any necessary additional information or if information is missing.

3. *Request time to think the offer over.* You may be pursuing other opportunities and other offers may be pending. Tell the employer who has made you the offer that you are flattered and ask them when they need to know of an acceptance. If you are a graduating student, you may be interviewing with many employers. Employers know this and in some cases, if they really want to hire you, may be open to negotiating extensions on offer acceptance deadlines.

4. *Negotiate as necessary.* It is often best to delay negotiating until your next contact with the employer. You need some time to digest the offer and weigh it against other offers or pending opportunities.

5. *If you accept the offer, write a letter of acceptance, restating the terms of employment.* Thank the employer and restate your excitement about starting the job.

6. *If you reject the offer, either do so at this time or when you next contact the employer.* You may want a bit of breathing room before rejecting the offer, so it is often wise to thank the employer and tell them you will get back to them in a few days. It is best to verbally reject the offer in a phone call and then follow that up with a courteous rejection letter that does not burn any bridges.

Understanding Job Offers

ob offers have these elements:

- A clear statement that says, "We are offering the job of (actual job title).
- A date, time, and place to begin work.
- A definite starting salary.
- A description of the working conditions, which should include hours and location of work, benefits, and moving and/or relocation allowance.

If you do not receive all of this information, ask the employer about these items before accepting the offer. It is vitally important you understand all elements of the job and work conditions before accepting the offer.

Know What You're Worth

Determining your worth is a necessary act. You must know both what the job is worth to the employer and what it is worth to you. Underpricing yourself results in pay below your worth; overpricing yourself may eliminate you from consideration. So what do you do? First, do your research.

Know What the Job Is Worth to the Employer

Pay rates vary widely for similar jobs depending on the industry, the employer, the economic factors, and the geographic location.

Keep away from people who try to belittle your ambitions. Small people always do that, but many great people make you feel that you, too, can become great.

—MARK TWAIN

Industry. The U. S. Department of Labor compiles statistics on the average weekly wage by occupation and by industry. Examine and compare wages across an industry to determine whether the amount an employer is offering is competitive within the industry and job category.

Employer. Salaries for identical jobs in the same industry vary depending on the employer. A grade school teacher may earn a higher salary in an exclusive private school than in a public school. Similarly, an accountant may earn a higher salary in a "Big Four" accounting firm than in a small, local accounting practice.

Economic factors. Some of the economic factors that affect local pay rates include the cost of living, the supply of and demand for qualified workers, state worker's compensation costs, housing availability, and employee benefits.

Geographic location. Salaries vary widely depending on geography. High wages may be offered to offset undesirable elements, while low wages may be acceptable because of desirable elements. For example, the isolation and difficult living conditions in Alaska command a higher wage than do more suitable geographic locations.

Know What the Job Is Worth to You

Only you can decide your worth. For example, a Bend, Oregon, doctor trades the pressures and high salary of Los Angeles for fewer dollars and the tranquility of a small community. People decide on different work situations and environments to meet their own needs and desires. Money is only one factor in their decision.

Know Your Lowest Acceptable Wage

Obviously, you need to know what you must earn to live, while saving a bit of your salary—that is your lowest acceptable wage. The best way to determine that figure is to prepare a bare-bones budget.

Job Offer Negotiations

here are many things to consider when you enter the negotiation stage of a job offer. Take time to consider what you need and what you want in the job and the salary. Here are some points to remember:

1. Be honest about your present salary if the employer asks.

2. Set an attractive salary goal. A 15- to 25-percent increase in salary is reasonable if you are moving "up" in responsibility level. If you are relocating to an area with a higher cost of living, you may need an even larger increase.

3. If the organization's "final" offer is below what you want, try to negotiate a review for a raise in three to six months.

4. Remember, money's not everything. You may be able to negotiate an extra week of vacation, a higher sales commission, fewer hours, a flexible schedule, a performance incentive, or stock options. Be creative in your bargaining.

5. The wage you get to begin work is the basis for all future raises. It is much easier to negotiate a higher wage at the beginning than it is to significantly increase your earning capacity later. Shoot for the highest possible wage at the start.

6. You have the most negotiating power once the employer has decided to hire you. The employer wants you and does not want to go through the whole hiring process again for someone else.

7. Never tell an employer you have another job offer at a higher wage unless it is true. This is not the way to negotiate. You may lose the offer if you aren't truthful.

Know the Negotiating Strategies

There are many different ways to negotiate salaries. If an employer states a pay range of, for example, $35,000–$40,000 annually, consider these options:

- Accept the $35,000 if it is appropriate for your skills, experience, education, and prior wages.
- Bridge the employer's offer by asking for $38,000–$43,000. This keeps you within the acceptable range and prevents you from being hired at the lowest wage.
- Ask what qualifies a person for the top rate. Demonstrate how you meet these requirements; then request the higher rate.
- Request a rate higher than $40,000 and provide evidence as to why you are worth more.

student profile

Mai. As the final days of August wane, Mai is excitedly anticipating her senior year in college. She just completed a three-month accounting internship with Life Promises. Her internship brought her into contact with a variety of functions and people at the company. She learned much about the medical products industry and the role of accounting in that industry. She is eager to compare what she learned to the advanced accounting and finance courses she will take her senior year.

Just then the phone rings. It is Beth, her internship supervisor. "Mai, we were thrilled to have you work for us this summer. We hope you learned a lot about our company and the industry. You did such great work that I want to offer you a full-time position pending your graduation in May. The starting salary is $42,000 and you will have full benefits. I'll be sending a letter to you with details of the offer. One thing, though, I have to know whether you will accept this offer by October 15."

Mai is both stunned and thrilled. She says thank you and tells Beth she will get back to her soon with her decision.

After hanging up the phone, Mai suddenly realizes she has a problem. She has plans to interview with many employers during her senior year. The employers she is especially interested in will be conducting interviews on campus during October and November. If she receives any job offers from those interviews, they will come in November and December.

She asks her friend Andre, "What should I do? I liked the internship and the company. But their deadline is so early, I won't be able to compare other job offers to theirs. I suppose I could accept their offer and still interview with other employers. If I get a better offer, I could just tell them that I got a better offer elsewhere."

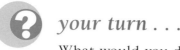

your turn . . .

What would you do if you were Mai? Write your strategy and suggestions below.

_____

_____

_____

_____

_____

_____

Counteroffers

Counteroffers are sometimes extended. Say you are given an offer by a potential new employer and you tell your current employer of the job offer and that you will be leaving. Or, maybe you have already accepted a job with a new employer when you tell your current employer you are leaving. Now, all of a sudden, your old employer believes you can do no wrong. You are the most perfect and necessary employee they have ever had. Your employer doesn't want to lose you or spend the time and money to replace you. Your current company makes you a counteroffer. Now what do you do?

Keep your eyes wide open before accepting the job, half-shut afterwards.

—BENJAMIN FRANKLIN

When you receive a counteroffer from your employer, carefully analyze it and the reasons you looked for a different job in the first place. If you are unhappy, will anything really change if you stay? Will the problems that exist be resolved? It is highly unlikely.

You should do what is best for you. If the counteroffer and job situation at your old employer are good, you might consider accepting the counteroffer and staying with your employer. Make sure that the counteroffer is in writing and that everything looks good concerning your future there. Be sure to honestly address the situation with your employer throughout the process, including why you'd like to stay.

Writing a Letter of Acceptance

If you accept an offer, write a letter of acceptance (see Chapter 6 on correspondence). This prevents misunderstandings and reemphasizes your excitement about the new job.

Writing a Letter of Rejection

It is possible to receive a job offer and find out that the job or organization is not suitable for you at this time. If this happens, handle it professionally with a gracious letter of rejection (see Chapter 6 on correspondence).

Writing a Letter of Resignation

If you are accepting the new job offer, leave your old job professionally by writing a letter of resignation. Show your appreciation to your old employer by taking the time to say thank you. Maintain a positive relationship (see Chapter 6 on correspondence).

Book and Internet Interviewing Resources

ome of the better books on interviewing include the following:

- *Job Interviews for Dummies*, Joyce Lain Kennedy
- *Knock 'Em Dead 2005*, Martin Yate
- *Nail the Job Interview: 101 Dynamite Answers to Interview Questions*, Caryl Rae Krannich
- *Sweaty Palms: The Neglected Art of Being Interviewed*, Anthony Medley
- *201 Best Questions to Ask on Your Job Interview*, John Kador
- *Vault Guide to the Case Interview*, Eric Chung and Mark Asher

Web sites that have good information on interviewing strategies include the following:

- Career Builder Network: www.careerbuilder.com
- Career Journal: www.careerjournal.com
- College Grad Network: www.collegegrad.com
- Monster.com: www.monster.com
- Quintessential Careers: www.quintcareers.com

Summary

Why should I hire you over all the others? This essentially is the question you need to answer to get the job offer. After all your pre-interview preparation—your research of the company, the job, and yourself; your questions; your dress; your promptness; and your routine—it still comes down to "Why should I hire you over anyone else?" Remember, the answer can vary by interviewer and by job. Sometimes, it is based only on your technical skills. Other times, your fit within the company is the predominant factor. Still other times, your ability to get along with coworkers is the determining factor.

In this chapter, we focused on the keys to preparing well for job interviews. Investing your time and energy in the preparation process is the key to interviewing well. Getting a job offer is the goal of interviewing. At that point, your decision-making process continues through the negotiation process over salary and benefits. Continue to act professionally throughout the closing stages of this process. It will pay off with a continuing positive impression to the employer and a good start in your new job.

Using the Job Description to Prepare for Behavioral-Based Interviewing

Think of the job description as a "freebie" in your preparation for an interview. It typically lists the job duties, background information on the employer, and key qualifications needed by applicants. It serves as the basis for the behavioral-based questions an interviewer will ask you. This exercise focuses on using a real job description to simulate your preparation for a hypothetical behavioral-based interview.

To Do

Find a job description in a career area that interests you or use a description of a job or internship you want to interview for. These can be found in the newspaper, through online job sites, on employer Web sites, or at your campus career center. Outline the job description using the following format and begin to develop answers to potential interview questions.

Qualification/skill/ability desired #1: _____

Interview answer for where and when I showed this ability (including results):

_____

_____

_____

_____

_____

_____

_____

_____

Qualification/skill/ability desired #2: _____

Interview answer for where and when I showed this ability (including results):

_____

_____

_____

_____

_____

_____

_____

_____

Qualification/skill/ability desired #3: _____

Interview answer for where and when I showed this ability (including results):

_____

_____

_____

_____

_____

_____

_____

_____

You may wish to do the same exercise for the parts of the job description that describe the employer in order to make the employer understand why you would fit in their organization.

This type of activity helps you streamline your preparation for a job interview. You still need to have a thorough knowledge of yourself and your employer, but this specific focus on the job description helps you prepare for the behavioral-based questions you are likely to be asked. Answering these questions, which are tightly linked to the job, helps you present yourself as an outstanding candidate.

File this exercise in your portfolio.

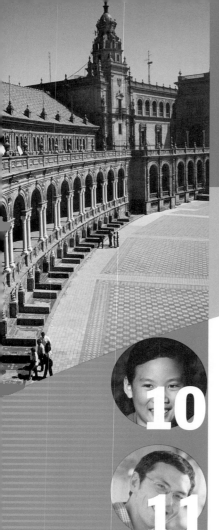

Balancing

YOUR CAREER & PERSONAL LIFE

IV

Growth, balance, and continuous lifelong learning are the goals of Unit IV. This unit revisits the primary aspects of your life: personal, social, professional, and financial. You will review the process of bringing a long-term balance into your life.

You are in charge of your future. You are an active participant—rather than a passive observer—in the progression of your life and career. In the following chapters, you will build a stronger pattern for continued growth and balance.

The Chapters

Chapter 10, Navigating: Your Professional Direction, begins with the transition to a new job. You will study work protocol and environment, and complete exercises on recording achievements and learning the policies about your place of employment. The goal of Chapter 10 is to prepare you for job success and help you manage your professional life.

All labor that uplifts humanity has dignity and importance and should be undertaken with painstaking excellence.

—MARTIN LUTHER KING, JR.

In Chapter 11, Cultivating Meaningful Connections: Personal and Social Relationships, you will look beyond the job to the other roles in your life. This chapter takes you through forming life habits, including a variety of hands-on exercises. You will have the opportunity to examine your relationships with the important people in your life. You will also explore your role as a citizen in the community. The exercises focus on helping you develop and maintain meaningful connections.

Chapter 12, Financing Your Life: Planning and Implementing, allows you to reexamine your financial goals and learn ways to achieve financial independence. This chapter is only an introduction to financial management—it is up to you to build on it and follow through.

To work for the common good is the greatest creed.

—ALBERT SCHWEITZER

Once you are hired, it is time to settle into the work and challenge of the "real world." Study the concepts of this unit, and put each of them into daily practice. The textbook is designed to guide you along the way, but ultimately it is up to you. You are in control of your own journey.

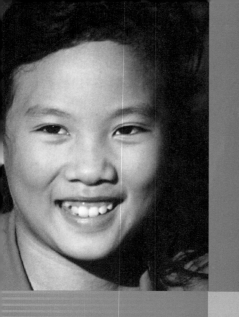

Navigating

YOUR PROFESSIONAL DIRECTION

chapter

10

learning objectives

1. To learn how to manage the transition to being a new employee

2. To understand the formal and informal structures of an organization

3. To realize the importance of ongoing professional development and how to find opportunities

4. To gain a better understanding of workplace issues, such as sexual harassment, discrimination, and diversity

5. To learn strategies to improve workplace attitudes and competencies

One doesn't discover new lands without consenting to lose sight of the shore . . .

—ANDRE GIDE

*The fundamental unit of the new economy is not the corporation but the **individual**. Tasks aren't assigned and controlled through a stable chain of management but rather are carried out autonomously by independent contractors. These electronically connected freelancers—e-lancers— join together in fluid and temporary networks to produce and sell goods and services. When the job is done, the network dissolves and its members become independent agents again, circulating through the economy, seeking the next assignment.*

—THOMAS MALONE AND
ROBERT LAUBACHER (1998)

Ultimately, you are in charge of your own career and professional development. Consider the adjoining quote from a *Harvard Business Review* article.

You are in charge of creating and managing your career. Granted, there are external factors that influence your career–life direction; however, you have a great deal of control over the choices you make in your life. This chapter addresses issues of professional management and provides suggestions on how to manage your work life. You may already hold a full- or part-time job. If so, integrate the concepts and exercises into your work experience. If you do not have work experience, envision a work scenario for yourself so that you can apply the concepts from this chapter. Let's begin with a student example.

student profile

Eric. I'll never forget Eric. The two of us worked together several years ago. Eric was college educated, had a great sense of humor, and had a good potential future. However, he had a major shortcoming: he did poor-quality work. He felt that the job he had wasn't important enough to do well, so he put minimum effort into his daily work. When I asked him why he didn't put in his best effort, he said, "When they value me enough to give me more money, then I'll do a better job. But since they don't appreciate my capabilities now, why should I put in extra effort now?" Needless to say, it wasn't long until Eric received news that he was being let go.

It is clear that Eric did not really understand some of the basic concepts and skills about managing his career. This chapter focuses on helping you succeed in the workplace rather than making the same mistakes Eric did.

New on the Job

Do you remember what it was like the last time you started something new? It could have been a new job or internship. What were your most significant concerns?

We have all been in new and unfamiliar situations. Perhaps it was the first day of college. Or maybe it was meeting a loved one's family members at a reunion or special occasion for the first time. In any event, you were likely nervous and excited. You also wanted to make a positive first impression. For anyone who has started a new job, these feelings are normal. This section provides some suggestions for successfully breaking into a new work experience.

Breaking in Gracefully

When you are a new employee or intern, many eyes are on you. It goes without saying that you want to make a good impression. Often, new employees want to make an immediate impact. Unfortunately, new employees may take on a project or assume too much responsibility before fully acclimating themselves to the organization. Not surprisingly, these attempts at making an immediate impact often have disastrous results. A wiser approach is to break into your work environment slowly and gracefully. Review the following suggestions:

You are now in a learning environment. Have a positive attitude and adopt a flexible approach.

Be a participant observer initially. As a new employee, take some time to observe how work is conducted at the organization. Ask colleagues about office policies and procedures. For example, Mark took a new job as a counselor on a college campus. It wasn't until he asked a colleague that he learned he needed to dial "9" before making an off-campus phone call. Finally, observe how staff members dress for work. Is there a dress code? For the first several days, it is better to overdress than underdress.

Get to know your colleagues. It is important that you become part of the team environment at your work site. Spend time getting to know your colleagues better. Take Julie, for example. When she took a job as an office assistant for a law firm, she made it a point to have lunch with a different staff member once a week. Julie wanted to learn more about her coworkers as well as about the organization.

Be ready and willing to learn. Regardless of your formal education or work experience, you are now in a new learning environment. The organization will likely train you to address the demands of your new job. Learning to learn becomes an important skill during the first few weeks because your learning curve may be steep and new material will come at you rapidly. Have a positive attitude and adopt a flexible approach.

Avoid forming cliques or romantic relationships. As mentioned earlier, try to get to know your colleagues, but acquaint yourself only "within reason." Establishing close ties with a small group of individuals or starting a romantic relationship with a colleague can have harmful effects on your new position.

Set some realistic goals for yourself during this breaking-in time. It is easy for new employees to have high expectations for themselves and others. Often, these expectations can be too high and can lead to disappointments. During the first few months, set some realistic short-term goals for yourself. Don't try to take on too much too soon. You may want to discuss your short-term goals with an immediate supervisor.

Getting to Know the Organization

Connecting. Assume that you are starting a new job or internship. A friend encourages you to "get to know" the organization. What do you think that means? How might you accomplish this goal?

You will no doubt be focused on your new job and all the excitement and energy that comes along with starting a new position. However, don't overlook the importance of knowing the organization by studying what takes place formally and informally. By observing the organization, you will be in a better position to navigate your way through the system. Also, your knowledge and insight will help you avoid certain pitfalls and take advantage of promising situations.

Establish a formal or informal mentor. Some organizations have a formal mentoring system in which a senior staff member is assigned to a new employee, while other organizations do not have a formal system. In either case, a more experienced staff member can show you the ropes of the organization. A mentor can help guide you through the transition of becoming a more established colleague. Don't underestimate the value of this mentoring relationship—a close mentor can even help advocate on your behalf if you are up for a promotion in the future. For example, Susan worked for a large retailer. She was eager to move to the next level after working there for three years. Her mentor, Judy, advocated for Susan, and she got the promotion she sought. Without Judy's help and guidance, Susan may not have been promoted.

Study the formal structure of the organization. How is the organization set up structurally? Is there an organizational chart? If so, what does it look like? Obtain this information during your first month as a new employee. It is true that many organizations are deviating from the traditional job descriptions and boxes on the organizational chart, but there is still some degree of formal structure at all organizations. This knowledge can help you learn about reporting lines and other related information.

Observe and analyze the culture of your organization. Organizational "culture" can be defined as "the way things are done around here." Each organization has its own unique culture. For example, what are the office rituals of your organization? Most organizations acknowledge special occasions or events in ways such as the following:

- Acknowledging the end of a busy week with a happy hour at a restaurant or bar
- Having food at staff meetings
- Celebrating staff members' birthdays
- Hosting holiday or other parties during the year

Another form of organizational culture involves work expectations. Some organizations have a work-at-all-costs culture—either stated or unstated. Promotions or bonuses might not be granted unless employees are putting in long weeks. For example, Bob left a prestigious firm as a consultant after five years. He was working 70-hour weeks and found little time for his partner and children. The company was known as a place where employees were expected to put in long hours if they were to be recognized. Many employees burned out, including Bob, due to the extensive evening and weekend hours. On the other hand, some employees enjoyed this fast-paced environment. They became workaholics, a status symbol they wore as a badge of honor for senior management to see.

personal **THINK PIECE**

Just the way it is. *What is the work culture like at your work site? If you are not currently working, think about an organization that you've worked for in the past or would like to work for in the future. Describe the culture.*

_____

_____

_____

Learn the politics of your organization. All organizations have politics. It is important that you become aware of what they are. Ed Holton, a professor and specialist on career transition, recommends that new employees become "organizational savvy—meaning learning how an organization really functions." Contrary to the stereotype of office politics, he believes that politics is not a dirty word. He provides three rules: "Rule 1: Don't try to play politics until you have more experience. Rule 2: Consider the political aspects of everything you do. Rule 3: Use the first year to learn good organizational political skills" (Holton, 1995).

Learn about the informal structure of the organization. What really happens within an organization (i.e., the informal structure) doesn't always follow the formal structure, so you should learn about the company's informal influence structure. For example, Jane is an assistant director at a consulting firm. The director, Pam, is often on the road developing new client contacts, so Jane essentially runs the day-to-day activities of the office.

Learn about the communication styles and methods at your site. With advanced technology, employees communicate with others in numerous ways—both inside and outside of the organization. As a new employee, you will need to learn how staff members communicate with others. Following are several questions you should ask your colleagues:

- How is formal communication handled? Is it via e-mail, written memos, staff announcements, or other reports?
- How is informal communication addressed? This includes face-to-face communication, staff meetings, telephone, e-mail, and the like.

At staff meetings, observe who leads the meeting, who speaks up most frequently or loudly, and whose opinions seem most respected. You can learn a great deal about the informal structure at these meetings.

Warning: Don't underestimate the power and the role of the grapevine at an organization. Be aware of what you say to others. There is an old but worthy saying that reads: "Loose lips sink ships." Be aware of who's around when you are discussing work, including on-the-job discussions, chats over the lunch break, and water-cooler exchanges. Remember to keep confidential information confidential.

Dressing Professionally

A new job is not the time to make a fashion statement. Observe how your colleagues are dressed and attempt to match your wardrobe choices to the culture of the work environment. Generally speaking, body art and other creative expressions of self (e.g., piercings) should be revealed cautiously (depending on the work organization). You want to be recognized and remembered for your diligent efforts and contributions to the organization—not the stud in your tongue and the multiple hoops around your earlobe.

Will You Fit In?

Dress and Fitting In

It is important to dress to fit the culture of an organization. According to David Schmier, president of a company that teaches job-finding skills, joining a company is really a lot like joining a tribe: "Quit selling yourself and start matching." This matching strategy includes decisions about what to wear to make a positive impression. Observe what other employees wear, or better yet, do some research before you interview at an organization.

Source: K. Maher (2003).

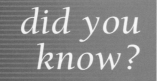

did you know?

According to the Association of Image Consultants, there are now over 1,000 image consultants in the United States, and more are setting up shop as a result of popular TV programs. About 75 percent of clients hire consultants in order to gain an edge in their careers.

You probably don't need to hire an image consultant, but it is important to pay attention to how you dress—especially when making a first impression.

Source: K. Maher (2004).

First-Day-on-the-Job Reminders

It is your first day on the new job or internship. No doubt you are nervous, excited, and perhaps relieved that you are beginning this new adventure. Here are some pointers to remember about this day, one of your most important days on the job:

- Dress appropriately for the job.
- Arrive early. This is a good idea so that you know exactly how long it takes to commute to the site.
- Ask about addressing superiors and coworkers. Some employees are on a first-name basis, while others may want to be addressed by their titles.
- Figure out how to use any office equipment. If you will use a computer, obtain a password and some instruction on how to use any office-specific software.
- Ask for a tour of the facility. This may include finding out where certain areas are located, including the cafeteria, human resources, facilities management, and so forth.
- Ask about your schedule. Are you responsible for maintaining your own schedule, or do others maintain it for you? Is there an electronic schedule?
- Start to develop relationships with your colleagues. Many organizations have adopted a team-based approach to problem solving. Your interpersonal skills will be important as you build effective relationships.

Are You a Team Player?

A resource that can be helpful to graduating students is a book titled *Graduating into the Nineties*. This book can assist all graduates whether they completed their degree in 1980, 1990, or 2005 and beyond. The authors provide some suggestions about managing relationships, including being a member of a team in your organization.

Tips for Becoming a Team Player

- Develop a "team" mentality.
- Participate in team activities—get involved in activities—both work and non-work related (for example, social events designed to build teamwork skills).
- Take pride in the team.

Traps to Avoid When Managing Work Relationships

- Forming cliques.
- Sex and race (in other words, comments and jokes about sex, race, ethnicity, religion, and the like do not belong in the work environment).
- Passing judgment.
- Brownnosing.
- Gossiping or breaking a trust.

Source: C. Carter & G. June (1993).

Committing to Your Professional Development

Are you committed? *What does it mean to you to be committed to your professional development? What strategies would you use to foster your own development at work?*

_____

_____

_____

_____

Whether you are a new employee or an established one, you should commit to your own professional development. This development is a lifelong, ongoing process for which you are responsible. To be flexible and competitive in tomorrow's changing marketplace, you must continue to learn and to develop new skills and knowledge. Professional development is no longer merely an option—it is a necessity if you expect to advance in your career. Here are some suggestions for managing your professional development:

- *Seek professional development.* Ask whether there is money designated for your professional development. Often, organizations will earmark a certain amount of funds for each employee to use at your discretion for your own professional development. Examples include tuition, software, books, training, and conferences.

- *Stay current.* Attend conferences, workshops, and training sessions. Regardless of your profession, advancements and developments take place continually. It is your responsibility to stay abreast of those developments. Conferences and workshops are wonderful opportunities to hear professionals talk about advances in your field. The events provide you with an excellent opportunity to meet other people.

- *Network.* Make an effort to network and meet people in your profession. This can help you advance in your career. Meeting the right person at the right time could lead to your next employment opportunity. Or, you may be able to help a colleague find her next position. Refer back to the information provided on networking and making contacts. Furthermore, attempt to connect with people outside your profession as well; expand your contacts by expanding your network.

- *Belong to a professional organization.* Does your occupation have a professional organization? It most likely does. For example, Kate belongs to a local professional association for career consultants that invites speakers to address various relevant issues. Kate has the chance to acquire this new information plus meet colleagues in the profession. The association also announces any job opportunities available at their work sites.

- *Read in your field.* We mentioned the value of reading in your field in an earlier chapter. Subscribe to journals and publications that are affiliated with your profession, and also read publications outside your profession. Review and save the articles that are specifically related to your work. Pass along articles of interest to your colleagues.

- *Continue to develop your technical and computer skills.* Your organization likely has some internal training available through human resources. Consult with human resources about taking advantage of these learning opportunities.

- *Make professional development fun.* Ongoing learning takes time and effort, but it can also be fun and inspiring. Embrace the learning process, and take pride in the fact that you are developing yourself for future opportunities. You are investing in yourself professionally and personally.

- *Learn a foreign language and travel outside your geographic "comfort zone."* You will learn more about other cultures and about yourself.

- *Stay involved with your alumni network.* The network back at your career development office on campus can be an invaluable way to stay connected for current students as well as graduates. In fact, you may be able to give back to the university. Review the examples below.

did you know?

Use the alumni network. Your college's alumni network is a valuable way for you to meet graduates who work in the professions that interest you. Check with your career center to see what resources might be available.

Many universities offer special networking events—including job shadowing, informational interviewing, and various workshops to help provide tips to students. Here are two such examples:

- Northwestern University started the Northwestern Externship (NEXT) program, which allows more than 600 students to job shadow an alumnus for a day. It is a great way to test out a career for a day. More than 400 alumni participate in the program.

- Colgate University in New York invited 80 alums back to campus for a long weekend so that they could provide recommendations for seniors who will be graduating in the spring. They offered numerous panel presentations, and students got the chance to meet one on one with professionals in a variety of career areas.

Ask your career counselor how you might get involved with the alumni network at your own school.

Source: P. Vogt (2005).

Getting in the Flow of Things

Another strategy for enhancing your professional development is to commit to work that you feel engaged in—personally, emotionally, and physically. When was the last time you were so engaged in an activity that you lost track of time? It could have been an activity related to school, work, or leisure. Psychologist Mihaly Csikszentmihalyi (1997) calls this state of being "the flow." He reminds us that work generally takes up approximately a third of the time available for living. Why not try to fill this time with work we enjoy?

your turn . . .

1. When was the last time you were in "the flow"? In other words, you lost track of time?

   _____

2. Was that activity work related?

   _____

3. If yes, what were you doing?

   _____

4. What was it you enjoyed about this activity? What made you lose track of time?

   _____

If your answer to Question 2 is no, is there a way you could incorporate this nonwork activity into a work-related activity? How so? Brainstorm your ideas. Csikszentmihalyi's book, *Good Business* (2003), encourages workers to find meaning in their work—a state where work becomes an extension of who we are and what we want to do.

Managing Workplace Issues: Sexual Attraction, Discrimination, and Harassment

Sexual Attraction

It is difficult to keep romance out of the workplace. Given the amount of time many individuals spend at the job, it isn't too surprising that some of them form close relationships with colleagues. Boundaries are often crossed, which in turn creates problems for those directly involved and potentially others who are not directly involved (e.g., family members or other colleagues). The authors recommend avoiding office relationships due to the high likelihood that these relationships will result in trouble. Despite the negative implications, however, employees inevitably get involved romantically with colleagues. When considering getting involved with another person at work, keep these thoughts in mind:

- It is difficult, if not impossible, to keep romantic relationships secret. Other colleagues will find out about the relationship regardless of your clandestine efforts.

Given the amount of time individuals may spend together on a job, it can be difficult to keep romance out of the workplace. Nonetheless, it is best to avoid office/work relationships.

- Romantic liaisons often misuse company time. How much time are you spending on your work as opposed to socializing? Romance can interfere with productivity and concentration.

- Assess the risks to your career. Sexual involvement can cost you your job and reputation depending on the organizational culture and the situation.

- Sexual relationships can result in an imbalance of power if one member of the relationship holds a higher title or supervises the other member.

- What is the company attitude toward employee romance? Is there a formal policy on relationships within the organization? What does the past history look like in terms of the way the company addressed other relationships between colleagues?

- Consider changing jobs, departments, locations, or employers if sexual attraction becomes an insurmountable challenge at your current workplace.

Sexual and Racial Discrimination

Even though it is prohibited by law, sexual and racial discrimination is still a common occurrence in the workplace. Your best line of defense is to know your rights and then discuss the situation openly with those involved. Be an active participant in any discussions, yet realize that there are outside factors affecting the hiring and promoting decisions. If you are passed up for a promotion, you have a right to question the decision; however, the decision may have had nothing to do with your gender, religion, race, ethnicity, or sexual orientation.

If you can't resolve this issue, speak to your supervisors or consult with the U.S. Department of Labor or a labor attorney. Taking the situation to court is not necessarily the best solution to the problem. Court battles can be long, costly, and ugly. On the other hand, if you feel you've been treated unjustly, it may be worth the fight. It is a choice you have to make for yourself, but weigh the costs carefully.

Sometimes the best solution is to find a different position in another work environment that is more suitable to your needs and preferences. Look at all sides of the issue when you are confronted with any form of discrimination and examine a variety of solutions. Your career and reputation may be at stake, so proceed with caution.

Sexual Harassment

Sexual harassment can be a threat to you and your company. It can occur in a number of ways. Most commonly, harassment occurs when an employer or colleague creates an uncomfortable and hostile working environment for another employee that often involves sexual demands or overtones that include suggestive comments. You should know the company policy and follow it. The same statements can be applied to other forms of harassment on the job—including issues relating to race, ethnicity, ability, and other forms of discrimination.

Employees have been protected by law since 1980 under Section VII of the 1964 Civil Rights Act. Federal law defines sexual harassment as the following: unwelcome sexual advances, requests for sexual favors, and other verbal or physical conduct of a sexual nature when:

- Submission to it is made a condition of employment.
- Submission to or rejection of it is the basis of employment decisions.
- It unreasonably interferes with work performance or creates an intimidating, hostile, or offensive working environment. (This includes suggestive comments or suggestive pictures or posters in an office.)

Confronting Sexual Harassment: What to Do

Below are six steps to follow if sexual harassment happens to you. Know the steps and follow each one if faced with a problem.

1. Tell the harasser the behavior is unwelcome and it should stop. Ignoring the problem usually doesn't discourage the harasser.

2. If the situation persists, report the problem to your supervisor, the personnel department, or the harasser's supervisor.

3. Keep a record. Document what the harasser does and says. Take note if there were witnesses, and record how you responded. Indicate to whom you reported the incident.

4. Discuss the situation with a counselor or someone whom you can trust. You may want to talk with an employee assistance counselor in the human resources department. Don't suffer alone. You may find that other people have had similar experiences.

5. File an official complaint with the organization using the company's grievance procedure. If no formalized system exists, write a letter to your boss. If this does not resolve the problem, inform your supervisor that you are going to take further action by bringing the situation to top management if necessary.

6. If the aforementioned steps fail, call the Equal Employment Opportunity Commission or a private attorney. You will be told what to do next. You may be encouraged to file a complaint. Be ready to do so if the behavior cannot be corrected.

Don't allow sexual harassment to exist. If you are confronted with sexual harassment, take action to have it stopped immediately. Sexual harassment doesn't go away if you ignore it—silence is permission. It needs to be addressed and resolved. If you are guilty of harassment, stop the behavior immediately. You and your organization cannot afford to be involved in a sexual harassment lawsuit.

Let's assume you are doing an internship or part-time job for an organization. Or perhaps you work full-time currently. Your task is to learn more about that organization. Play the role of researcher and attempt to find answers to the following question: What are the organizational policies at your place of employment?

Step 1. Obtain written information from the human resources office at your work site. If you are not currently employed, ask an employed family member or friend to obtain a copy for you. Many human resource offices publish a brochure or booklet outlining the organization's policies.

Step 2. Review the brochure, reading the policies on harassment, relationships, and discrimination.

Step 3. On a sheet of paper, respond to the following questions:

1. Is there a policy on sexual relationships or dating within the organization? If so, what is it? If there is no written policy, is there an "unofficial" rule against it? You may need to ask a colleague. What does the policy say about discrimination (e.g., sexual, racial, etc.)?

2. Is there a policy regarding harassment? What are the steps outlined in the brochure for your organization?

3. What does the organization say about issues of equal opportunity?

4. In your opinion, why do you think human resource departments publish this information? Why is this information important for you to know?

File this exercise in your portfolio.

An ethical dilemma. *You are a male employed by a male-dominated organization. In fact, there are only a few females in the entire department. You notice that two male colleagues continually harass one of the female workers. They frequently make crude jokes and discuss sexually related topics in front of the female worker. You don't participate in these activities, but you observe them on an ongoing basis. The female worker is visibly upset by the comments and has repeatedly asked the male workers to stop. How might you address this situation? What action, if any, would you take?*

Managing Issues of Diversity in the Workplace

In Unit I, we discussed the changing world of work in terms of diversity. As you may recall, we outlined trends in diversity and discussed issues of cultural competence. Clearly, managing diversity in today's workforce is no easy task, and the challenge will only get more daunting in the post-9/11 future. However, there are strategies and suggestions that workers can use to help manage diversity. It is crucial that all employees, regardless of title or industry, work harmoniously with others irrespective of race, ethnicity, gender, sexual orientation, status, class, or ability. Following are some suggestions you can follow to increase your awareness of diversity issues:

- Attend diversity training workshops and seminars at your place of employment. Training fosters your development and understanding of diversity issues and gives you a perspective on your organization.

- Participate in any programs that acknowledge and embrace diversity sponsored by your organization. For example, one organization held a ceremony over the lunch hour honoring Martin Luther King, Jr., on his birthday. If you are a student, attend the various cultural events sponsored by the student cultural centers.

- Focus on being inclusive, and use language that is inclusive in your discussions with colleagues. For example, realize that during the holiday season not everyone celebrates Christmas. Be sensitive to these issues of inclusiveness at all times, especially in written and verbal communication.

- Go beyond tolerance; embrace diversity. Tolerance of others who are different is simply not enough. Tolerance implies that "I will put up with these differences, but I won't go much further." Get to know your colleagues who are different. Don't make assumptions about others based on stereotypes, generalizations about a culture, media accounts, and other outside sources.

The following suggestions are aimed at career counselors and other helping professionals but can be applied to a wider audience, including employees and students.

- Increase your self-awareness. Learn more about your own diversity. All of us have a unique ethnicity.

- Learn to value difference.

- Increase your knowledge of other cultures.

- Seek opportunities for cultural immersion.

- Develop improved intercultural communication skills.

- Work for social change—"Work to eliminate all forms of racism, sexism, classism, and all the other 'isms' that prevent social justice and create barriers to the development of human beings."

Source: L. S. Hansen (1997).

Improving Your Workplace Attitudes and Competencies

 t the beginning of this chapter, we outlined several strategies to help ease the transition into your new position. In this section, we will discuss developing good work habits. These suggestions are applicable to all employees—both new and seasoned. The more you learn about working well with others and doing a good job, the more likely you will reach your full potential. Following are several strategies to make your work more rewarding.

Mediocrity costs; how much can you afford?

—UNKNOWN

Do Your Best

You always want to put forth your best effort. The following story is told of a graduate student working for Dr. Henry Kissinger (Heistand, 1986):

> Upon completing his first written assignment, he took and left it in Dr. Kissinger's office, expecting a critique. A few days later he returned to pick it up. Dr. Kissinger said, "Is this the best job you can do?" The young man winced and said, "Maybe I could change a few things. I'll take it back and see what I can do." He reworded the piece and brought it in again. When he returned a few days later, Dr. Kissinger asked, "Is this really your best work?" "I could probably improve it a little," the student said, retrieving it once more. This time, the student spent hours pouring over it, working it word by word, sentence by sentence, paragraph by paragraph, and honing it until it was the best he could do. Again, he left it at Dr. Kissinger's office. The student

returned several days later. Dr. Kissinger asked, "Are you going to tell me this is your best effort?" "Yes, sir," responded the young man. "This is the best job I can do." "All right," Dr. Kissinger said. "I'll read it now." (p. 9)

What is the moral of this story? What does it mean to you? The message of the story is evident. Always try your best right from the beginning. From the authors' perspective, doing one's best is not always winning—it's persevering, picking oneself up, and trying again. It's continuing on in the face of adversity. It's always striving to reach excellence.

Honest Abe	Doing his best did not mean winning to the man who said: "I do the very best I know how—the very best I can and I mean to keep doing so until the end." This man failed in business, was defeated in eight major political elections, and suffered a nervous breakdown at 36, he was defeated over and over. This man lost many times but was elected president of the United States of America in 1860. This man was Abraham Lincoln. He did his best even though he lost often.

Be Enthusiastic

Talk to successful people and you will find that enthusiasm is the core of their being—enthusiasm for what they are doing, for who they are, and for what they believe.

Nothing great was ever achieved without enthusiasm.

—RALPH WALDO EMERSON

Make what you do a passion, not merely a job. Regard each day as important, and maintain a daily interest in your work. Assume two individuals work at the same job: one works with boredom, waiting for the day to end, and the other works with concentration and enthusiasm, finding excitement in the work. Which one is going to do a better job? Which one is going to get ahead?

Show Appreciation to Colleagues

Pave your path to success with recognition and praise of others. People respond positively to you when they are honestly recognized and rewarded. Here are some tips to consider:

- Remember people's names and acknowledge them. People tend to feel appreciated when recognized—even if it is a simple "hello" as a gesture.

- Take time for personal correspondence. Write notes of thanks or congratulations to your coworkers or to your boss. If you see an interesting article in the paper about a relevant issue or topic, clip it out and send it with a note. You never know when you may need to reach out for help.

- Offer timely rewards for improvements and achievements. Praise and compliments build rapport and foster good relationships at work.

- Give credit where credit is due with team members.

Support Your Ideas with Numbers

Being able to statistically measure what you have done or plan to do gives your ideas validation. Numbers provide a basis for measurement, allowing you to quantify your accomplishments. When you use numbers, employers listen and proposals get approved.

The deepest principle in human nature is the craving to be appreciated.

—WILLIAM JAMES

You don't have to be a financial wizard or an accountant to use numbers effectively. Consider these ideas:

- Take a class in statistics, business finance, or accounting. Learn the basics of accounting, cost accounting, and statistical presentations.

- Develop an understanding of financial reports and how each one reflects and affects the organization.

- Make tasks measurable. Everything the organization does is eventually represented in numbers. Ask questions when you don't understand what the numbers mean.

- Represent your numbers in pictures and stories. Create a graph or chart to visually show what you mean.

- Understand the big picture, not just your area. Find out how your department or job fits in with and affects other departments and the whole organization.

To get ahead, be enthusiastic about your job. Work with concentration and a positive attitude.

Even if you are not a numbers person or do not directly work with numbers on a daily basis, it is wise to understand how to use numbers to prove or discredit a point. Experience and intuition serve you, but when it comes to selling your ideas or making your point, numbers speak loudest. When you make a proposal, support your idea with numbers. Organizational decisions are almost always based on numerical projections.

Begin to See Yourself as an Independent Worker

According to an article in *The Christian Science Monitor*, there is a rise in the number of independent workers in the marketplace. Staff writer Stacy Teicher (2004) says, "measuring growth in freelancing is difficult because it's not fully captured in government employment surveys. In 2001, the Bureau of Labor Statistics (BLS) found that there were 5.4 million contingent workers (those who say their jobs are temporary). It also reported categories that can overlap with that group: 8.6 million (6.4 percent of the workforce) defined themselves as independent contractors, 633,000 were contract company workers, and 1.2 million were temp-agency workers" (p. 14).

 your turn . . .

1. Do you see yourself as a freelancer?

_____

_____

2. What type of work might you do on a contract basis?

_____

_____

3. What are the advantages of working as a freelancer? What are the potential disadvantages of this work choice?

_____

_____

_____

Continue to Develop Workplace Skills for the Future

You have a good idea of what skills employers are currently seeking for new graduates. But what about the future? How can you prepare for tomorrow's jobs?

Do You Have *Hyper-Human Skills?*

Currently, we live in a service-oriented economy. However, some pundits believe that know-how service workers and some knowledge work will be reduced or eliminated by automation and electronic systems in the future. Richard Samson contends that service workers are likely to plunge to less than 2 percent of the workforce by the end of the century. However, hyper-human service workers may skyrocket to over 90 percent. So, what exactly are hyper-human skills? They are interpersonal skills that cannot be replaced by automation. Examples include teaching, cultural understanding of clients, persuasiveness, intuitiveness about client needs, direct care giving, innovation, design, and creativity.

Dan Pink, author of *A Whole New Mind* (2005), contends that these skills are right-brain abilities and traits (i.e., compared to left-brain, logical thinking traits). It will be these skills and qualities that are essential and will dominate work in the future.

Can you think of any other hyper-human skills that might not be replaced easily in the future? Identify two or three skills in this category that you possess. What skills might you be able to develop in the future?

Source: R. W. Samson (2004).

Your Action Steps: Creating the Career Management Section of the Portfolio

The Career Management section of your portfolio is a place to keep records of your achievements and your list of special projects and improvements. Below is a summary of the documents maintained in this section and suggestions for their use.

Performance Review

- Review your work performance three months after accepting a new position.
- Review your work performance annually or anytime you feel it's necessary.
- **File the review in your portfolio** until the next review.

Record of Achievements

- Maintain a chronological and detailed file of special projects and achievements.
- Each time you complete a project, make a record. Keep specific details. For example, if you saved the organization money, include the dollar amount.

During the first year at your job, keep track of all the special projects you complete. They do not have to be major projects. You will find it amazing how many tasks you do when you begin to keep a record. The objective of Exercise 10.2 is to analyze and record your achievements. If you are currently employed, use your present position to complete this exercise. If you are not currently employed, use a previous job you held or a volunteer experience. Review this list before every performance review. Type it up and take it with you to the review.

If you do not keep an accurate record, you will forget the minor yet important improvements you have made during the year, and you will not be able to see your growth and contributions to the organization.

10.2 Tracking Your Achievements

Step 1. On a sheet of paper, write down the achievements you made in the last month. Attempt to quantify those accomplishments.

Step 2. Write down your achievements from the past six months. Again, use numbers whenever possible.

Step 3. Write down your achievements from the past year.

Step 4. Answer the following questions.

 follow-up questions

1. Were you surprised at how much you accomplished over the past year? Explain.

_____

_____

_____

_____

2. How might you be able to use this list as a resource in the future?

_____

_____

_____

_____

3. How might this activity help you in your future career–life planning?

_____

_____

_____

_____

_____

File your list of achievements in your portfoilo.

Generalist or Specialist?

Is it better to be a generalist or a specialist? In recent years, a great deal of attention has focused on issues of globalization and the offshoring of jobs. How might this impact your work choices?

According to Forrester Research (cited in Cohen & DeLong, 2005), it is estimated that by the year 2018 over 3.3 million jobs in business processes are likely to go offshore. This may negatively impact wages and the economy of jobs that remain in the United States. So, who wins out given these trends? According to economists Cohen and DeLong (2005), "the new environment is likely to pit those who are most flexible—most able to shift jobs or careers, most able to absorb unexpected blows, best positioned to benefit from unforeseen opportunities—against those who are less so. The contours of such a divide seem predictable: young versus old, generalist versus specialist, people with savings versus those who depend on their next paycheck" (p. 116).

Most fields include both specialties and generalist opportunities. For example, accountants can serve as generalists doing multiple roles or they can specialize in a certain area of interest.

On a sheet of paper, respond to the following questions:

1. In your opinion, is it better to be a generalist or specialist?

2. Write down several areas or jobs within your tentative discipline or area of interest.

3. Think of several specialties within your tentative area of study.

4. Think of several generalist options within your tentative area of study.

Source: S. Cohen & J. B. DeLong (2005).

10.4 Influences on Career Decision Making and Professional Development

Often, your professional development will be impacted by others, including outside influences. Who or what is influencing you? Our career decisions are also influenced by external factors, either consciously or unconsciously. Influences can be people in our lives, or other outside events or circumstances. Consider the following influences. Think about the messages you receive from each source.

Write a brief statement or two about the messages that you are getting from each. You may be surprised by your own responses.

1. Parents or guardians

   _____

   _____

2. Peers

   _____

   _____

3. Media (television, movies, etc.). Often, we are influenced by images we receive from the media—and we don't always realize the impact these messages have on us!

   _____

   _____

4. Mentors

   _____

   _____

5. Other people whom we admire

   _____

   _____

Now, jot down a few sentences about what sources and messages are the strongest. Which ones are the most positive? Least positive?

_____

_____

_____

How might you continue to find support and guidance from the most positive sources? Write your response below.

_____

_____

_____

_____

Summary

This chapter addressed numerous workplace issues and provided strategies to help you manage your work life, including suggestions to improve the professional zone of your life. We considered such topics as preparing to enter a new job; getting to know your colleagues and the organization; issues of sexual harassment, attraction, discrimination, and diversity; and other helpful on-the-job tips. You also completed a series of exercises that helped you apply the concepts discussed.

In the following chapters, we will turn our attention to managing the other area of our lives—the personal, social, and financial.

REFERENCES

Carter, C., & June, G. (1993). *Graduating into the nineties: Getting the most out of your first job after college.* New York: Noonday Press.

Cohen, S., & DeLong, J. B. (2005, January/February). Shaken and stirred. *The Atlantic Monthly, 295*(1), 112–117.

Csikszentmihalyi, M. (2003). *Good business: Leadership, flow, and the making of meaning.* New York: Viking.

Csikszentmihalyi, M. (1997). *Finding flow: The psychology of engagement with everyday life.* New York: Basic Books.

Hansen, L. S. (1997). *Integrative life planning.* San Francisco: Jossey-Bass.

Heistand, A. (1986, December). The Kissinger critique. *Writer's Digest,* p. 9.

Holton, E. (1995, Fall). How to earn an outstanding rating while new on the job. *Journal of Career Planning and Employment,* 51–52.

Laporte, B. (2005). *Goal achievement through treasure mapping: A guide to personal and professional fulfillment.* St. Paul, MN: Heart Lifter Publications.

Maher, K. (2003, December 16). Career journal: Corporate culture shapes hiring decisions: Learning company values can help job candidates make the right impression. *Wall Street Journal,* p. A.7.

Maher, K. (2004, July 13). The jungle. *Wall Street Journal,* p. B.6.

Malone, T. W., & Laubacher, R. (1998). The dawn of the E-lance economy. *Harvard Business Review, 76*(5), 144–152.

Pink, D. (2005). *A whole new mind: Moving from the information age to the conceptual age.* New York: Riverhead Books.

Samson, R. W. (2004). How to succeed in the hyper-human economy. *The Futurist, 38*(5), 38–43.

Teicher, S. (2004, August 2). Freelancing in your future? Rise of independent workers highlights challenges facing today's US labor market. *The Christian Science Monitor,* p. 14.

Vogt, P. (Ed.). (2005, January). Seniors absorb tips from alums in real world seminars and students get chance to shadow alums across the country. *Campus Career Counselor,* p. 4.

Cultivating Meaningful Connections

Personal Goals, Life Balance, and Relationships

learning objectives

1. To explore life habits beyond paid work

2. To discover ways to relieve stress and anxiety

3. To learn how to create a personal mission statement

4. To discover the value of interpersonal relationships, including family and community

5. To review time management strategies

chapter

11

*Language exerts hidden power,
like a moon on the tides.*

—RITA MAE BROWN

Coauthor Connie Harris shares the following story. "Several years ago I attended a presentation about writing positive, present-tense statements for each major goal in your life. I wrote down five specific sentences, but with no time frames. Each sentence expressed a long-term desire as having already been achieved. Looking back, I should have laughed at my audacity. Logically, there was no way these desires could become reality.

"After writing my affirmations, I repeated them to myself several times each day. When I had fears and doubts about my future, I read my affirmation card and repeated each sentence aloud. I did this over a period of several years. As time passed, the goals materialized. Within seven years of having written those statements, most were realities. Here are the stories of three of them.

"My first affirmation was, 'I am a college graduate.' What an improbable goal! I needed to work full-time, had no way of financing a degree, and lived hundreds of miles from any university. But one day, I saw my answer—an off-campus degree program. Five years after writing my goal, I graduated with top honors from one of the top private colleges in the nation. I worked full-time and personally paid all of my education expenses. Coincidence? Perhaps.

"Another affirmation was 'I motivate and influence people in positive directions.' This also happened. Within seven years of writing down this goal, I had changed career paths, from accountant to personnel director to college instructor. I moved from data and numbers to people.

"The third affirmation was 'I travel worldwide.' Since scripting this sentence, I have visited all 50 states, 9 provinces in Canada, 7 states in Mexico, and more than 50 other foreign countries."

From broad affirmations, Connie's deepest desires came true beyond her wildest imagination. Out of her first attempt to set life goals and write affirmations developed the main life areas and the goal planning forms you find in this book. In this chapter, you will review the goals you considered in Unit I. So, let's get started.

Be not afraid of life. Believe that life is worth living, and your belief will help create the fact.

—WILLIAM JAMES

Beyond the Job: Life Habits

Life extends far beyond any job. To succeed, you must find a balance in all that you do. Your daily living habits affect your job, health, finances, home, and family. Managing all of the roles in your life is no small task. Furthermore, there are some areas that tend to tip the scale of balance, areas of continued growth that you need to work on. Imagine that you are your own business (remember your commercial or product from Chapter 5?). You are in control of managing your time, your career, and the choices you make in life. And you need to manage *You, Inc.* through your planning.

Unmanaged segments of your life can cause stress. We have all experienced various forms and degrees of stress in life. By managing time, money, people, communication, health, and education, you can positively manage stressors. Following are some habits to form for life.

You must be the change you wish to see in the world.

—MAHATMA GANDHI

Believe in Yourself

Never underestimate the power of positive thinking. No job is too big, no goal unobtainable when your belief systems are intact. If you want to achieve a specific goal, see yourself as having already accomplished it. Your potential is probably greater than you realize. Like an iceberg, only 2 percent is visible—the rest is hidden. You have what you need to succeed because it lies within you. Begin by taking the first step now.

The more you think well of yourself, the easier it is to give up destructive habits—habits you use to punish yourself for not being good enough. Not only do we have negative opinions but we beat ourselves unmercifully for our perceived imperfections. This doesn't mean that you should stop trying to improve; it just means that you should look upon yourself as a person who is evolving.

- *Treat yourself as you would your best friend.* There are two sides to you—your worst side and your best side. You have within you the potential to be calm, poised, assured, confident, and powerful. You also have the potential to be the opposite: nervous, afraid, unsure, weak, and limited. Which of these two sides do you prefer? Orient your beliefs and select experiences that support your positive feelings.

- *Form an ideal picture of yourself and accept that as real instead of creating a picture that is less than ideal.*

- *Nourish your ideal self.* The more you think well of yourself, the more automatic your thinking and actions become. Yoga masters teach that the brain is like soft clay and therefore subject to impressions. As you repeat a thought many times, the impression or groove that develops becomes deep. Use this thought repetition to give you the power to feel good about yourself and to think positive, healthy thoughts.

Introspection. *What positive feelings do I currently have about myself?*

_____

_____

What one negative feeling do I have about myself? How will I go about changing it?

_____

_____

Slow Down and Take the Time to Enjoy Life

To really enjoy life, take pleasure daily in life's small successes. If you don't experience the feeling of happiness in your everyday life, you are unlikely to experience it in the future. Take pleasure in the journey, the small steps along the way to the greater destination. Life is not perfect, and there will be highs and lows. However, enjoying life's daily pleasures can help make the lows more tolerable.

Taking time to have fun is a normal, healthy part of life. Consciously schedule relaxation time into your life.

In our society, it is easy to get over-involved in work commitments. For many, the work seems to never end. Despite our hectic work lives, it is important to take time to relax and remove ourselves physically and emotionally from the work environment. A balanced life can literally help protect your life. Workaholism in many countries, including the United States and Japan, can lead to premature death among overambitious workers. Taking time to have some fun is a normal, healthy part of life. You may need to consciously schedule relaxation time into your life, and it is vital that you do it.

Most of us can relate to the stress of managing overwhelming schedules. In fact, statistics indicate that we are not taking the time to relax. Rather we are working at a greater pace. According to one study:

> "People are working more hours and working more quickly," said Bob Drago, a labor studies professor at Penn State University. On average, U.S. workers put in 47.1 hours per week, compared with 43.6 hours in 1977. Almost two-thirds of Americans want to work less, he said. (Gage, 2000, p. 1c)

Are you spending enough time devoted to relaxation? About how many hours do you spend working, studying, and so forth per week? In the space below, list three activities you could incorporate into your daily schedule to help you relax.

1. _____

2. _____

3. _____

Relieve Stress

The following information may surprise you: "On an average workday, about a million employees are absent due to stress-related problems, costing American businesses more than $200 billion annually in absenteeism, worker's compensation claims, health insurance costs and lowered productivity. Fully 40 percent of employee turnover is stress-related" (Epstein, 2000). At times, the pressures and demands of life may seem like too much. Instead of reaching for the aspirin bottle, try one of these instant stress relievers:

- *Say "no thanks."* We often feel we must say "yes" to opportunities or new work projects offered to us. However, you do have the option of saying "no." By having predetermined life goals, you control what you say "yes" to.

- *Practice relaxation techniques.* You may have used this breathing technique before a big exam or prior to another anxiety-producing situation. Breathing deeply can help relax you and relieve stress. Breathe in through your nose and out through your mouth. Concentrate on the changes in your body.

- *Take a walk.* Use your lunch hour to take a short walk outside. Get out of your work space if possible. One colleague who works at a university walks over to the on-campus art museum to relax over the lunch break.

- *Visualize a favorite place.* Where is your favorite destination? Perhaps it is a warm, tropical environment or an exotic, adventurous mountain setting. Right now, in your mind, visit that place.

- *Laugh often.* Laughing can serve as a powerful stress reliever. Reach for the joke book on your bookshelf. Read the cartoons on the bulletin board. Share a joke (even a dirty one) with a friend. A good laugh will refresh you.

- *Change your focus.* Put your concerns to the side. Plan a pleasant event, a vacation, dinner with friends, or an outing with your family.

- *Exercise.* You may feel too tired to lift a finger, but if you do some physical exercise, you'll feel renewed. In fact, public health experts now recommend that you get 60 or more minutes of physical exercise *daily*. Take a brisk walk. Go to the gym and work out. You will notice the difference—both physically and emotionally. Not only does exercise relieve stress, but it is also good for your overall health.

Get Active

According to a report from the *New England Journal of Medicine* (Olshansky et al., 2005), life expectancy in the United States may well drop over the next 50 years, mainly because of the increase in obesity rates. According to scientists, obesity will kill more people than cancer or heart attacks. It could decrease the average life expectancy for obese people by 12 to 15 years. The effects of increased obesity could impact the incidence of other health-related ailments such as diabetes, heart attacks, and strokes. It is important to get active and stay in shape!

personal **THINK PIECE**

What do you do to relieve stress? *The previous suggestions are just several ways to reduce stress. What other options would you add to the list? What are your favorite activities to help reduce tension? Write your responses below.*

_____

_____

_____

_____

Consider a Return to the Simple Life

A favorite quote from actress Lily Tomlin reads, "Even if you win the rat race, you are still a rat." Do you ever feel as if you are in a race? Many overworked individuals compare their hectic lives to being on a nonstop treadmill—the treadmill of life.

Do you have a choice in the matter? Of course you do. And more and more individuals are making the choice to slow down and return to a simpler lifestyle. And they are doing it out of personal choice, not necessity. Many Americans are opting to scale back and lead simpler lives. Some of these overworked individuals decided to get away from the "earn and spend" mentality that permeates our society. They opted for less hectic jobs, smaller homes, less expensive cars, and fewer luxury items that they don't really need. Do you know anyone who has selected this lifestyle? If you are interested in learning more about this trend and way of life, take a look at some of the resources available to readers:

- *Choosing Simplicity: Real People Finding Peace and Fulfillment in a Complex World* (2000) by Linda Breen Pierce and Vicki Rubin
- *Simplicity: The New Competitive Advantage in a World of More, Better, Faster* (2000) by Bill Jensen
- *Slowing Down to the Speed of Love: How to Create a Deeper, More Fulfilling Relationship in a Hurried World* (2003) by Joseph Bailey and Richard Carlson

Living leisurely allows work-life balance, allowing us time for work, school, and family.

Explore the Role of Leisure in Your Life

Often, we overlook the importance of leisure in our lives. Our lives are hectic and seemingly out of control much of the time (perhaps you can relate?). However, leisure can be (and should be) an important aspect of our lives. Consider the following statements (O'Brien, 2005) about leisure and choosing a leisurely lifestyle:

- Living leisurely implies working and living under control.
- Living leisurely encourages us to work at a moderate pace (compared to a crazy pace).
- Incorporating leisure does not imply being sloth-like or taking a lazy approach to life.
- Living leisurely allows work–life balance; we have time for school, work, and family.
- When we live leisurely, we take care of our bodies and ourselves.
- Living leisurely is primarily a state of mind; it is a way of life that is imbued in our actions and thoughts.

Emulate Successful People

Find someone who is successfully doing what you want to do, and then model some of the qualities you admire in that person. Modeling can be an effective way to improve your abilities and move you in the direction you want to go. If you have the opportunity to find a mentor, by all means pursue it! Mentors are wonderful resources that can really assist you with your life and career planning process. How can they help you?

Ragins (1997) lists two primary functions of mentors. First, mentors provide career development behaviors that involve coaching, sponsoring advancement, providing challenging assignments, protecting proteges from adverse forces, and fostering positive visibility. Second, they provide a variety of psychosocial roles, including such functions as personal support, friendship, acceptance, counseling, and role modeling.

Supplement mentoring relationships by reading biographies of successful people. You may find admirable traits that inspire you. Incorporate those traits into your life.

---

personal **THINK PIECE**

Whom do you admire? *Quickly and spontaneously write down the names of three people you most admire. Then, jot down what you most admire about them. You may want to include at least one famous person.*

1. _____

_____

_____

_____

2. _____

_____

_____

_____

3. _____

_____

_____

_____

Even monkeys sometimes fall out of trees.

—PROVERB

Learn to Admit Mistakes

No matter how hard you try, you will still make errors at times. When this happens, take responsibility for the mistake. Admit your miscue and move on. Dwelling on mistakes and past errors will immobilize you. The key is to learn from your mistakes and then move forward.

My goal is this: Always to put myself in the place in which I am best able to serve—wherever my gifts find the best soil, the widest field of action. There is no other goal.

—HERMAN HESSE, *JOURNEY TO THE EAST*

Find a Worthy Purpose

What is your purpose in life? Refer back to the opening story in this chapter. The co-author states the following affirmation: "I motivate and influence people in positive directions." This affirmation became her purpose, her life's work. What is your worthy purpose? Find it and pursue it relentlessly. Some people create a personal mission statement that helps guide them and their life choices. Consider writing your own personal mission statement.

What is your worthy purpose? What gifts do you bring to your work? Respond briefly below.

_____

_____

_____

Maintain Balance and Harmony

If you are under extreme stress, if you don't have time for the important aspects of life, you are probably out of balance. To come back into harmony, look at the main areas in your life and find those areas that need attention. Annually review your short- and long-term goals, making sure they are in harmony with one another. Make sure your life's desires are represented in your goals and affirmations.

Setting Personal Goals and Managing Time

Strive to stay on target with your life goals. (Refer back to our discussion of goal setting in Chapter 2.) Review the previous year's goals and your progress. Then, write new goals. To maintain balance and harmony in the different areas of your life, review and revise your life goals annually. The beginning of the year is a good time for this project.

The following exercises will help you set long-term and short-term personal goals and better manage your time in order to achieve those goals.

11.1   Establish Long-Term Personal Goals

Use this opportunity to review your personal goals. Goals within the personal area include physical, mental, spiritual, and emotional goals. What are your long-term goals in these areas? Use a worksheet like the one in Figure 11.1 to record your personal goals and related affirmations.

Next, compare your long-term goals and affirmations with your mission statement and make sure they are in harmony with each other. Ask yourself:

- Am I taking good care of my physical health? My mental health?
- Are there certain technical skills I want to develop?
- What can I do to improve my spiritual life?
- What other areas of self-improvement do I want to work on?

If any of these questions relate to areas you wish to attend to, it is time to evaluate where you are presently and where you want to go in the future. Recall our discussion in Unit I on the importance of identifying potential barriers and then planning how to overcome them. Your social support system (friends, family members, and loved ones) can help you reach your goals.

figure **11.1**   *Example of a list of personal long-term goals.*

GOALS AND AFFIRMATIONS: Long-Term   Date: 01/01/xx

PERSONAL	GOALS	AFFIRMATIONS
Physical Weight, Pulse, Blood Pressure, Cholesterol Level, Personal Appearance	Weigh 138 pounds. Get cholesterol to 198. Improve personal appearance; have it professional and understated.	I am physically, mentally, and spiritually fit. I eat only healthy food. I enjoy exercising daily. I celebrate today by being my best. I weigh 138 pounds. I always take time to play and rest.
Mental Education, Self-Improvement, Technical Skills, Special Knowledge	Become more computer literate. Improve speaking and presentation ability. Obtain a bachelor's degree in psychology, then a Ph.D. Learn more about diet and nutrition so I can be healthier.	
Spiritual Emotional	Be at peace with my past and myself. Always be enthusiastic. Always be in balance with my personal values. Set the best example possible for others.	

11.2 Establish Short-Term Personal Goals

Short-term personal goals include health management—your physical, spiritual, emotional, and mental health. Balance is again the key. To manage these aspects of your life, you must plan for them. Because diet and exercise are critical, neglecting your personal being is shortchanging yourself. Consider these health tips:

The health of the people is really the foundation upon which all their happiness and all their power as a state depend.

— BENJAMIN DISRAELI

1. Exercise daily, if possible.

2. Breathe deeply.

3. Meditate and worship regularly to quiet your mind.

4. Build strong and stable emotional bonds.

5. Feed the mind. Read inspirational books and listen to motivational tapes. Think positive thoughts. Attend continuing education classes.

6. Develop lasting friendships. Take time for family and visit friends. Meet new people. Keep in touch.

Now, review your long-term goals and affirmations and write short-term goals for the coming year (see the example in Figure 11.2).

figure **11.2** *Example of a list of personal short-term goals.*

GOALS AND AFFIRMATIONS: Short-Term   Date: 01/01/xx

PERSONAL	GOALS	AFFIRMATIONS
Physical Weight, Pulse, Blood Pressure, Cholesterol Level, Personal Appearance	Lose 15 pounds (now weigh 153 pounds). Eat low-fat foods, get cholesterol to 198. Walk 4 miles 5 days a week.	I am physically, mentally, and spiritually fit. I eat only healthy food. I celebrate today by being my best. I weigh 138 pounds. I enjoy walking every day. Water is my drink of choice. I always take time to play and rest. I like myself and enjoy being me. I take time to meditate every day. I value and honor myself.
Mental Education, Self-Improvement, Technical Skills, Special Knowledge	Enroll in master's degree program. Take computer class. Join Toastmasters. Learn a new word every week.	
Spiritual Emotional	Smile a lot. Meditate 20 minutes each day. Do breathing exercises each morning.	

In reviewing your goals, ask yourself:

- Are my personal goals in balance with the rest of my life?

_____

_____

_____

_____

- Have I set reachable goals?

_____

_____

_____

_____

- Are my affirmations in the first person, present tense, and positive?

_____

_____

_____

_____

- Have I identified my key desires?

_____

_____

_____

_____

File your long-term and short-term goals in your portfoilo.

To be successful, you must effectively manage your time. It is your only nonrenewable, irreplaceable resource. Time management begins with plans, "to-do" lists, and action. Following are some time-saving strategies to help you manage your time more effectively.

Your tools for time management (see Figures 11.3, 11.4, and 11.5) are:

- Monthly planner form
- Weekly planner form
- Daily "to-do" list

Use Your Monthly Planner

Looking at your short-term personal goals and affirmations, fill in your priorities for each month. Next, take your long-term personal goals and affirmations and fill in your priorities for each month. Figure 11.3 shows a sample monthly planner.

Priorities are important activities. Unfortunately, they usually get put aside for less important but more pressing activities. Truly important activities include those listed on the following page.

figure **11.3** *Example of a monthly planner.*

PRIORITY TASKS	MONTHLY PLANNER					Month of: *January 20xx*	
	SUNDAY	MONDAY	TUESDAY	WEDNESDAY	THURSDAY	FRIDAY	SATURDAY
Review and revise long-term goals and affirmations.		1 Review and revise long-term goals.	2 Compile resume.	3 Complete resume.	4	5 Have resume copied.	6 Write short-term yearly goals.
Write short-term yearly goals. Complete taxes. Review and update all financial reports.	7 Review help wanted ads.	8 Make networking phone calls.	9 More phone calls.	10 Mail ten resumes.	11 Mail ten resumes.	12 Go to birthday party for Ronnie.	13 Review and update budget and financial papers.
Do a budget and a 6-month cash flow.	14 Review help wanted ads.	15	16 Follow up on calls.	17 Attend ACEG meeting.	18 Lunch with mentor.	19 Go to beach.	20 Spend weekend with family. Relax.
Eat healthily. Exercise daily.	21 Visit Jane and Bill while at the beach.	22 Calls to follow up on resumes.	23	24	25 Job shadow Sarah.	26	27
Birthdays 12 Ronnie 21 Jane 31 Julie	28 Begin taxes.	29 Job shadow Jackson.	30	31 Call Julie for birthday.			

Affirmations *I celebrate today by being my best. I like to listen. Exercise is fun for me.*

- Life planning and goal setting
- Exercise
- Building and strengthening relationships
- Eating healthily
- Self-examination

Use Your Weekly Planner

Viewing the week in its entirety allows you to see a larger picture and aids in your planning. List your priorities at the left. They are your most important activities. Write the most important affirmations for the week at the bottom of your weekly planner. Next, check your monthly calendar and transfer your priorities to your weekly schedule. Figure 11.4 shows a sample weekly planner.

The daily to-do list can be used in conjunction with your weekly planner. You can prioritize the items that need to be accomplished on a daily basis.

figure **11.4** *Example of a weekly planner.*

WEEKLY PLANNER   **Week Ending:** January 6, 20xx

PRIORITIES	TIME	SUNDAY	MONDAY	TUESDAY	WEDNESDAY	THURSDAY	FRIDAY	SATURDAY
Review and revise long-term goals and affirmations.	6:00 AM		Review l-t goals	Swim	Walk	Swim	Walk	
	7:00							
Write short-term goals.	8:00							Write annual goals
	9:00							
Eat healthily.	10:00							
Exercise daily.	11:00							
	12:00 PM			Toastmasters		Lunch with Alex		
	1:00							
	2:00							
	3:00							
	4:00							
	5:00							
	6:00 on			Terry's school play at 7 p.m.				

Affirmations I celebrate today by being my best. I like to listen. Exercise is fun for me.

Figure 11.5 shows an example of a daily to-do list. Perhaps you use similar lists presently as a way to accomplish your goals.

Time Management Tips

It is likely that you've received advice about time management in the past—perhaps from many sources. Listed below are some "friendly" reminders for managing your own time more efficiently. What tips would you add to the list?

1. Plan your time.

2. Use a weekly or daily planner.

3. Act; don't just think.

4. Complete all items on your to-do list.

5. Begin and complete projects on time.

6. Delegate work. Train others to do some of your work.

7. Be on time to work, meetings, and events.

8. Do your most important work during your peak energy hours.

9. Schedule and take relaxation time, free from worry and stress.

10. Periodically update, in writing, your professional and personal goals.

11. _____

12. _____

13. _____

14. _____

15. _____

figure **11.5**

Example of a daily to-do list.

TO-DO LIST   Date: June 6, 20XX

1. Do laundry

2. Contact Tom and Rick regarding Friday night plans

3. Make reservations at the restaurant

4. Change oil in car

5. Do research on paper for class

6. Purchase birthday gift for Mom

7. Send bills

8. Buy extra stamps

Managing and balancing your personal life is no easy task. We provided some suggestions in this chapter to assist you with the process. More importantly, you have generated some ideas of your own. Remember, this balancing act is a lifelong, ongoing process. Learning some helpful strategies now will help in the future.

Personal and Community Relationships

*H*IRED! has focused primarily on you as an independent individual. We've stressed throughout the textbook the importance of taking responsibility and being an active participant in your career–life decision making. It is important that we explore the value and significance of the relationships you have with family members and friends—your social support system. As you will recall from a previous chapter on goal setting, your social network can serve as an invaluable resource as you work toward your personal long- and short-term goals. Also, strong social relationships help provide balance in your life. Other social relationships could include professional relationships at work and community relationships. This section focuses primarily on personal and community relationships.

Who and What Is Important to You?

We all play multiple roles at any given time in our lives. The key is to recognize our priorities and maintain some sense of balance—no easy task. If you are in school at this time, your primary role may be that of "student," especially if you are attending full-time. On the other hand, if you are a nontraditional student with a family of your own plus a full-time job, the "student" role may not be the major role in your life.

How do various roles fit into your life? One of the co-authors, Michael Stebleton, remembers when he was an undergraduate, working diligently toward a degree. So much of his time was spent on academics that he often overlooked the importance of maintaining close relationships with the people that really mattered to him. It wasn't until his "student" role temporarily ended that he saw the value of the effort needed to sustain those relationships.

11.4 Who Is Important to You?

In this exercise, think of at least three people in your life who are important to you. Write their names down in the space below. Next, jot down a short description of what you value from your relationship with each person listed. Your list could include family members, friends, teachers, mentors, and others.

Name of Person   **What You Value**

1. _____   _____

2. _____   _____

3. _____   _____

Now, ask yourself: "How much attention and time am I currently giving to each of these relationships?" All meaningful relationships need to be fostered and attended to over time. In the space below, give a brief "progress report" on the current status of your relationships with the three individuals you listed above. Are you devoting enough energy to each relationship? If not, how might you improve on each?

Name of Person   **Status of Relationship Currently**

1. _____   _____

2. _____   _____

3. _____   _____

How can I improve or maintain the quality of these relationships?

1. _____
   _____
   _____

2. _____
   _____
   _____

3. _____
   _____
   _____

File this exercise in your portfolio.

We have talked about the importance of maintaining balance throughout this textbook. Clearly, it is an ongoing and arduous process. Each of us has to make daily decisions about how to best use our time. One way to facilitate this balancing act is to actively assess priorities. This assessment is not a one-time event, rather, it's a process. Time is limited. How do you wish to use your time? The scenario described in the following box illustrates the importance of balance in one's life.

A Lesson in Life Role Balance

What are the Big Rocks in Your Life?

One day an expert in time management was speaking to a group of business students and, to drive home a point, used an illustration those students will never forget.

As he stood in front of the group of high-powered overachievers, he said, "Okay, time for a quiz." Then he pulled out a one-gallon, wide mouth mason jar and set it on the table in front of him. Then he produced about a dozen fist-sized rocks and carefully placed them, one at a time, into the jar.

When the jar was filled to the top and no more rocks would it inside, he asked, "Is this jar full?" Everyone in the class said, "Yes." Then he said, "Really?" He reached under the table and pulled out a bucket of gravel and dumped some gravel in and shook the jar, causing pieces of gravel to work themselves down into the space between the big rocks. Then he asked the group once more, "Is the jar full?" By this time the class was on to him. "Probably not," one of them answered. "Good!" he replied. He reached under the table and brought out a bucket of sand and started dumping the sand in the jar and it went into all the spaces left between the rocks and the gravel. Once more he asked the question, "Is this jar full?" "No!" the class shouted. Once again he said "Good." Then he grabbed a pitcher of water and began to pour it in until the jar was filled to the brim. Then he looked at the class and asked, "What is the point of this illustration?"

One eager beaver raised his hand and said, "The point is no matter how full your schedule is, if you try really hard, you can always cram some more things in it!"

"No," the speaker replied, "that's not the point. The truth this illustration teaches us is: If you don't put the big rocks in first, you'll never get them in at all."

What are the big rocks in your life? Time with loved ones? Your faith, your education, your dreams? A worthy cause? Teaching or mentoring others? Remember to put these BIG ROCKS in first or you'll never get them in at all. So, tonight, or in the morning when you are reflecting on this short story, ask yourself this question: What are the "big rocks" in my life? Then, put those in your jar first.

—Author Unkown.

personal
THINK PIECE

What are the big rocks in your life? *After reading the lesson in life-role balance, ask yourself this question: What is really important to me? Respond briefly below.*

_____

_____

_____

_____

Exploring the Role of Citizen

The role of citizen is an important one. What does it mean to be a good citizen? What might this role mean to you? There are no right or wrong answers to these questions. For some individuals, the citizen role might include being involved in community affairs, taking an active role in politics, or voting in local and national elections. Other individuals may view the citizen role in terms of serving the community through volunteer work. This section focuses on the latter view of citizenship—giving to others through community service and volunteer work.

Life's most urgent question is, "What are you doing for others?"

—MARTIN LUTHER KING, JR.

You may wonder, how I am ever going to find time to do community service work—especially given my already hectic schedule? Serving the community does not have to be a time-consuming commitment. In fact, your time commitment can involve serving only a few hours per week or month. Recent statistics indicate that more than half of the nation's teenagers do some type of volunteer activity. The number of college students who volunteer is equally impressive. There are numerous groups that can help you find service opportunities. Listed below are some suggestions to get you started in the right direction:

- Look in the daily paper. There are numerous organizations that could use your help.

- Access nonprofit organization resources. For example, the United Way publishes a resource called "First Call for Help," which includes a thorough listing of social service agencies and the services they provide.

- Surf the Internet. Look under "community service," "volunteer," and other key search words.

Volunteer work allows you to help others while gaining experience, developing skills, and meeting new people.

- Explore your own neighborhood. Likely, there are ways to get involved by just walking outside your back door. Get involved in community organizations.

Clearly, the primary reason for serving is to help others, to give back to your community in some way. Secondary reasons for volunteering your time and energy to a cause may include the following:

- Doing volunteer work in an area that you may pursue as a possible career allows you to do some "reality testing" to see if you enjoy that type of work.
- You will develop interpersonal and communication skills.
- You will meet new people, and you may make some network connections.
- Volunteering permits you to get applied experience working with others. Depending on your course of study, you can integrate your classroom knowledge with "real life."
- Serving others makes you and them feel good, plus it can be fun.

How Does Service Work Fit into My Career–Life Planning?

It may seem challenging to actively make decisions about your career, or search for a job while still serving others in the community. In fact, the act of serving others may inevitably be more rewarding to you than finding the "best job" or the "right career."

Social Capital and You	Putnam and Felstein (2003) write about a concept called *social capital*. Social capital refers to various social networks, mutual reciprocity, assistance, and trust that you have with others (e.g., neighbors, colleagues, even people that you don't know). They state that communities with high social capital tend to be stronger and more satisfying (e.g., lower crime rates). Contributing individuals help create communities that have higher social capital. How involved are you in your community? What can you do to contribute to the social capital in your own life?

Benefits of Social Relationships

Being involved in social relationships helps one's physical health and in many cases prolongs life. For example, men who are married tend to outlive men who remain single. Companionship, in general, whether from a loved one, a family member, or a pet, tends to have a beneficial impact on physical, emotional, and psychological health. Why do you think this is so?

We are meant to be social creatures. Despite our need to be strong individuals, we also have a strong need to love and to be loved. Isolation and alienation tend not to be beneficial to overall health. Psychologist Abraham Maslow developed a hierarchy of human needs. The two basic levels include physiological needs and safety needs. The next level includes belongingness and love needs, which involve affection from and acceptance by family, friends, and other loved ones (Maslow, 1968). Clearly, the need to be "rugged" individuals is matched by our needs to love and to be loved by others.

The Value of Family

Families take multiple forms. The traditional "Leave It to Beaver" family with the two perfect children and the white picket fence is a relic of the past. Today, it doesn't matter what a family looks like. In some cultures, the nuclear family is more prominent, while in others the extended family is central. Many children in our society are growing up in single-parent families, and two mothers or two fathers are rearing some children. The makeup of the family should not matter. What matters is the love and affection that family members give to one another. All of us need some form of support from family and loved ones—especially in times of need.

The Importance of Family

Below is an excerpt from a popular nonfiction book, *Tuesdays with Morrie,* by Mitch Albom. Morrie Schwartz is a retired professor who has ALS, or Lou Gehrig's disease. He is dying. A former student, Albom, reconnects with his old professor, and they meet each Tuesday afternoon to discuss life's greatest lessons. During one of their meetings, the topic turns to the importance of family:

Morrie responds, "The fact is, there is no foundation, no secure ground, upon which people may stand today if it isn't the family. It's become quite clear to me as I've been sick, if you don't have the support and love and caring and concern that you get from a family, you don't have much at all. Love is so supremely important. As our great poet Auden said, 'Love each other or perish.'"

"Love each other or perish." I wrote it down. Auden said that?

"Love each other or perish," Morrie said. "It's good, no? And it's so true. Without love, we are birds with broken wings."

Morrie also talked about the value of a meaningful life, "Remember what I said about finding a meaningful life? I wrote it down, but now I can recite it: Devote yourself to loving others, devote yourself to your community around you, and devote yourself to creating something that gives you purpose and meaning." (Albom, 1997)

Social Management and the Portfolio

Your task is to think about managing your social life. Provided below are some tips to help you with this ongoing process.

TIPS FOR MANAGING THE SOCIAL AREA OF YOUR LIFE

- Set goals to help manage your social relationships.
- Make it a point to socialize frequently.

- Use e-mail. It's an inexpensive and quick way to stay in touch with family and friends—especially those who live in a different state or country.

- Attempt to remember special events such as birthdays and anniversaries. There are personal electronic organizers to help you with this objective. Acknowledge those special events.

- Have meaningful conversations with family and friends. Tell them how important they are to you in your life.

personal **THINK PIECE**

What suggestions do you have? *It may seem a bit assuming for us to provide "tips" for improving your relationships. What suggestions do you have for managing your social zone? Describe several below.*

1. _____

2. _____

3. _____

4. _____

5. _____

Stay on target with your life goals. Review the previous year's goals and your progress. Then, write new goals. To maintain balance and harmony in the main areas of life, review and revise your life goals annually. The beginning of the year is a good time for this project. **Keep your completed goals form in the Social Management section of your portfolio.** Having a place to keep the form gives you easy access for periodic review and revision.

11.5 What Exactly Is "Work"?

Is "work" more than your paid job? Economist Charles Handy seems to think so. Handy (2002) defines work "in terms of how he spent his time and not how he got paid." Other career development theorists agree that the "worker" role is just one of life's several roles that comprise a more holistic "career."

What other types of work might be meaningful and necessary? In addition to paid, or fee work, Handy identifies other types of work:

- *Home work:* labor required to maintain a home
- *Gift work:* time devoted to charities, religious involvement, and volunteer organizations
- *Study work:* time spent being a student; keeping up to date in one's field and upgrading skills

follow-up questions

1. What types of work (according to Handy) are you involved in?

   _____

   _____

   _____

   _____

2. How might "paid work" fit into the other types of work in your career?

   _____

   _____

   _____

   _____

3. Do you feel that your various aspects of work are in balance with each other? If not, what might you do to try to balance these types of work?

   _____

   _____

   _____

   _____

   _____

   _____

File this exercise in your portfolio.

Establish Long-Term Social Goals and Affirmations

At times life is like walking a tightrope. You take one step at a time, but if you lean too far in any one direction, you may fall. Return to the work you did in Unit I. Review your long-term goals and discover whether you are focused and balanced.

Using your goal-setting skills, write your long-term social goals and affirmations.

_____

_____

_____

_____

_____

_____

_____

_____

Then, compare your overall goals with your long-term social goals and make sure they are in harmony with each other. Ask yourself the following questions:

- Are you leaving enough time for family and friends?

- Are you spending so much time on your education goals that you are letting other responsibilities slide?

- Are you spending so much time socializing with your friends that you are not concentrating enough time on school or managing your finances?

If any of these situations (or related ones) describe your circumstances, it is time to evaluate where you are, where you want to go, and how and when you want to achieve your goals. Describe what you want and where you want to be. What changes do you feel you should make to your long-term social goals? This type of planning provides you with a life direction and focus and helps guide your daily decision making.

File this exercise in your portfolio.

11.7 Establish Short-Term Social Goals and Affirmations

Life is a relationship.

— RICH FIELDS

Your social relationships affect all other areas of your life. When you are in balance and harmony with the people you live and work with, you are free to concentrate on the other areas of life. Your relationships will be enriched when you nourish and attend to them. On the other hand, they become unhealthy when neglected and ignored. Accept others for what they are, not for what you want them to become.

Review your long-term social goals and affirmations. Using a separate chart, write short-term, or yearly, goals and affirmations. You may wish to divide your social relationships into three categories: personal relationships, professional relationships, and community relationships. Figure 11.6 shows a sample list of social short-term goals and affirmations.

Ask yourself these questions:

- Are my relationships in balance with the rest of my goals?
- Do I set enough time aside for family and friends?
- Is there time to serve my community?
- Are these goals and affirmations what I want today?
- Are there any changes that need to be made? (If yes, revise your goals and affirmations. If no, continue on.)

---

figure **11.6**   *Example of a list of short-term social goals.*

GOALS AND AFFIRMATIONS: Short-Term   Date: 01/01/xx

SOCIAL	GOALS	AFFIRMATIONS
Personal Relationships Spouse/Partner, Significant Other, Family, Friends, Neighbors	Listen attentively to my partner and kids. Visit friends regularly. Write a friend once a month. Seek ways to show appreciation. Remember birthdays.	I am happy. I am a loving, caring person. I enjoy listening to others. I volunteer gladly. I enjoy my work.
Professional Relationships Work, Business Organizations, Professional Organizations, Other	Remember birthdays. Conduct annual reviews. Have quarterly luncheon with boss. Join Personnel Manager's Association.	
Community Relationships Religious, Political, Community, Social	Join and get involved in chamber of commerce. Volunteer at library. Serve on school board.	

Summary

It is important to take care of yourself and to develop meaningful relationships with others in your life—including your community. In this chapter, we discussed the importance of managing your personal life, life beyond paid work, and building interpersonal relationships. In particular, we explored the value of relationships with friends, family members, and other loved ones. Additionally, you examined your role as citizen through active involvement in a volunteer or community service opportunity. In the next chapter, we will discuss another important aspect—financing your life.

Return to old watering holes for more than water—friends and dreams are there to meet you.

—AFRICAN PROVERB

REFERENCES

Albom, M. (1997). *Tuesdays with Morrie.* New York: Doubleday.

Covey, S. R. (1989). *The seven habits of highly effective people: Restoring the character ethic.* New York: Simon & Schuster.

Epstein, R. (2000). Stress busters. *Psychology Today, 33*(2), 30–35.

Gage, A. (2000, February 17). As work week lengthens, calls for relief rise. *Pioneer Press,* p. 1c.

Handy, C. (2002). *The elephant and the flea: Reflections of a reluctant capitalist.* Boston, MA: Harvard Business School Press.

Maslow, A. H. (1968). *Toward a psychology of being* (2nd ed.). New York: Van Nostrand.

O'Brien, T. (2005, March 18). Degree of leisure in life affects health, well-being. *Pioneer Press,* p. E3.

Olshansky, S. J., Passaro, D. J., Hershow, R. C., Layden, J., Carnes, B. A., Brody, J., et al. (2005, March 17).

A potential decline in life expectancy in the United States in the 21st century. *New England Journal of Medicine, 352*(11), 1138–1145.

Putnam, R., & Felstein, L. M. (2003). *Better together: Restoring the American community.* New York: Simon & Schuster.

Ragins, B. (1997). Diversified mentoring relationships in organizations: A peer perspective. *Academy of Management Review, 22*(2), 482–521.

Financing Your Life

PLANNING AND IMPLEMENTING

learning objectives

1. To gain a better understanding of the importance of financial planning

2. To learn about the rules of money

3. To highlight strategies for making your money work for you

4. To review the value of preparing and maintaining a budget

5. To encourage you to explore your own relationship with money

If you would be wealthy, think of saving as well as getting.

—BENJAMIN FRANKLIN

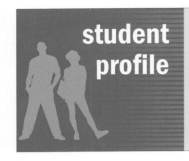
Mai. As Mai left her finance class she remarked to her friend Justin, "Until now, I never realized how money works. There are so many options beyond paying bills and basic savings. My parents never invested in the stock market or bought real estate except for their house. Any savings they had they put into a bank account. I want to become a savvy money manager."

You, too, can improve your financial status by following some of the suggestions in this chapter. By developing an accurate picture of your financial state and financial goals, you can move toward financial independence.

Where Will You Be Financially at Retirement?

In the past, many American workers could expect to comfortably retire at the age of 65, with the company pension plan nicely padded and Social Security payments beginning. Individuals could retire and be set for life. Well, times have changed, to say the least. There are at least five recent trends that make the traditional "retire at 65" goal less attainable.

There is something about making your own money and having control over your life that cannot be duplicated. Knowing that you can take care of yourself, no matter what happens, is so important that it should be a right.

—REBECCA MADDOX,
INC. YOUR DREAMS

- Most Americans are living longer. Men and women can expect to live into their eighties and nineties. Individuals need to be financially prepared to live another 20 or 30 years beyond the age of 65. The number of Americans age 100 and older doubled over the past decade to 70,000 and is expected to double every 10 years as the century proceeds (Wilcox Dovel, 2000). Seniors are concerned about outliving their retirement funds— a realistic concern given advances in medical technology and health maintenance.

- The Social Security system will eventually default unless changes are instituted. Under the current system of contributions, investment returns, and payout, the system will go bankrupt somewhere between the years 2040 and 2060. The ratio of workers to beneficiaries went from 5 to 1 in 1960 to 2 to 1 in 2005.

- Defined contribution plans, where employment length was a major determinant of benefits, have largely been phased out except in a few industries. More control and decision making has been handed over to the individual employee through 401(k) plans. With most American workers no longer staying with one organization throughout their career, retirement plans have become and will continue to be more flexible, with key financial decisions being turned over to each worker and retiree.

- Many seniors will work for pay after "retirement." Retirement will become more of a process than an event.

- Aging baby boomers are looking forward to different work experiences after age 65. Many healthy boomers are looking forward to second careers, called "bridge careers," of the type that allow them to give back to their community.

personal **THINK PIECE**

When do you expect to "retire"? *Do you see "retirement" for you as a process or an event? How do you envision your own retirement? Consider living conditions, family issues, spending patterns, travel, and other financial issues important to you. Write your thoughts below.*

_____

_____

_____

_____

did you know?

An International Longevity Center/Harris Poll found that one-fourth of 25- to 29-year-olds expect to retire before they're 55. But by the time people reach their forties, reality hits home and fewer than 10 percent think 55 is a realistic goal (Franklin, 2000).

Regardless whether you plan to retire at 65 or never plan to officially retire, you need to have a financial plan. Unfortunately, many people do not save money on a regular basis. This chapter can only begin to plant some ideas about financial planning. It takes an understanding of how money "works," as well as spending and saving wisely.

The Fundamentals of Wealth

Americans are notorious as "accumulators" of things. They are spenders, not savers. Nevertheless, the formula to accumulate wealth is very simple. Save more than you spend and invest the difference wisely. Following are some general outlines of these fundamental practices:

A part of all I earn is mine to keep.

—GEORGE S. CLASON

1. Acquiring money

- Live off less than you earn.

- Pay yourself first! Aim at saving 10 percent of your income every month. The remainder is what you can spend for the month.

2. Managing money
   - Despite what you think, when you buy "on sale" items you are not saving; you are spending.
   - Don't become greedy and don't throw all your eggs into one "can't miss" investment.
   - If you fall off the savings bandwagon for a month, don't beat yourself up. Just get back to it the next month.
3. Growing your money
   - Invest your earnings in a high quality mix of money market accounts, mutual funds, stocks, and bonds, starting with safer investments first and adding riskier, higher-return investments only after you build a strong foundation.
   - Invest for your retirement in tax-deferred investments including IRAs and employer retirement plans.
   - Ask for financial advice, but only from people you trust and who are knowledgeable about finances.
   - Let your money grow through reinvesting dividends and interest. Withdrawing these funds only keeps you where you are financially. Instead, build a money market or bank account that you can use for withdrawals if needed.

   Here are several other tips for managing your finances and improving your financial situation:

   - Compile a budget and a balance sheet with your assets and liabilities.
   - Establish a long-term financial plan and review it annually.
   - Pay off your credit card balances every month.
   - Have an emergency cash fund equal to six months' salary.
   - Look for ways to save money: buy in bulk, use mass transit, carpool, limit frivolous purchases, look for bargains, pack a lunch for work, and so forth.
   - Start contributing to a tax-deferred retirement savings plan.
   - Think about buying a home and building equity rather than renting.
   - Increase your knowledge about taxes by taking a tax strategy class.
   - Be "bank-wise": shop for an interest-paying, free or low-cost checking account and avoid ATM fees whenever possible.

Investment classes can help you understand today's complicated financial world. Study investment options with an eye toward the future.

- Study investment strategies with a view toward the future. Investment classes can help you understand the complicated and option-filled financial world of today.

At the end of the chapter you'll find a list of books and online services that can help you build your financial smarts.

The Importance of Starting Early

Let's suppose that John and Dave were high school friends. They had similar jobs and each had a family. Their incomes for 40 years were identical, but their financial planning differed. Here is what each did:

> John began investing at age 35 and saved $5,000 a year for 10 years for a total of $50,000. At age 65, John's $50,000 was worth $337,606.

> Dave began investing at age 45 and saved $5,000 a year for 20 years, or a total of $100,000. At age 65, Dave's $100,000 was worth $228,810.

This example assumes an average growth rate of 8 percent. The big lesson is this: let time assist your accumulation of wealth. By starting early, John's nest egg at retirement was much larger than Dave's, despite the fact he actually invested less principal.

personal **THINK PIECE**

Exploring your relationship with money. *What value do you place on money? How much does money motivate you? Reexamine the first chapter's discussion on exploring values. We all have an emotional or psychological relationship with money. We may have been shaped through our family experiences, good or bad. In the space below, write down your response to the question, "What is my relationship with money—having it, earning it, and spending it?"*

_____

_____

_____

_____

Education as a Wise Investment

The authors firmly believe that education of any kind is the best investment you can make irrespective of your current age. Although college tuition has increased dramatically in recent years, formal education beyond high school does pay off for you. Also, numerous financial

Education is an investment in your future. Your lifetime earnings will reflect your education and your willingness to undertake lifelong learning.

aid options are available for students, including loans at manageable interest rates. Consider the following statistics summarizing mean annual income by educational attainment for workers age 25 and over (*Occupational Outlook Quarterly*, 2004):

EDUCATION AND INCOME

- Doctorate, $70,148
- Professional degree, $67,964
- Master's degree (MA, MS), $55,326
- Bachelor's degree, $46,800
- Associate's degree (AA, AS), $34,944
- Some college, no degree, $32,344
- High school graduate, $28,808
- Less than HS graduate, $20,592

These earnings are based on a yearly salary. You can imagine what the difference is in lifetime earnings between those with a college degree and those without! Especially in today's information-based economy, the value of and need for a college education shouldn't be overlooked.

personal **THINK PIECE**

What do the numbers mean to you? *What inferences do you make from the data on median annual household income by educational attainment? How might this data affect you and your career–life decision making?*

_____

_____

_____

_____

Show Me the Money

Students and Money

A survey of college students (Kadison & DiGeronimo, 2004) reveals interesting facts about their perspective on money and finance. Here are some of the findings:

- Students feel a need for a financial return on their education. Post-9/11, many feel the need to pursue an idealist motive, but often they cannot justify

(Continued)

(Continued)

taking a lower salary. Students wonder: What is their role in the emerging global state/world? If they want to get involved, how should their role and involvement unfold?

- Career choices are often influenced by the student's degree of indebtedness. "They may face the need to sell their souls to feed the bank." This creates undue stress.

- Average student debt is $18,000 to $19,000. They feel "economic times are uncertain" (as of this writing). They hold multiple credit cards ranging from $3,000 to $7,000 in debt.

- More students are putting tuition and fees on credit cards to help fund education. 25 percent of all students interviewed reported they used credit cards to pay for some part of tuition and fees.

- 30 percent of students are very or extremely concerned about their current level of personal debt including student loans.

- The pressure to work to meet college expenses affects degree completion time and academic performance.

- Earn now, serve later: Many students tentatively plan to earn money after graduation in order to pay off debts and then change careers and serve others—to do something they really want to do.

Organizing Your Finances

As you progress in your work life, keep all of your investment accounts and vehicles in an organized system. You may want to use an electronic accounting program such as Quicken to help you. Following are some additional suggestions to help you organize your financial life:

- Use a filing system to keep documents organized. Save important documents, such as tax-related paperwork, and label them clearly. The IRS can provide information on record keeping.
- Keep your account numbers for all investment vehicles in a safe place.
- Annually review your investments and make changes if necessary.
- Update and balance your checkbook on a regular basis.

- Consider paying your bills online through automatic withdrawals from your checking account.
- Throw out old, outdated receipts and documents. The IRS has information on document retention.

Factors Underlying Wealth Accumulation

Stanley and Danko (1996) wrote a best-selling book titled *The Millionaire Next Door*. They studied individuals who had accumulated wealth. Their analysis identified seven factors or common denominators that characterize the affluent:

1. They live well below their means.
2. They allocate their time, energy, and money efficiently, in ways conducive to building wealth.
3. They believe that financial independence is more important than displaying high social status.
4. Their parents did not provide "economic outpatient" care.
5. Their adult children are economically self-sufficient.
6. They are proficient in targeting market opportunities.
7. They chose the right occupation.

Workplace Investment Plans

Most financial advisors recommend investing your retirement savings into tax-deferred accounts, including such employer sponsored plans as 401(k)s, 403(b)(7)s, SEPs, and Keoghs. A major benefit gained from this type of investment is that your account earnings grow faster than they do in taxable investments. When you invest in one of these programs, your taxes are deferred until you draw out the earnings during your retirement. You save on taxes in the short run; you may also save taxes at withdrawal time because you are likely to be in a lower tax bracket during retirement.

Discuss options and advantages with a certified financial planner.

Developing a Budget and Long-Range Financial Plan

Having an ongoing financial plan allows you to achieve your financial goals within set time frames. It also helps you make alternate plans when life doesn't go as planned. Knowing where your money comes from and where it goes is an integral part of career–life planning. Maintaining financial goals and records is essential to preserving a healthy, balanced life.

figure **12.1**   *An example of short-term financial goals.*

SHORT-TERM FINANCIAL GOALS

Date: 01/01/xx

AREA	GOALS	ACCOMPLISHED?
Liquid Assets Cash, money market funds, annuities, cash-value life insurance, other	Maintain $10,000 cash fund Balance checkbook monthly Pay off credit card balances monthly Review status quarterly	
Marketable Investments Stocks, mutual funds, bonds, commodities	Monitor stocks and funds for performance Save 4% for additional education	
Nonmarketable Investments Real estate, IRAs, retirement funds, business interests	Save 6% for retirement	
Personal Assets Home, vehicles, home furnishings, jewelry, collectibles	Purchase newer vehicle	

Ask yourself these questions:

1. Have I set attainable goals?
2. Are the goals specific and measurable?
3. Do I have specific plans to attain these goals?
4. Will I commit and hold myself accountable to this plan?

The figures shown in this chapter are also included on the planning disk that came with this book. These worksheets can help you outline an annual budget and focus on long-range financial goals.

- Figure 12.1 Short-term financial goals
- Figure 12.2 Long-term financial goals
- Figure 12.3 Assets and liabilities
- Figure 12.4 Income and expenses
- Figure 12.5 Budget worksheet

Once you have completed the worksheets, file them in your portfolio.

figure **12.2**   *An example of long-term financial goals.*

LONG-TERM FINANCIAL GOALS   Date: 01/01/xx

AREA	GOALS	ACCOMPLISHED?
Liquid Assets Cash, money market funds, annuities, cash-value life insurance, other	Sufficient cash reserves for emergencies	
Marketable Investments Stocks, mutual funds, bonds, commodities	Grow investment portfolio with blue-chip investments	
Nonmarketable Investments Real estate, IRAs, retirement funds, business interests	Own duplex for additional cash flow Grow retirement funds steadily	
Personal Assets Home, vehicles, home furnishings, jewelry, collectibles	Own comfortable home Replace car periodically Own valuable art	

Ask yourself these questions:

1. Do these financial goals still fit my desires and lifestyle?

2. Have I looked at the big picture financially?

3. Have I accounted for family needs: education, retirement, housing changes, and so on?

figure **12.3**   *Assets and liabilities worksheet.*

Update and review your assets and liabilities annually to measure your financial progress.

ASSETS	ACTUAL AS OF 12/31/__	PROJECTED AS OF 12/31/__
Liquid Assets:		
Marketable Investments:		
Nonmarketable Investments:		
Personal Assets:		
TOTAL ASSETS		
LIABILITIES		
Short-term (<1 year):		
Long-term (>1 year):		
TOTAL LIABILITIES		
NET WORTH		

figure **12.4**   *Income and expenses worksheet.*

CATEGORY	MONTHLY PLAN	YEARLY PLAN	ACTUAL YEAR
INCOME:			
Salary and wages			
Interest and dividends			
Self-employment			
Other			
TOTAL INCOME			
EXPENSES:			
Housing (mortgage or rent)			
Utilities			
Phone			
Insurance			
Transportation			
Loan payments			
Food			
Clothing			
Personal hygiene			
Medical			
Licenses and fees			
Repairs and maintenance			
Recreation and entertainment			
Education, memberships, subscriptions			
Contributions and donations			
Gifts			
Taxes			
TOTAL EXPENSES			
TOTAL INCOME			

figure **12.5** *An example of a budget worksheet.*

EXPENSES		MONTH		YEAR
Housing	$	495	$	5,940
Utilities (Phone, Electricity, Gas, Water, Garbage)		125		1,500
Furnishings Maintenance and Upkeep		10		120
Food, Beverages, and Other Grocery Items		390		4,680
Clothing and Upkeep		50		600
Personal (Health and Beauty Aids)		25		300
Transportation (Gas, Oil, Maintenance)		125		1,500
Insurance: Life *currently paid by employer				*
Insurance: Medical, Dental, Vision *currently paid by employer				*
Insurance: Long-Term Disability *currently paid by employer				*
Insurance: Automobile		50		600
Insurance: Property and Household		70		840
Insurance: Personal Liability *Included in household insurance				*
Insurance: Other				—
Savings and Other Investments		100		1,200
Retirement *Employer contributes 6% of gross wages to retirement		50		600
Recreation and Entertainment		50		600
Education		25		300
Contributions and Gifts		100		1,200
Dues, Subscriptions, and Memberships		5		60
Loans and Interest Payments		235		2,820
Licenses and Fees		10		120
Property Taxes		100		1,200
Net Before Payroll Taxes	$	**2,015**	$	**24,180**
Federal Income Taxes				
Other Federal Taxes (FUTA, etc.)				
State Income Taxes *Estimated Taxes		864		10,368
Other Taxes (State Worker's Compensation, Unemployment, City)				
Social Security (FICA and Medicare)				
Total Budget Requirements	$	**2,879**	$	**34,548**
Rate per Hour (Divide year total by 2,080 hours)				$16.61/hour

Summary

In this chapter, we examined various aspects of money and how you deal with it. We offered suggestions concerning money management. We also introduced short- and long-term financial planning and discussed the importance of investing in your education.

Books and Internet Resources

- *Ernst & Young's Personal Financial Planning Guide*, Martin Nissenbaum, 2004
- *Jane Bryant Quinn's Smart and Simple Financial Strategies for Busy People*, Jane Bryant Quinn, 2006
- *The Millionaire Next Door*, Thomas J. Stanley and William D. Danko, 1996
- *The Money Book for the Young, Fabulous and Broke*, Suze Orman, 2005
- *Personal Finance for Dummies*, Eric Tyson, 2003

Some of the better Web sites include the following:

- SmartMoney.com: www.smartmoney.com
- Money.com: money.cnn.com
- Morningstar: www.morningstar.com

REFERENCES

Current Population Statistics. (2004, Fall). *Occupational Outlook Quarterly*, www.bls.gov.

Franklin, M. B. (2000, January). Bailing out at 55. *Kiplinger's, 54*(1), 110.

Kadison, R., & DiGeronimo, T. F. (2004). *College of the overwhelmed: The campus mental health crisis and what to do about it.* San Francisco: Jossey-Bass.

Maddox, R. (1996). *Inc. your dreams.* New York: Penguin Books.

Stanley, T., & Danko, W. (1996). *The millionaire next door.* New York: Pocket Books.

Wilcox Dovel, M. (2000, January). Do you feel rich? *Kiplinger's, 54*(1), 79.

Conclusion

Ideally, *HIRED!* has thoroughly prepared you for the many facets of work in the next millennium. However, the textbook is only one tool to assist you along your life and career journey. As we mentioned in the introduction, the exercises in the book are designed to complement other career assessments that you complete as part of the life and career exploration process. Concepts regarding work and career have changed significantly in recent years. Loyalty to and security from a particular job are no longer realistic expectations. Instead, your willingness to learn and flexibility are now paramount.

We can predict that in future years there will be other changes in the world of work. Your ability to adapt to these ongoing changes will be more important than the actual changes. Change is inevitable. The following quote from Dr. Robert P. Larsen, Counseling Center, University of Illinois-Urbana-Champaign, illustrates best how you can thrive in a world of change:

> The progress of your career and life can be compared to a mariner piloting a sailboat. You can't control the winds (unchangeable reality) but you can learn to handle the sails skillfully (changeable reality) so you can reach your destination or goal. You have to accept that sometimes the winds will be active and sometimes they will be quiet. But you trust that the winds will come back. As with the winds, you can't always get what you want from your career when you want it. But with a positive attitude, realism, patience, and persistence you can nearly always get more of what you want.

We hope that this guide has helped you learn to handle the sails skillfully so that you can reach your destination. Good luck to you!

Index

Results, resume and, 183
Resumes, 172–196 (see also
    Portfolio)
    action words in, 184
    checklist for, 191
    chronological, 175–176, 177
    content of, 179–184
    defined, 173–174
    drafting, 189
    e-resumes, 192–195
    field-testing, 190
    functional, 176, 178
    job description and, 203
    paper/printing, 185
    recipients of, 175
    samples, 177–178, 188, 195
    stylistic tips for, 186
    tailoring, 187, 203
    themes of, 173
    three C's of, 174
    tips for writing, 194
    types of, 175–179
    visual appeal of, 185–186
Retirement, preparing financially,
    318–319
Review, performance, 285
Rewards, for goal achievement, 48
Rich text format, of e-resume, 193
Ricki, profile, 45
Rico, Gabriele Lusser, 8
Risk taking, 52
Riso-Hudson Enneagram Type
    Indicator, 31
Robbins, Anthony, 215
Roles, life, 52–55

Safety, personal, 86
Salary:
    determining, 258–259
    education and, 321–323
    lowest acceptable, 259
    range, 227
Salutation, in letter, 146
Samson, Richard, 284
School associates, as networking
    contacts, 211
School, options for, 76–81
Self, your ideal, 293
Self-analysis, 7–38
Self-assessment, 7–38
    inventories, 10–37
    lifelong dreams and, 16
    of achievements, 24
    of experience, 35–36
    of interview, 252–256

of natural talents, 22
of passions/interests, 12–17
of personality, 30–32, 34–35
of skills, 18–24 (see also Skills)
of values, 25–29
of workstyle preferences,
    30, 33
portfolio and, 136
Self-awareness, 2–28
Self-confidence, 293
    portfolio and, 135
Self-Directed Search, 31
Self-employment, 87
Self-knowledge, see Self-awareness
Selling yourself, 138
Sensing/intuition, personality
    and, 30
Serial interview, 225–226
Service industries, occupations
    in, 85
Service work, 308–309
Sexual attraction, 276–277
Sexual discrimination, 276–278
Sexual harassment, 277–278
Shirts, 250
Shoes, 250, 251
Short-term goals, 45–46
    financial, 325
    personal, 300–301
    social, 314
Simple life, returning to, 296
Skills:
    advantages and, 36
    assessment of, 18–24, 67
    cataloging, 182–184
    data/people/things and, 18
    developing technical/
        computer, 275
    hyper-human, 284
    portable, 107
    portfolios and, 131
    resume and, 182–183
    sought by employers, 21
    transferable, 19–20, 107
    workplace, 284
Slowing down, 293–294
SMART goal setting, 44
Social:
    assistance, occupations in, 85
    capital, 309
    goals, long- and short-term,
        313–314
    management, 310–311
    personality type, 34
    relationships, 305–310

Social Security, 318
Sophocles, 42
Specialist, 287
Stalnaker, Stan, 130
Standard and Poor's Register of
    Corporations, Directors, and
    Executives, 70
S.T.A.R. model of portfolios, 127
Statistics, 283
Strategies, negotiating, 260–261
Strengths, summarizing your,
    231–232, 236
Stress, 292, 294–295
Strong Interest Inventory (SII), 67
Structure, of organization,
    270, 271
Student:
    clubs, 212
    debt, 322–323
    exchange, 66, 102 (see also
        Study abroad)
Students:
    Hispanic, 53
    older, 53
Studio arts and design
    portfolio, 127
Study abroad, 4, 66, 100, 102,
    103–104
Study, work, 312
Success, emulating, 297
Suits, for interviews, 249–250, 251
Summary of the World, 95
Super, Donald, 52–53
Systems thinking, 20

Tailoring resume, 187, 203
Talents, assessing your natural, 22
Tamika, profile, 76
Teamwork, 21
Technical skills, 275
Techno-literate skills, 20
Technology, career trends and,
    83–84
Telecommuting, 87
Telephone, see Phone
Temperament, 3
Temporary employment, 219
Temporary workers, 87
Terrorism, 86
Text format, of e-resume, 192–193
Thank you letter, 116, 144,
    151–153
    follow-up, 256
    sample, 152
Things, interests and, 14–15